Moving to

Kiss the Blue Screen of Death Goodbye!

Moving to *Linux*®

Kiss the Blue Screen of Death Goodbye!

Marcel Gagné

✦ Addison-Wesley

Boston • San Francisco • New York • Toronto • Montreal
London • Munich • Paris • Madrid
Cape Town • Sydney • Tokyo • Singapore • Mexico City

The publisher offers discounts on this book when ordered in quantity for bulk purchases and special sales. For more information, please contact:

> U.S. Corporate and Government Sales
> (800) 382-3419
> corpsales@pearsontechgroup.com

For sales outside of the U.S., please contact:

> International Sales
> (317) 581-3793
> international@pearsontechgroup.com

Visit Addison-Wesley on the Web: www.awprofessional.com

Library of Congress Cataloging-in-Publication Data

Gagné, Marcel.
   Moving to Linux: kiss the blue screen of death goodbye!/Marcel Gagné
      p. cm.
   Includes bibliographical references references and index.
   ISBN 0-321-15998-5
   1. Linux. 2. Operating systems (Computers) I. Title

QA76.76.O63G345 2003
005.4'469—dc21   2003052198

ISBN: 0-321-15998-5

7   8   9   10
First printing, [July 2003]

Dedication

This book is dedicated to Sally Tomasevic,
my wife,
my partner,
my best friend,
and the love of my life.

Contents

Contents

Acknowledgments

Some time after completing my first book, *Linux System Administration : A User's Guide*, I said something akin to, "This was an amazing amount of work! I must have been crazy to do this." As it turns out, I may have been wrong. Either that, or the craziness I suspected at the time has taken permanent hold of my senses. With this book, which you now hold in your hands, I've learned that even a difficult undertaking can be exciting, rewarding, and fun, a feeling that I hope will echo in the words and pages that follow.

Nevertheless, I'm not sure that this is something I could have done on my own. Sure, I spent the hours writing the words, testing each command, and taking screenshots, but I was never alone. My wife, Sally, as well as my friends and family — all have played a part in the creation of this book. Their confidence, support, and love helped to keep me going even while I was revisiting my *"madness"* theory. I'd like to take a moment to recognize some of these people.

First and foremost, I have to thank my beautiful wife, Sally Tomasevic, first reviewer of everything I write. She is my inspiration and my strength.

Special thanks to my friend Robert J. Sawyer, who told me he desperately wanted this book — "I want you to write a book called **Kiss the Blue Screen of Death Goodbye** for me and people like me who want to move to Linux but don't know where to start." Well, Rob, here it is.

Many thanks to Richard Curtis, my agent. Thanks also to Mark Taub, my editor, and to everyone at my publisher, Addison-Wesley.

Sincere thanks to those people who reviewed my book along the way. They are (in alphabetical order by last name) Henry Ferlauto, Peter Halasz, Mark Halegua, Michael Jarvis, Carolyn Sinclair, and Sally Tomasevic. The process of reviewing is hard work and I truly appreciate their efforts, sharp eyes, and suggestions.

Finally, I would like to recognize and thank the Linux community: the developers and software designers, the members of Linux user groups (including my own WFTL-LUG), the many who share their experience on Usenet, and all those unnamed folks who give free advice under pseudonyms in IRC groups.

Thank you all.

chapter

1

Introduction

Welcome to the Linux universe, one and all!

Linux has finally hit the mainstream; so much so that the first question I get from people these days is no longer, "What is Linux?" but rather, "What do I have to do to get Linux on my system?" For those who may want some clarification nevertheless, Linux is a fully multitasking operating system based on UNIX, although technically, Linux is the kernel, the master program that makes running a Linux system possible. That kernel, by the way, was written by a young Finnish student named Linus Torvalds. On August 25, 1991, Torvalds posted this now famous (perhaps legendary) message to the Usenet group comp.os.minix:

```
From: torvalds@klaava.Helsinki.FI (Linus Benedict Torvalds)
      Newsgroups: comp.os.minix
      Subject: What would you like to see most in minix?
      Summary: small poll for my new operating system
      Message-ID:
<1991Aug25.205708.9541@klaava.Helsinki.FI>
      Date: 25 Aug 91 20:57:08 GMT
      Organization: University of Helsinki
      Hello everybody out there using minix -
      I'm doing a (free) operating system (just a hobby,
won't be big and professional like gnu) for 386(486) AT
clones. This has been brewing since april, and is starting
to get ready. I'd like any feedback on things people
like/dislike in minix, as my OS resembles it somewhat (same
physical layout of the file-system (due to practical rea-
sons) among other things).
      I've currently ported bash(1.08) and gcc(1.40), and
things seem to work. This implies that I'll get something
practical within a few months, and I'd like to know what
features most people would want. Any suggestions are wel-
come, but I won't promise I'll implement them :-)
                Linus (torvalds@kruuna.helsinki.fi)
      PS. Yes - it's free of any minix code, and it has a
multi-threaded fs. It is NOT protable (uses 386 task switch-
ing etc), and it probably never will support anything other
than AT-hard disks, as that's all I have :-(.
```

Much has happened since then. Linus somehow captured the imagination of scores of talented programmers around the world. Joined together through the magic of the Internet, they collaborated, coded, tweaked, and gave birth to the operating system that is now revolutionizing the world of computing.

These days, Linux is a powerful, reliable (rock-solid, in fact), expandable, flexible, configurable, multiuser, multitasking, and completely free operating system that runs on many different platforms. These include Intel PCs, DEC Alphas, Macintosh systems, PowerPCs, and a growing number of embedded processors. You can find Linux in PDA organizers, digital watches, golf carts, and cell phones. In fact, Linux has a greater support base (in terms of platforms) than just about any other operating system in the world.

What we call the Linux operating system is not the work of just one man alone. Linus Torvalds is the original architect of Linux—its father, if you will—but his is not the only effort behind it. Perhaps Linus Torvalds's greatest genius lay in knowing when to share the load. For no other pay but satisfaction, he employed people around the world, delegated to them, worked with them, and asked for and accepted feedback in a next generation of the model that began with the *GNU project*.

GNU, by the way, is a recursive acronym that stands for "GNU's Not UNIX," a project of the Free Software Foundation. This project was started in 1984 with the intention of creating a free, UNIX-like operating system. Over the years, many GNU tools were written and widely used by many commercial UNIX vendors and, of course, system administrators trying to get a job done. The appearance of Linus Torvalds's Linux kernel has made the GNU dream of a completely free, UNIX-like operating system a reality at last.

Is Linux Really FREE?

In a discussion of what *free* means in relation to software, you'll often see the expressions "free as in speech" or "free as in beer." Free, in this case, isn't a question of cost, although you can get a free copy (as in *free beer*) of Linux and install it on your system without breaking any laws. As Robert A. Heinlein would have said, "There ain't no such thing as a free lunch." A free download will still cost you connection time on the Internet, disk space, time to burn the CDs, and so on.

Walk into a computer software store and you'll see copies of Mandrake, SuSE, and Red Hat on the shelves, so this free software can also cost you money. On the other hand, those boxed sets come with documentation, support, and CDs, the latter saving you time and energy downloading and burning discs. Furthermore, there are boxed sets of varying prices, even within a distribution. For instance, you can buy a Red Hat personal or professional edition. The differences there may be additional software, documentation, or support.

Linux is distributed under the GNU General Public License (GPL), which, in essence, says that anyone may copy, distribute, and even sell the program, as long as changes to the source are reintroduced to the community and the terms of the license remain unaltered. Free means that you are free to take Linux, modify it, and create your own version. Free means that you are not at the mercy of a single vendor who forces you into a kind of corporate servitude by making sure that it is extremely costly to convert to another environment. If you are unhappy with your Linux vendor or the support you are getting, you can move to the next vendor without forfeiting your investment in Linux.

In other words, "free as in speech"—or freedom.

The GPL

The GNU GPL permits a distributor to "charge a fee for the physical act of transferring a copy, and you may at your option offer warranty protection in exchange for a fee." This is further qualified by the statement that the distributor must release "for a charge no more than your cost of physically performing source distribution, a complete machine-readable copy of the corresponding source code." In other words, the GPL ensures that programs like Linux will at best be free of charge. At worst, you may be asked to pay for the cost of a copy.

You should take some time to read the GNU GPL. For your convenience, I've reprinted it in Appendix A of this book.

So What Do I Gain?

No operating system is perfect, and nothing comes without some hassles, but as time goes on, Linux is getting closer and closer to perfection. These days, Linux is even easier to install than your old operating system, and you don't have to reboot time and again as you load driver disk after driver disk. I won't bore you with everything I consider an advantage but I will give you a few of the more important points.

Security

Say goodbye to your virus checker and stop worrying. Although Linux is not 100% immune to viruses, it comes pretty close. In fact, to date, most so-called Linux viruses do not exist *in the wild* (only under tightly controlled environments in *proof-of-concept* labs). It isn't that no one has tried, but the design model behind Linux means that it is built with security in mind. Consequently, viruses are virtually nonexistent in the Linux world, and security issues are dealt with quickly and efficiently by the Linux community. Security flaws are well advertised. It isn't unusual for a security hole to be discovered and a fix created within a few short hours of the discovery. If something does present a risk, you won't have to wait for the next release of your operating system to come along.

Stability

The stability of Linux is almost legendary. Living in a world where people are used to rebooting their PCs one or more times a day, Linux users talk about running weeks and sometimes months without a reboot. *"Illegal operations"* and the *"Blue Screen of Death"* are not part of the Linux experience. Sure, programs occasionally crash here as well, but they don't generally take down your *whole* system with them.

Power

Linux is a multitasking, multiuser operating system. In this book, I concentrate on the desktop features of Linux, but under the hood, Linux is a system designed to provide all the power and flexibility of an enterprise-class server. Linux-powered Web site servers and electronic mail gateways move information along on the Internet and run small to large businesses. Under the friendly face of your graphical desktop, that power is still there.

Money

It is possible to do everything you need to do on a computer without spending any money on software—that means new software and upgrades alike. In fact, free software for Linux is almost an embarrassment of riches. In Chapter 7, I'll show you how to install (or remove) additional software on your Linux system.

Freedom from Legal Hassles

When you run Linux, you don't have to worry about whether you've kept a copy of your operating system license. The GNU GPL, which I mentioned earlier, means you are legally entitled to copy and can legally redistribute your Linux CDs if you wish.

Keep in mind, however, that although Linux itself can be freely distributed, *not all software* that runs on Linux is covered by the same license. If you buy or download software for your system, you should still pay attention to the license that covers that software.

What Do I Lose?

Nothing ever seems to be perfect. By moving to Linux you gain a great deal, but I would be doing a disservice if I did not mention the disadvantages.

Hardware and Peripheral Support

The hardware support for Linux is, quite honestly, among the best there is. In fact, when you consider all the platforms that run Linux, its hardware and peripheral support is better than that of the Windows system you are leaving behind. Unfortunately, there are some consumer devices designed with Windows specifically in mind. Consequently, certain printers or scanners may have limited support under Linux because the manufacturer is slow in providing drivers.

On the upside, you'll find that where you always had to load drivers to make something run in your old OS, Linux automatically recognizes and supports an amazing number of peripherals without you having to do anything extra or hunt down a driver disk. Furthermore, the Linux community is vibrant in a way that few businesses can ever hope to be. If you have your eye on a hot new piece of hardware, you can almost bet that some Linux developer somewhere has an eye on exactly the same thing. Chances are it won't be long before your dream device is part of standard Linux.

We'll talk about devices and device drivers later in the book.

Software Packages

There is a huge amount of software available for the Linux operating system; unfortunately, most of it is not commercial. On the one hand, you can download *thousands* of games, tools, and Internet and office applications to run on your system. Much of it will cost you nothing more than the time it takes to download it.

On the other hand, commercial, shrink-wrapped software, including those hot new 3D games at your local computer store, is still hard to come by. As Linux grows in popularity, particularly on the desktop, this is starting to change.

That said, there is software available for Linux that makes it possible to run Windows software. I'll talk more about that in the next chapter.

A Step into the Unknown

Let's face it. For some, moving to Linux is a step into the unknown. Things won't be exactly as they were with your old operating system, and for the most part, this is a good thing. You will have to do a little relearning and get used to a different way of doing things.

Even so, if you are used to working in your Windows graphical environment and you are comfortable with basic mousing skills, writing the occasional email, surfing the Web, or composing a memo in your word processor, moving to

Linux won't be a big deal. Your Linux desktop is a modern graphical environment, and much of what you have learned in your old operating system can be taken with you into this new world.

Some Tips on Using this Book

My intention in creating this book is to provide a simple move from your old OS to Linux. I'll cover things such as installation shortly, but the majority of the book has to do with working (and playing) in your new Linux environment. I want to show you how to do the things you have grown used to doing: surfing the Net, writing emails, listening to music, printing, burning CDs, and so on. Furthermore, I am going to tell you how to take those Word documents, Excel spreadsheets, and music files you have collected over time and start using them with Linux. In short, my plan is to have you move as effortlessly as possible from your old OS to Linux.

Working your way through the chapters, you'll notice that I am constantly inviting you to try things. That's because I believe the best way to learn anything is by doing. Yes, you're going to learn to work with a new operating system, but it doesn't mean you can't have fun. As everyone knows, all work and no play will make anyone pretty dull. Later on in this book (in an effort to avoid dullness), I'll take you into the world of Linux fun and games.

Quick Tips and Shelling Out

Throughout the book, I will occasionally provide you with boxed asides, "Quick tips" that should serve as little reminders or simpler ways to do things.

You'll also notice boxes that start out with the phrase "Shell out." Although I intend to concentrate on working with graphical tools and in a graphical way, much of the power of Linux comes from working with the command line, or the *shell*. The "Shell out" boxes will guide you in working with the shell.

Learning to wield the command line is akin to getting a black belt in a martial art or earning a first aid certificate. It doesn't mean that you are going to run out and take on all comers or that you are going to be facing daily crisis situations. What working with the shell does is give you the means and the confidence to step outside the confines of the graphical environment. The shell is power, and it is always there for you, so you should not fear it.

Meet Your Desktop

Modern Linux distributions come with powerful, easy-to-use graphical environments. There are many such environments, and in time, you will learn about them. Part of that freedom I spoke about is the freedom to do things your way, and that extends to the type of graphical environment you may want to work in. The most popular desktop environments today are the K Desktop Environment (KDE) and GNOME, but WindowMaker, IceWM, and others have quite a following, as well. *My* personal choice is KDE, but I often switch to other desktops when the mood takes me.

Although much of what you do with GNOME or KDE is pretty interchangeable, it makes sense in a book like this to pick one and run with it. Consequently, we will concentrate on the KDE desktop, primarily version 3.1 (although much of what I cover is very similar to what you would see in release 3.0).

KDE comes with most major distributions, including SuSE, Red Hat, SCO, Mandrake, and others. I recommend KDE because it is more mature, beautiful, and better developed than the alternatives (yes, some of this is partly my opinion). It sports a clean, consistent, and integrated set of tools, widgets, and menus. Because of all these things, KDE is also much easier and friendlier to work with. In fact, many Linux companies install KDE as the default.

When you become comfortable with KDE and Linux, I invite you to experiment with other desktop environments. *Exercise your freedom to be yourself.*

Help Me!

Once you are done working with this book, I am confident that Linux will be your operating system of choice for the foreseeable future. That doesn't mean you won't have questions that aren't answered in this book. To that end, I give you a Web site address that will link you to the support pages for this book on my own Web site:

```
http://www.marcelgagne.com
```

My site has links to a number of other resources, including many articles I have written on using and administering Linux, links to other information sites, and much more. Click on the KBSODG link, and you'll be transported to the support pages for this book.

I also run a few mailing lists for readers, which you'll find under the WFTL heading. WFTL is a short form I've used for years now. It stands for "Writer and Free Thinker at Large" (computer people love acronyms). It's also the hierarchy for the lists I'm talking about. One of those lists is the WFTL-LUG (a LUG is a Linux User Group), an online discussion group where readers can share information, ask questions, and help each other out with their various Linux adventures. I invite you to join any of the lists I offer there. There is *no cost*, and you can unsubscribe at any time.

If you check under the Linux Links menu of my Web site, you'll find a useful list of additional links to Linux information sources. One of these is the Linux Documentation Project (LDP).

The Linux Documentation Project

The LDP is a dynamic community resource. On your Linux distribution CD, you probably have a collection of documents known in the Linux world as *HOWTOs*. These are user- or developer-contributed documents that are maintained and updated by one or more individuals. You can find the latest version of these documents at the LDP site:

```
http://www.tldp.org/
```

The mandate of the LDP is essentially to provide a comprehensive base of documentation for all things Linux. If you've been looking high and low for information on installing that bleeding-edge FTL radio card on your PC and still haven't found what you are looking for, try the LDP. The LDP also makes a point of offering the latest versions of the man pages, as well as user guides that tend to cover more ground than standard HOWTOs.

Linux User Groups

A few paragraphs back, I made passing reference to Linux User Groups, or LUGs. Let's put technology aside for a moment and explore something else you may have heard about: the Linux community. Yes, there really is a Linux community. All around the world, you will find groups of enthusiastic Linux users gathering for regular meetings, chatting over beer and pizza, and sharing information. This sharing of information is part of what makes Linux so friendly.

LUGs tend to run electronic mailing lists where informal exchanges of information take place (just as I do with my online LUG). New users are welcomed, and their questions are happily answered. These users range from newbies getting their feet wet to seasoned kernel developers. Should you find yourself stuck with nowhere to turn, seek out your local LUG and sign on to the mailing list. Today, someone helps you. As you grow more knowledgeable in administering your Linux system, maybe you will return the favor.

Locating a LUG in your community is as simple as surfing over to the Linux Online Web site (`http://www.linux.org/`). Once there, click the User Groups button, and you are on your way. The list is organized by country, then by state or province, and so on.

About the CD

Included with this book is a full-featured Linux distribution called *Knoppix*.

Knoppix is a Debian-based Linux distribution that runs entirely from your PC's CD-ROM drive (though slower than if you actually install Linux). That's right. You can run Linux on your system without having to change your system or uninstall Windows.

 Note The version of Knoppix included with this book is *not* the official version but one that has been slightly modified by this humble author. I wish to express my admiration and thanks to Klaus Knopper, the creator of Knoppix, for his fine work, but any questions regarding the included disk should be directed to me.

This CD is full of great software, some of which I will be covering in this book. You'll have access to email applications, Web browsers, word processors, spreadsheets, games, and more. In fact, you should be able to follow along with this book and do many—*though not all*—of the things I talk about without having to install Linux at all. The bootable CD is a fantastic introduction, but there are limitations.

The first limitation is one I have already mentioned, but it bears mentioning again. The CD does run *much slower* than a hard-disk install, so keep in mind that the performance you experience from the CD is not indicative of the performance you can experience from a Linux hard-disk install. At their fastest, CD-ROM drives are no match for even the slowest hard disk drive. Furthermore, because this bootable Linux does not install itself on your hard drive, you are limited to the packages on the CD. In other words, you can't add or install any new software. If you are truly ready to make the move to Linux, consider installing a full distribution, a topic I will cover in the next two chapters.

Want to Try Linux Right Now?

Loading Knoppix is easy.

Take your CD and insert it into your CD-ROM drive. Shut down Windows, and select Restart. Make sure your PC is set to boot from the CD. Knoppix boots up to a nice, graphical screen with a simple `boot:` prompt, from which you can simply press <Enter> and let Knoppix do the rest; this is an amazingly simple *install*.

Quick Tip Many systems are set to boot directly from the CD-ROM drive if a bootable CD is found there. If your system does not, you may have to change the BIOS settings on your PC to allow this. This is generally done by pressing <Delete> or <F2> to enter Setup as the system is booting (you will usually see such a message before the operating system starts to load). Because the menus vary, it is impossible for me to cover them all, but look for a menu option that specifies the boot order. You'll see something like A: first, then C: (i.e., your floppy drive, then the hard disk). Change the boot order so that it looks to the CD first, save your changes, then restart your system.

The boot process is all text, but it is certainly colorful because Knoppix identifies devices, disks, sound cards, and so on in different colors. At some point, the screen will go dark as your video card is configured and X, the Linux graphical user interface, is started. If the screen doesn't respond instantly, don't panic. Give it a few seconds. If nothing has happened even after you've waited a while, it is possible that your video card is one of the rare ones not included in the distribution. Never fear, most (if not all) modern cards support VESA. Reboot and type the following at the boot prompt.

```
knoppix xmodule=vesa
```

Once the system has booted, you can start playing with Knoppix. You can speed things up a bit right off the bat by letting Knoppix create a *swap file* in your Windows partition. This won't hurt anything on your system. All it does is allow Linux to use some of your disk space as though it were real memory. That is what we mean by *swap space*. Doing this is easy. Click on KDE's program launcher (the big K in the lower left-hand corner), and move your cursor up to the KNOPPIX entry in the menu. There are four submenus here; one of them is Configure; under that menu, you'll see an entry labeled *SWAP file configuration*. Click this option, and you'll get a nice little warning that you are about to create a file named *knoppix.swp* on your existing DOS (Windows) partition. Click Yes, after which you'll be asked for the size of your swap file in megabytes. What qualifies as a good size depends on how much real memory you already have, but taking the default is probably a good bet.

While we are busy looking at the Configure menu, notice that you can configure a printer and sound card, as well (both local and network connected).

Before I move on, I'd like to point out one final item on this KNOPPIX menu, *Save KNOPPIX configuration*. As you go along, you'll be making some changes, such as configuring printers or setting up your network. Using this menu option, you can save all of these configuration details to a diskette. The next time you boot Knoppix, make sure the diskette is in your drive and enter this command at the boot prompt:

```
knoppix floppyconf
```

One of the other items under the KNOPPIX menu is Network/Internet. From here, you can setup an ADSL/PPPOE connection (for your local phone company's high-speed service), a dial-up modem, a network card, and so on. For network access, simply choose whatever makes sense for your setup, and answer the questions that follow. I will be covering Internet access and network tools later in the book.

I'm going to leave the discussion of Knoppix right here. Using this bootable Linux and this book, you should be able to get a pretty good handle on Linux without sacrificing your system but at some point, you will want to go further. Although you could just skip to Chapter 4 and continue with your introduction to Linux, you might still want to read the other two chapters. They discuss where and how to get a full Linux distribution and how to install it.

It's My Philosophy

I have a philosophy. All right, I have *many*, and this is just one of them.

Every once in a while, people tell me that desktop Linux is just crazy, that it is just too complicated for *the majority of people*.

I don't know about you, but I am tired of being told that people can't learn to use something that is both good and powerful. With a certain amount of training and a little proper guidance, *anyone who is familiar with a computer can learn to use Linux*.

That isn't to say that working with Linux is difficult (it is not), but as you go along, you will be learning new things. This book is meant for users at every level of experience. It is meant to be read for fun, as well as for reference. And because I'll ask you to try things throughout this book, it's a training guide, as well.

I'm delighted and thrilled that you've decided to join me in *Moving to Linux*. It's time to kiss the Blue Screen of Death goodbye!

Resources

Linux Documentation Project

http://www.tldp.org

Linux.org List of LUGs

http://www.linux.org/groups/index.html

Linux User Groups Worldwide

http://lugww.counter.li.org/groups.cms

Marcel (Writer and Free Thinker at Large) Gagné's Web site

http://www.marcelgagne.com

chapter

2

Ready . . . Set . . . Linux!

Ready for some serious fun?

Your Linux adventure is about to begin. To really get going, though, you need to deal with two major things. First and foremost, you need to get a copy of Linux. You may have chosen to try things out using the bootable Knoppix CD, but at some point (perhaps even now), you may want to do a proper hard-disk install.

The second thing we will need to take care of is important only if you have Windows on your system and there is data you need to preserve and migrate. Let's start with the first step.

Getting Linux

This one is actually the easy part.

One way to get Linux is to buy a copy. Head down to your local computer software store and ask for your favorite distribution. Alternatively, visit your favorite vendor's Web site, whether it be Mandrake, SuSE, Red Hat, or any of the many different distributions listed on the DistroWatch (`http://www.distrowatch.com`) Web site and order one online. Incidentally, DistroWatch also lists the top 10 major distributions at any given time.

Which distribution should you get? Well, every Linux vendor does things a little differently. If you think of this in terms of cars, it starts to make sense. Every single car out there is basically an engine on wheels with seats and some kind of steering mechanism so that drivers can get to where they want to go. What kind of car you buy depends on what else you expect from a car, whether that is comfort, style, the vendor's reputation, or any great number of other choices.

 Recommendation You *really* want me to suggest something? Let me start by saying that I think it is a wonderful thing that so many Linux distributions exist. Aside from creating a rich OS landscape, it furthers creativity and fosters innovation in software design. This can only be a good thing. However, if you *push* me for a suggestion and you are *just getting started* with Linux, I would probably suggest Mandrake first. It's an excellent, well-engineered, and beginner-friendly Linux.

You might be asking the question, *If I can get a free copy of Linux, why would I want to pay for one?* As it turns out, there is more than one answer to that question. The first is that buying a boxed set usually gets you some amount of technical support from the vendor. If you are feeling nervous about your first Linux installation, this might be a good reason. Second, the boxed set usually contains some kind of manual or manuals *specific* to that version of Linux. That will inevitably lead to another question as to what makes this Linux different from that one. Finally, in purchasing a boxed set, you are supporting the company that put leather on the seats or tinted the windows. It's a way of saying, "Thanks for all the hard work."

Because it is possible to get a free copy of Linux, you don't have to shell out the dollars if you don't want to. At most, you'll need a fast Internet connection, a CD burner, and some blank CDs—or a helpful friend who has these.

Getting a Free Copy of Linux

The idea of free software—a free operating system in particular—takes some getting used to, but it happens fast. When you are working with other operating systems, getting and trying new releases involves some kind of cash outlay. In the case of Linux, the most you need is a spare machine on which to play. Consequently, you can load one version of Linux, take it for a spin, then load another and see whether that feels any better to you.

If you have a high-speed Internet connection (and a CD burner), you can visit any of the vendors' sites listed at the end of this chapter and download their latest and greatest. Remember, though, that although you may download their latest Linux free of charge, technical support may still be an extra cost.

If you don't like the idea of visiting each and every one of those sites, a visit to LinuxIso.org (`http://www.linuxiso.org/`) may be in order. This site provides you with a one-stop shop for the more popular Linux distributions with ISOs (CD-ROM images) available for download.

Package Managers and Updates

Package managers often have a great deal to do with what people end up choosing in terms of a distribution. In this book, I'll be talking about installing software using RPM, and every distribution I mentioned above uses RPM as the package manager, so the information you take with you will work with any of these releases. I have also developed a great respect for the power and simplicity of Debian's apt-get program. In fact, you now get apt-get for RPM-based systems.

The method of update is also worthy of consideration. Many vendors now provide an option for updating and patching your system online. As long as you have a fast Internet connection, you are all set. Finally, here's the great disclaimer of the decade: Linux, like all dynamic, living things, is evolving and changing. It is a moving target and, consequently, the details of a specific distribution will change over time. In the next chapter, I'll cover three major distributions and their installation procedures to give you an idea of what you can expect to see. For now, let's talk about what you are going to need in preparation for getting Linux on your system.

Dual Booting

As much as I would like to think that each and every one of you is more than ready to say goodbye forever to your old operating system and hello to Linux, I know that for many this is a *very big* jump. If you are still feeling a little insecure about simply breaking free and running Linux, I'm here to tell you that you can get the best of both worlds. It is called *dual booting*.

Dual booting refers to the technique of making a home for both operating systems on your machine. When you start your computer, a small program called a *boot loader* offers you a menu of choices from which you can decide to boot Linux or whatever other operating system you have installed. That boot loader, for the most part, is called *Grand Unified Bootloader* (GRUB). A second and still very common boot loader is called *LILO*, the Linux Loader.

When you load Linux on a system that already has Windows installed, your new system is smart enough to recognize the existence of this other operating system. You'll find that an entry for both your operating systems will magically appear in your boot loader menu.

Preserving Your Data

When you've been using a computer for a long time, you amass a lot of data. Forget software—*the data is the most important thing on your system*, and you need to get it backed up. Whether you dual boot or not, I want to stress that you are going to be doing some major changes to your hard disk. Please don't take any chances with your data. Make a backup.

Because Windows backup programs aren't necessarily going to be helpful in getting your data onto a Linux system, you should copy the various word processing documents, spreadsheets, graphics (all those pictures you took with your digital camera), music files, and anything else that you will want later onto some kind of media, whether it is a ZIP drive, diskettes, or a CD.

If you have large amounts of data, it might make sense to keep a Windows partition around long enough to copy from one to the other. Most of the major Linux distributions will not only notice the existence of your Windows partition, they will also provide you with an icon on your desktop so that you can easily access that data. Although this may seem like a great way to avoid backing up your data, *please* don't ignore this step. In fact, if you haven't been backing up your system, your system has been *living* on borrowed time. *If in doubt, back up*.

A Linux-Only System

This is by far the easiest alternative because you don't have to worry about keeping an intact copy of something else on the system. This represents quite the leap because there is no going back (without reinstalling from scratch). If you go down this road, you have access to all your disk space, and Linux uses disk space more efficiently. You can also kiss those proprietary licensing issues goodbye (not to mention the Blue Screen of Death).

When you are ready to install, simply choose the option that will overwrite the entire system. The installation process will take care of the rest for you. It's that simple.

Windows on Linux

Under Linux, it is possible to run a number of Windows applications without having Windows installed at all. This is done with Wine. I'm not talking about the fermented beverage some of us are quite fond of, but a package that runs on Linux. Allow me to paraphrase from the Wine Web site . . . *Wine Is Not an Emulator*. Wine is a compatibility layer, a set of APIs that enable some Windows applications to operate on a Linux system running the X window system (the Linux graphical environment).

Wine will not run every Windows application, but the number of applications it is capable of running is increasing all the time. Some commercial vendors have ported certain Windows applications to Linux by making some of the code run in Wine. This has sped up the normal production cycle and made it possible for them to get their programs to Linux users faster.

 Wine Tip When it comes to Wine (the software), younger is most definitely better. A well-aged Wine (the software) will not be as good at running your Windows software as a brand new Wine. As for wine (the beverage), aging is certainly a good thing, but there are limits. As a rule, reds can age longer than whites, but it all depends on the variety. Consult your local wine vendor or pick up a good book on the subject.

Many Linux distributions include a version of Wine on the CDs, and some let you select Windows compatibility applications as part of the installation procedure. Keep in mind that the newer your Wine, the better. For the latest and greatest on Wine development, visit the Wine Web site (http://www.winehq.com/). A great deal of Wine development is being done at CodeWeavers (http://www.codeweavers.com/). Its version provides an installation wizard to guide you through the installation and configuration process for Wine. It makes the whole process extremely simple.

VMware

The Wine project has done some impressive work, but it will not run all Windows applications. Sometimes you just need to run the whole shebang, and that means a *full* copy of Windows. Because you don't want to boot back and forth between Linux and Windows, it would be great if you could run Windows entirely on your Linux machine. This is the philosophy behind VMware—and it doesn't stop there.

VMware enables you to create virtual machines on your computer. Complete with boot-up BIOS and memory checks, VMware virtualizes your entire hardware configuration, making the PC inside the PC as real as the one you are running. Furthermore, VMware enables you to run (not emulate) Windows 95, 98, 2000, NT, FreeBSD, or other Linuxes. For the developer or support person who needs to work (or write code) on different platforms, this is an incredible package. Yes, you can even run another Linux on your Linux, making it possible to test (or play with) different releases without reinstalling on a separate machine. VMware knows enough to share your printers, network cards, and so on. You can even network between the "real" machine and the virtual machine as though they were two separate systems.

All this capability comes at a price, however. Aside from the dollars that you spend on this package (and it can be well worth it), there is a considerable price in performance. VMware is a hungry beast. The more processor power and memory you have, the better. A Pentium III with 96 or more megabytes should be your starting point. Unlike Wine, you do need a licensed copy of Windows (or whatever OS you are installing) to run.

VMware comes in a variety of packages and price points. Visit the VMware Web site (http://www.vmware.com/) for details.

Win4Lin

Another alternative still requires a licensed copy of Windows. Netraverse (http://www.netraverse.com) sells a package called *Win4Lin*. This is a package designed to let you run Windows on your system but unlike VMware, *only* Windows (95, 98, and ME at this writing). It is, however, somewhat less expensive than VMware. Once again, remember that because you aren't *emulating* Windows but actually running a copy, you still need that licensed copy of Windows.

Win4Lin's magic is performed at the kernel level. Consequently, this requires that you download a patched kernel equivalent to what you are currently running or that you patch and rebuild your own. If you have compiled custom drivers into your kernel, you are going to have to go through the process again to get Win4Lin going.

What I have found interesting is that Windows installs and loads much faster under Linux than in native mode. Win4Lin works very well indeed and requires surprisingly little in terms of resources. I have run it on a Pentium 233 notebook with 64MB of RAM and found that it was reasonably peppy. You do take a performance hit, but it feels minor and should not distract you under most circumstances.

Breaking Free!

You may not need to go through any of these hoops to preserve your old operating system. As you go through this book, you may find that all of your needs are met just running Linux. There are plenty of applications as slick and as capable as anything in the Windows world.

Why go back and forth when you can just go forward? On that note, let's turn the page to Chapter 3 and get Linux installed on your system.

Resources

CodeWeavers

http://www.codeweavers.com

Debian

http://www.debian.org

DistroWatch (for a great distribution roundup)

http://www.distrowatch.com

Linux.org

http://www.linux.org

Mandrake

http://www.mandrakelinux.com

Red Hat Software

http://www.redhat.com

Slackware Linux

http://www.slackware.org

SuSE Linux

http://www.suse.com

VMware

http://www.vmware.com

Win4Lin Web Site

http://www.netraverse.com

WINE Project

http://www.winehq.com

chapter
3

The Installation

Somewhere back in the introduction, I mentioned that I would be basing a great deal of the desktop on KDE version 3 (both 3.0 and 3.1). From the Linux installation perspective, this implies that you are planning to run a modern Linux distribution and not some disks you've had lying around for the last three years. An up-to-date release of your favorite distribution, whether it is Red Hat, SuSE, Mandrake, or something else is essential.

A modern Linux installation is easy. I will go so far as to say that it is even easier than installing Windows. For the most part, you boot from your CD-ROM drive, click Next a few times and you are running Linux. Okay, perhaps there is a bit more to it than that, but not much. Linux will, for the most part, auto-detect nearly all devices on your machine and automatically configure things optimally.

Getting Ready for Your Installation

If your machine has Windows already, installed and you have documents, spreadsheets, pictures, or music files that you wish to keep, now would be a good time to back those things up, either on diskette or burned to a CD-ROM. Even if you plan on preserving your Windows installation for a dual-boot system, it's always prudent to have a good backup if you are going to be doing major work on your hard disk. You might also want to take advantage of all the hard work that was done in pre-installing Windows and make notes on all the hardware in your machine—the type of network and video cards and anything else you can think of. You do that by clicking the Start button, selecting Settings, Control Panel, then double-clicking the System icon. Now walk through the hardware profiles and take some notes. Odds are you won't need it at all, but you can never have too much information.

The average Linux installation takes about 30-60 minutes, although I have seen it take as little as 5 minutes on a really fast system. That's a fully network-ready, configured, all-set-to-work machine with no rebooting every few minutes to load another driver. It doesn't get much easier than this.

That said, unless you are feeling particularly adventurous, I would highly recommend that you read through this chapter once before actually starting.

Hardware Considerations

Before we move on, let's talk hardware. The sad truth is that not every device will work with Linux. You should not think of this as being strange, or somehow representing a weakness in Linux. After all, Linux is not unique in this. In fact, Linux may be fairly unique when it comes to the sheer number of devices and platforms that it supports. Linux will run on Intel-based systems as well as Alpha, RISC, and Macintosh. IBM's entire line of computers, from small, desktop PCs to large mainframe systems such as the S/390, run Linux. Then there are MIPS, SPARC, and StrongARM. You can also find Linux embedded in microchips, running on portable MP3 players, PDAs, cell phones, even on digital watches. That's incredible hardware support!

From the perspective of your computer, it is highly unlikely that Linux won't install and run well. Should something be unsupported, it would probably be some Windows-only modems, printers, or scanners. To find out whether or not your computer and its associated devices will work with your Linux installation, the first place to look is your Linux vendor's Web site. Another great hardware resource is the Hardware HOWTO. You can always find the latest version by surfing on over to the LDP's Linux Hardware Compatibility HOWTO page (http://www.tldp/HOWTO/Hardware-HOWTO/).

As Linux gains in popularity, you'll find that hardware vendors are increasingly interested in tapping into this ever-growing market. I've had the experience of being on site, adding hardware to a customer's system (Ethernet cards come immediately to mind), and finding that the system did not have the drivers. I quickly visited the Ethernet card manufacturer's Web site and found precompiled drivers ready and waiting for me. With the incredible growth of Linux, it won't be long before these issues will be a thing of the past.

Dual Booting Revisited

In the last chapter, I mentioned dual-booting, a means by which you can run both Linux and Windows on one machine. At boot time, a menu lets you start one *or* the other. Let's pretend for a moment that you still want to run Windows from time to time. Perhaps you want the comfort of knowing that you can go back to your old operating system to do certain things. This is where dual-booting comes into play. There are a couple of ways to do this and I will get to those in a moment. Please note, however, that doing this will require a little more up-front work.

One dual-boot scenario involves a completely separate disk that you can dedicate to a Linux installation. Although this is an ideal situation, most people will have a single disk with Windows already loaded. If you have a large disk, there is a good chance that there are already two partitions. One will be a C: drive and the other a D: drive. What you want to do is erase the D: drive and use it for Linux. If you are going to follow this route, make sure you back up any documents or copy them into folders on your C: drive.

Unfortunately, Windows is just as likely to be taking up the entire partition table. The trick is to *shrink* the existing Windows partition, thereby creating some space on which to install Linux. To do this, you must defragment your disk in Windows before going ahead and resizing your partitions. You do this by clicking the Start button and then selecting Programs | Accessories | System Tools | Disk Defragmenter.

Resizing the partition is your next step. Once again, there are two ways of doing this. Some recent distributions such as Mandrake or SuSE will automatically detect a Windows-only disk and offer to shrink the partition for you. Alternatively, you can do this with a little DOS program called *FIPS*, which you can find on your Linux distribution CD. On Debian, check the tools directory. On Red Hat or SuSE, check the dosutils directory.

In most cases, there will probably be a directory called `FIPS` or `FIPS20` with a number of files inside, including the `FIPS.EXE` program itself.

A Sample FIPS Session

 Warning When doing anything this drastic with your drives, *always* make a backup. In fact, no matter what you do with your system, always make regular backups.

Let's pretend that you've already run your defragmenter and that you have plenty of space on your hard drive. Start by creating a DOS/Windows boot diskette. This is generally done by typing the following command from the DOS/Windows command prompt (after inserting a blank diskette into the diskette drive).

```
FORMAT A: /S
```

The "/S" tells DOS/Windows to transfer the system to the boot diskette. You will also want to have a second boot diskette handy in order to do this a second time. You'll need it to back up your boot sector. I'll explain why in a moment. Next copy the FIPS.EXE utility and its associated files from the CDROM drive to the first diskette:

```
COPY D:\DOSUTILS\FIPS20\*.* A:
```

Remember that the path to the FIPS20 directory may vary depending on your distribution CD. Now, shut down Windows and boot from the FIPS diskette. When the boot completes, you should be at a DOS prompt. This is where the split occurs. Now, run the FIPS command:

```
FIPS
```

FIPS will display a partition table showing you how the disk space has been allocated. FIPS will ask which partition you want to split. Given that we are taking these steps, there is only one partition; that makes it easy. Enter the partition number and press <Enter>. As a precaution, FIPS will ask you whether you want to make a copy of your boot sector on the remote chance that disaster strikes. You probably want to answer Y (yes) to the question. This will require a second, pre-formatted diskette. Put in your second diskette and answer Y to the next question; *"Do you have a bootable floppy disk in drive A: as described in the documentation (y/n)?"* Since you have just inserted the diskette, press *<Enter>*.

Now the fun begins. FIPS will display your partition table. Using the left and right cursor (arrow) keys, change the size of the partition (you'll see the numbers changing each time you press the keys). When you are happy with your changes, press <Enter>. FIPS will ask you to confirm the changes. You can still change your mind at this time. If everything looks good, press <c> to continue, then type y when asked if you are *"Ready to write the new partition scheme to disk?"*.

When FIPS completes, you will reboot your system. You might want to reboot into Windows first just to make sure that things are working properly. If everything looks as you want it to, pop in your Linux installation CD, shut down Windows, and reboot the system.

Windows XP Considerations

Before we get into those details, please take note of the following statement.

 Important Note Although the install tools included on the distribution CDs are very good at determining the presence of a Windows 95, 98, or ME partition and shrinking those for you, most *can not* shrink a Windows XP NTFS partition. At the time of this writing, there was one **exception** to the rule— **Mandrake 9.1** included a tool that could resize NTFS partitions, but it was the only one.

What that means, unfortunately, is that FIPS and the magical tools included as part of the Linux install CD won't work here. Once again, there are two possibilities. One is to get your hands on a product called *PartitionMagic* (http://www.partitionmagic.com/), an alternative to using FIPS. It's a nice, friendly, commercial package that enables you to modify partitions on the fly, including NTFS partitions such as those found on Windows XP systems.

The second option is to back up your data, reformat your hard drive, and reinstall Windows XP from scratch, this time making sure that only half (or a third or quarter) of your disk has been allocated to Windows. Please be sure that you are completely comfortable with the idea of reinstalling XP before you proceed.

There is a third option, of course. Install Linux and forget about XP.

An Installation Comparison

Modern installations offer a nice, graphical process and for the most part, installing Linux today is a point-and-click experience with help every step of the way. Of course, a graphical installation makes a lot of assumptions that you might not necessarily want. Should all else fail, try the text-based installation. Most distributions still provide one, and I don't see that changing anytime soon.

A Very Generic Install

Every installation is similar in many ways, though the order of the steps may vary slightly. After booting, you get a nice welcome screen usually followed by a request for the language you want to install in. Hot on the heels of this is some kind of basic peripheral selection, namely for your keyboard and mouse. You'll also be asked for the time zone you live in. Every installation will (somewhere near here) ask you for options on partitioning and formatting your drive. For most users, the defaults should be fine and your Windows partition (if you opted for a dual boot system) will be detected and set aside. This is also the point where you are asked to select a boot loader and to confirm the operating systems you want to be able to launch at boot time. Once again, this is particularly important if you are setting up a dual boot system.

After all these preliminary steps are taken care of, it is time to load your software. Some kind of default collection will be offered (ie: workstation, server, etc.) at which point your system starts to load. There may be one or more CDs to load depending on how much you asked for. Once this is over, it is time to configure your network connection, followed by the graphical window setup, also known as the X window system.

You will then get your first introduction to *Linux security*. The installer will ask you for an administrative user (root) password and provide you with the opportunity to create one or more additional users for day-to-day use. Under normal circumstances, the root user should not be used except to install software, or to update and administer your system in some fashion. The separation of administrative from *regular* users is one of the ways Linux protects your system from accidental or malicious damage.

Usually, that is pretty much it. The system will reboot and you'll be running Linux.

Note Installers tend to make fairly intelligent choices as you go. Nevertheless, you should still check to make sure that what is selected is what is indeed correct.

Remember that until you have actually formatted your drives, you can still change your mind about a great many of the decisions you made along the way. Just click the Back button (or use the <Tab> key to move to it) and reenter the information the way you intended.

Of course, my generic install is just that; generic. In order to give you an idea of just what you can expect when you go through the real thing, I have gone through *three different installations* using some of the more popular Linux distributions and detailed them for you here.

Note As of this writing, Mandrake 9.1 has just been released. RedHat 9 and SuSE 8.2 are expected shortly. I mention this because the screens you see may not be precisely as I describe here—not a great deal, but some things will be a bit different. That's why I want you to look at these install examples *as* examples. They are meant to prepare you for what you will experience during an installation.

The PC on which I did these installs already had Windows XP running. Half of the 60 gigabyte disk drive was unallocated. Actually, it was set up as a Windows D: drive but there was nothing on it and I simply deleted the drive. Let's start this look at Linux installations with one of the most popular distributions among Linux desktop users, Mandrake Linux.

Warning Almost any modern PC can boot from a CD-ROM and this is the easiest way to do this. If your system will not boot from the CD, you can create a boot diskette. If this is a problem for you, put your first Linux CD into the drive and use Windows Explorer (the file manager) to look for a directory called "boot" on the CD. There will be a boot disk image there (the name may vary) and instructions on how to create the diskette.

A Mandrake Linux Install

With this Mandrake install, I used version 9.0.

Reboot your system with the installation CD in the drive. Mandrake boots with a graphical screen with two options. Pressing <F1> will allow you to choose between text and low resolution install modes, while the default is the standard graphical install. Press <Enter> and you are on your way.

Basic hardware detection takes place at this time and the installer is loaded into memory. In a few seconds, you'll be at the main install screen. Mandrake uses a kind of drag racing metaphor for its install (Mandrake 9.1 does away with the lights, but the steps remain more or less the same). Down the left hand side of the screen is a series of lights that change from red to orange to green as you go through the various steps. Looking at the labels, it is very easy to see exactly what is going to happen during the process.

The first of these steps is to select a preferred language for installation and there are many. Select your language of choice or click OK to accept *United States English* and continue. On the next screen, read the license agreement (where you learn about the GPL and related licenses) and click Accept. Notice that the *"Choose your language"* light went green while the *"Select installation class"* light went from red to orange. Get the idea?

On the next screen, you'll be given the choice between a Recommended and an Expert install. Unless you are already feeling comfortable with this, click Install to accept the Recommended install. Then, the Mandrake install automatically detects your hard drive, mouse, and keyboard and those respective lights go green. Now it is time to set up your file systems. The options here involve erasing the entire disk, doing your own custom disk partitioning, or using the free space on the Windows partition. This is quite *interesting* because it makes it possible to automatically resize the Windows partition, making use of the free space in order to install Mandrake. You might remember from my earlier discussion that the only caveat is that Windows disk must be defragmented first. Remember also that this will not work with NTFS file systems (see earlier comments in this chapter).

The default option is to *"Use free space"* and that is probably what you should choose. Click OK to continue and the partitions will be created and formatted and a list of available packages will be pulled from the install disk. Now it is time to decide what kind of a system you want. You will be looking at the *Package Group Selection* screen. A standard Mandrake install is a Workstation install and that's where the emphasis is placed with the defaults. *Office Workstation* is automatically selected as is *Internet Station*. That means you get your word processors and spreadsheets as well as email clients and Web browsers. If I assume correctly, you will probably want to play games and music in which case you should click on *Game station* as well as *Multimedia station*.

Now, once again, I am going to point out that if you want to be able to compile programs (for those bleeding edge new programs), you should also click on *Development*. I would also recommend *Configuration* and *Console tools* to help with system configuration.

Before you move on, look over on the right and you'll notice a section called *Graphical Environment*. Notice that Mandrake knows that people will benefit from having both KDE and GNOME environments available and these are selected by default. If you would like to experiment with even more desktop environments at some future time, you might consider checking on *Other Graphical Desktops*. This loads WindowMaker, IceWM, and others.

Click OK and the package installation will begin. You'll be treated to a little slide show about Open Source software, Mandrake products, and information about the various things that come with your Mandrake system. In short, the show tells you why you are going to love working with Mandrake Linux. Depending on the choices you made, you may need to switch the CD at some point.

When the installation completes, you'll be asked to choose a root password after which you will have the opportunity to create one or more normal users. You really only need to create one at this time. Notice that the Mandrake install lets you choose a representative icon for your users. Just click on the icon and select one that suits you. *I particularly like the cat*. After entering your information, click *Accept user*, then click *Done* (unless you are adding multiple users, of course).

Mandrake will then ask you to choose your default Window manager. KDE is displayed as the default and that will do nicely. Click Yes to continue and you'll be taken to the *Network Configuration Wizard*. The install will try to determine if you are connected to an ADSL line, a cable modem, or a local LAN. Click OK to accept the choice (assuming it is correct). If you are on a LAN, you will now have a chance to enter your network and IP address information.

You then have the opportunity to configure a printer. Click Yes and the *Printer Setup Wizard* will appear. The Mandrake install can try to autodetect printers connected both locally and on the network. Network connected printers include Unix/Linux printers as well as printers connected to machines running Windows. You have the option of skipping network detection—if you have no shared printers on your network, you should. You might want to send a test page, just to make sure things are working correctly. If so, you can click Yes to the question *"Did it print properly?"* Unless you have more than one printer, you can click No when asked to configure additional units.

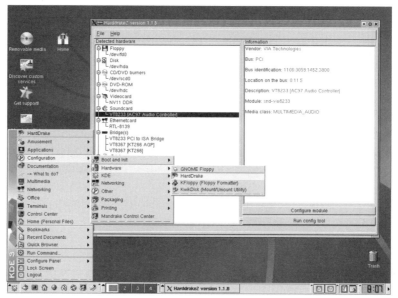

FIGURE 3-1   Mandrake 9.0's desktop.

The next screen is a summary screen. The install process tells you what mouse, keyboard, time zone, printer, and sound card have been configured. If everything looks good, just click OK. Almost there . . . now, it is time for your X window configuration. Mandrake should autodetect your video card and monitor resolution, but you do have the option of changing these as well. When you accept the settings, these settings will automatically be tested. You can click Yes to accept on the test screen.

You should now be at the last orange light—*Install system updates*. Ideally, you should have a live Internet connection at this point and high speed access because the packages can be *substantial*—downloading the updates can take a long time if your only connection is a dial-up modem. What Mandrake does here is provide you with a chance to load and install any updates and security fixes that may have been released since the OS first came out. Click Yes to start the update.

That's it. You are done. Click OK to reboot and make sure that you take the CD out of the drive when it is ejected.

Putting On The Red Hat

The version I used for this install was Red Hat 8.0.

Start by putting in the CD-ROM and rebooting your system. The boot menu will appear giving you the option of choosing either a graphical or text install. For almost every system out there, the graphical install will be just fine. All you need to do is click or press Install and the system will start booting. The system will identify devices and you'll see a number of messages scroll by.

A few seconds later, you'll see an interesting message. RedHat's install has a *media check* option. Here's the idea. You have your installation CDs, but you don't know for sure if there is some kind of surface defect that will make installation impossible. Isn't it better to find out before you start on all this work? You can choose to test each CD in your set before you proceed or you can simply skip the step.

After the media check option, the graphical install screen will appear. This is just a welcome screen and you can simply click Next and continue on. On the following screen, select the language you would like to use for the installation. I selected English and clicked Next again. What follows then is the keyboard selection screen. Once again, I selected the default of *U.S. English* and clicked Next which brings us to the mouse selection screen.

On the mouse selection screen, the installer will do an autodetect and make a selection. Make sure that the mouse selected is more or less what you have. Notice the *"Emulate 3 buttons"* option at the bottom of the screen. If you do not have a three button mouse, select this because the Linux graphical X window system makes use of all three buttons. Clicking the left and right button simultaneously is the same as clicking the middle button on a three button mouse.

The next screen is for installation type. The default option is *"Personal Desktop"* which RedHat suggests is *"Perfect for personal computers or laptops."* Most people will want to accept the default and click Next.

On the next screen, you can accept the default to allow the install to automatically partition your disk. After clicking Next, you will be given some choices on *Automatic Partitioning*, to decide how the installer would make use of the available space. The default is to *"Remove all Linux Partitions on this system"* and this is probably the right choice. If you want to double check the decisions made by the installer, make sure that you check off the option to *"Review (and modify if needed) the partitions created."*

A warning box will appear, letting you know that all data will be erased. Click OK. Depending on the size of your hard drive, you may get a warning to this effect—*"Boot partition /boot may not meet booting constraints for your architecture. Creation of a boot disk is highly encouraged."* We'll talk about a boot disk later.

The *Boot Loader configuration* is next. RedHat installs the GRUB boot loader by default, but it is possible to change it to LILO. Both work very well and in the end, it is your choice. I have personally grown to like GRUB quite a bit, but I still use LILO on other systems without a care. At this point, you also have the option of setting a password on the boot loader. Home users don't have to worry about this, but some network installations may want the additional security of having to enter a password when the system is booted. Before you move on, you may want to have a look at the labels the installer assigns. I mention this because if you are setting up a dual boot system, it will be identified as DOS. When you are happy with your choices, click Next.

The following screen is for network configuration. If you do not have a network card installed, you can skip to the next step. If your Internet connection is through a DSL or cable modem connection, that will likely be the case. The default is to boot and pull an address via DHCP and this is what you would choose. If your PC is on a home or corporate network with fixed addresses, you will want to click Edit, check off the *"Configure using DHCP"* and enter your address information. If you are in an office, check with your systems administrator for this information. Otherwise, enter your IP address and netmask, then click OK. Enter your hostname, gateway, and DNS information, then click Next.

The next section is very appropriate; the *Firewall Configuration* screen. There are many options here and you should take the time to read what each one offers. Network security is extremely important as the incidence of cyber-attacks continues to rise. Linux PCs aren't as susceptible to viruses, particularly if you don't run as the root or administrative user, but that doesn't mean you should let your guard down. If you are a single user on a home PC that is connected to the Internet, choose *High* and click Next.

What follows is yet another language selection screen (*Additional Language Support*). That's because the OS can support multiple languages and you can change that default at a later time. Unless you have another language at your disposal, leave the choice as it is and click Next. On the next screen, you will be asked to enter your time zone (in my case, I chose *America/Montreal*). When you are done, click Next.

When you arrive at the next screen, you will get your first taste of Linux's multi-user nature with the Account configuration. This is where you set your root password (root is the administrator login) and create other accounts. You should create at least one non-root account here before you continue on to the next screen, *Package selection*. If more than one person will be sharing this PC, you can enter their information here as well. You'll also have the opportunity to do this after the system is installed.

The packages selected for the *Personal Desktop* are as follows:

```
Desktop shell (GNOME)
Office Suite    (OpenOffice)
Web browser (Mozilla)
Email (Evolution)
Instant messaging
Sound and video applications
Games
```

Since I will be concentrating on KDE as the desktop, make sure that you click "*Customize the set of packages to be installed*" before you go on. Click Next and you will be on the *Package Group Selection* screen. You'll notice that packages are ordered into categories such as Desktops, Applications, and so on. Make sure that you check off the *KDE Desktop Environment* under Desktops. Then, click Details and make sure that *all* KDE packages have been selected before you click OK.

 Note For the most part, you can leave everything else as is, but there is one other thing you may want to consider here. Despite the fact that most *desktop users* will not want to compile packages, I think that the lure of trying out something that is leading edge or unusual will be more than even home users will be able to resist as they get familiar with their systems. That's why you might want to chose to install the development tools (gcc, perl, python, etc) as well as X Software Development, GNOME Software Development, and KDE Software Development.

When you are done here, click Next. This is the last step before the installation takes off on its own. You'll be given a final opportunity to change your mind before committing to this installation. Click Next and you are on your way.

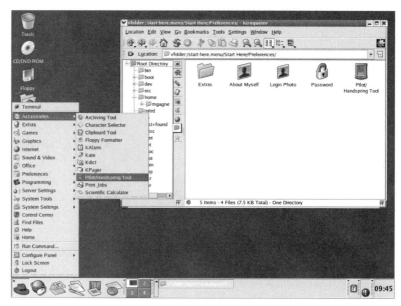

FIGURE 3-2   RedHat 8.0 desktop.

Your partitions will be formatted and a progress bar will keep track of where you are in the installation. As the install progresses, you will be treated to some images hyping various things such as the new desktop design called *Bluecurve*, the included products such as Ximian Evolution, Mozilla, and the OpenOffice.org suite—all packages that I will discuss later in the book. Incidentally, this is usually a good time to take a break and grab something to drink. From time to time, you'll need to change CDs (there are three). When the installation completes, you will be given the opportunity to create an emergency boot diskette. Follow the instructions to do so and label the diskette *"Linux emergency boot diskette."*

When the diskette creation is done, click Next and you'll see the *Graphical Interface (X) Configuration*. The install will autodetect your video card, then suggest a resolution (such as 16 bit, high color at 1024x768). When you click Next again, it will be time to select your monitor type. Once again, the installer will autodetect it. If, for some reason, the autodetect fails to find your monitor, then select it from the list. When you click Next past this screen, you will have the opportunity to *Test Setting*. I highly recommend that you *do not skip* this step. After confirming that your video settings are okay, click Next and you will be informed that the installation has completed. Click Exit and the system will reboot.

Note Make sure you take out the CD-ROM when it is ejected.

On first boot, Red Hat Linux will autodetect your printer. There will also be a handful of final settings such as date and time and so on. This is a good time to register with the Red Hat Network so that you can do online updates. Aside from being a free service, this is the Red Hat way to keep your system secure and up to date.

Finally, you'll be at the login screen. *Make sure* that we are on the same page by clicking "*Session*" (at the bottom of the login screen) and selecting KDE before you log in.

A SuSE Install

For my SuSE install, I used exactly the same machine and started from the same place. Note that I was using SuSE 8.1 for this. My copy of SuSE 8.1 came with both multiple CDs and a single DVD. The advantage of the DVD, assuming you have a DVD drive, is that you do not have to swap disks.

Reboot your system with the CD (or DVD) in the drive. You now have the option of selecting various install modes. If this is a new installation, simply press <Enter> or wait and the system will begin the installation.

The first screen you'll see after this is a welcome screen. It also happens to be the language selection screen. The default is *English* but you can certainly choose something else. Click Accept and the install process will begin analyzing your system for peripherals. All of these choices are shown to you on a single page—the keyboard, mouse, partitioning, software install, booting, and time zone info are all there on one screen. Notice the *blue underline* on each setting, much like a Web page. Look at the suggested settings to make sure that things look right. If you need to change something, click the blue link. For instance, to change your time zone from the default of *US/Pacific*, click *Time zone*, select from the list, and click Accept.

I would like you to look at *Partitioning and Software* in particular. If you do have a Windows partition, you should see it listed as /windows/C--that will be its mount point unless you would like a different name. The software choices are the *KDE Desktop Environment, Office Applications* (this is OpenOffice.org), *Help & Support Documentation*, and *Graphical Base System* (the X window system).

You might recall that I suggested that the lure of playing with some leading edge software might be overwhelming at some point. You can prepare for that here by clicking on the blue *Software* link. On the screen that follows, click the *Detailed selection* button. On the left hand side of the next screen, you'll see a number of categories for additional software. If you do want to compile your own programs, you'll want to select the *C/C++ Compiler and Tools*. I'm also pretty sure you'll want the *Games and Multimedia* packages. If I am right, choose those as well.

Finally, there's the GNOME desktop environment. Even though I am concentrating this book on KDE, you might recall that I said it is a good thing to experiment with another desktop environment. In the end, you might like GNOME better than KDE. In the Linux world, you have a choice. Furthermore, it doesn't hurt anything to load it at the same time. When you are done, click Accept to go back to your *Installation Settings* screen. Have a final look and click Accept. You'll be given a final warning regarding installation. If you are ready to start, click *"Yes, install."*

Your drive will be formatted, your Linux system will load, and you'll see a progress bar at the top right. After a little while, the basic installation will complete (you'll get a message to that effect) whereupon you remove the CD, and press <Enter>.

This is where the SuSE installation is different. If you are installing from CD, you'll be asked for additional CDs to complete the package installation. If, on the other hand, you were using the DVD to install, you'll immediately jump to final configuration. The first of these steps is account creation starting with setting the root password. The root account is used for administrative functions such as installing software. You do not want to run as root under normal circumstances since root is essentially *all powerful*.

After selecting a root password, click Next and create at least one user login. The SuSE install is interesting here in that it allows you to redirect all of root's mail directly to a user account. Check off the box that says *"Forward root's mail to this user"* when you are creating your personal user id. You can choose to create additional users at this time, or simply click Next to continue.

Finally, you will get to the X window graphical configuration to lock in your video settings. The dialogue here may vary depending on what kind of video hardware you have, or whether your card is 3D accelerated. *Just make sure that you test out the final settings before moving on.* Even if the information looks right, click the Change button and you'll have an opportunity to test your settings. Video settings work perfectly 99.99% of the time. It's just good to be sure beforehand. When you are done here, click Accept.

The SuSE installer will write these settings to disk, then do some final hardware settings, starting with your printer configuration. Make sure that your printer is plugged in and turned on, then click Yes when asked whether you want YaST2 (the installer) to detect your printer.

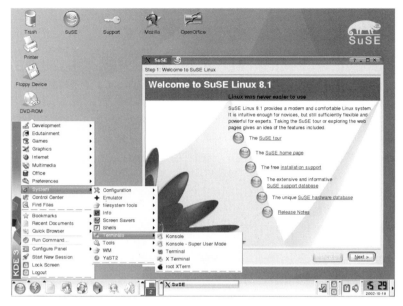

FIGURE 3-3   SuSE 8.1 desktop.

After a few seconds, YasST2 will return to the *Installation Settings* screen for your connected peripherals and hardware. This includes ethernet cards, printers, modems, sound cards and so on. Make sure that things are as you expect them to be and change them if necessary. For instance, if your network card is connected to a cable modem, the DHCP settings are probably exactly as you want them to be. However, if you are on an existing network, you will probably want to change your interface to reflect your network's addressing scheme.

When you are happy with the changes, click Next. YaST2 will finish writing all of these settings to disk and finish bringing up the system. Seconds later, you'll be at your login screen and ready to go.

Not So Tough Installs

As you can see, installing Linux isn't difficult but it does vary from distribution to distribution. The thing to remember is that every distribution has similar steps such as language, keyboard, and mouse selection. All will ask you about how to deal with disk partitions and offer to do it for you if you would rather keep it simple. For the most part, it's just a matter of accepting the defaults and clicking Next.

Starting and Stopping Linux

This sounds like such a simple thing that you might wonder why I am spending any time on it at all. After all, you turn on the power switch, sit back, and watch Linux come to life. Depending on the installation, you may have more than one boot option. The default will almost certainly be to take you into Linux. If you opted for a dual-boot system, you may have to select Linux from the boot menu.

The lesson here is simply this: because you do have options, take the time to read what's on the menu.

Warning All right. Here is *rule number one* when it comes to shutting down your system. Never, ever simply power off the system. You must do a *proper* shutdown. Oh, and get an uninterruptible power supply (UPS) so that your system doesn't shut down accidentally. *You do not need a UPS* to run Linux. However, if you don't want a random power fluctuation or a three-second power outage to take down your system, the added protection of a UPS makes sense.

Linux is a multiuser, multiprocessing operating system. Even when it appears that nothing is happening, there can be a great deal going on. Your system is maintaining disk space, memory, and files. All this time, it is busy making notes on what is happening in terms of security, e-mail, errors, and so on. There may be open files or jobs running. A sudden stop as a result of pulling the plug can damage your file systems. A proper shutdown is essential. Even in the world of your old OS, you still had to do a proper shutdown—Linux is no different.

There are a few ways of shutting down your system. You start by logging off from your system. Make sure that you've closed all your applications and saved anything you might have been working on. Now, right-click on the desktop and select Logout from the popup menu. You should get something that looks similar to the screen shown in Figure 3-4.

This particular logoff screen is from a SuSE system, but the types of options will be similar regardless of what system you are on. At this point, select *"Turn off computer."* There's rarely any need for a *"Restart computer"* in the Linux world—when you shut down, it's usually because you intend to power off the system.

FIGURE 3–4   Logoff screen.

Shell Out You can also log out from the command line, but it must be done from the root login. From a terminal window, switch to root with "`su - root`" (you'll be prompted for the password), and type the following:

```
shutdown -h now
```

When shutdown is called with the -h option, it is another way of saying, "Shut the system down and keep it down." On some systems (and with proper hardware), this option will power off the system after it is down. Another option is to type the following:

```
shutdown -r now
```

The -r option tells Linux to reboot immediately after a shutdown. A reboot option is usually used after a kernel rebuild.

And Now . . . Linux!

Congratulations! You have installed your Linux system, and learned how to bring it up and shut it down (properly). Now you are ready to get to really know your Linux system. As you turn to the next chapter, the fun really begins.

To paraphrase from *Casablanca*, one of my favorite movies, *this will be the beginning of a beautiful friendship*.

Resources

FIPS Home Page

http://www.igd.fhg.de/~aschaefe/fips/fips.html

Mandrake

http://www.mandrakelinux.com

PowerQuest (for Partition Magic)

http://www.partitionmagic.com

Red Hat Software

http://www.redhat.com

SuSE Linux

http://www.suse.com

chapter
4

Getting Your Hands Dirty

Welcome to the multiuser, multitasking, multieverything world. Linux is designed to run multiple users and processes concurrently. What that means is that your system is capable of doing many things, even while it appears to be idle. This is the reason so many businesses and organizations use Linux as a Web server, email server, file server, print server . . . well, you get the idea.

From the perspective of the individual user, this means that all users in your family (or office) can have desktop environments that are truly theirs and theirs alone. Your desktop can be configured and modified to let you work the way you want to, with different backgrounds, icons, colors, or themes, depending on your mood. It also protects your personal information from others, meaning that the kids can change their desktops and reorganize things but you won't be affected when you log in.

I'll have you logging in very shortly, but for the moment, I want to say a few words about your new desktop.

Getting to Know You . . . KDE

Linux is extremely flexible. Linux makes it possible to run in a number of different desktop environments. The plus side of this is that *you* decide how you want to work. Your system works the way you want it to and not the other way around. The down side is exactly the same. Let's face it, being told what to do is often easier, even if it means getting used to working in a way that you may not particularly like at first—not necessarily better, but easier.

On that note, at some time when you've gotten comfortable with your Linux system running the KDE desktop, I'm going to ask you to be brave and experiment with some of these other environments, such as GNOME, WindowMaker, IceWM, or one of the many other desktop environments available to the Linux user. You may find yourself totally taken with a different way of doing things. All your programs will still work as they did, but the *feel* of your desktop—the *experience,* if you prefer—will be all yours. For now, we'll stick to KDE.

KDE is the most popular desktop environment in the Linux world, and deservedly so. It is beautiful, slick, mature, powerful, and easy to use. It is also loaded with great applications for email, surfing the Web, playing movies, burning CDs, writing documents, working with spreadsheets, and so on. KDE also features a great collection of games that should keep you busy for some time.

A Few Words about X

In a few seconds when I start showing you around your desktop, what I am telling you now will fade into the background of your memory, but I still think you should know. KDE, that great-looking desktop system, is the friendly face that rides above your Linux system's real graphical engine. That engine is called the *X window system, XFree86,* or simply *X.* What KDE, your desktop environment, does is provide control of windows, borders, decorations, colors, icons, and so on.

When you installed your system, you went through a graphical desktop configuration step of some kind. What you were setting up at that time wasn't KDE or GNOME, but X.

X is what the desktop—and every graphical program you run—*really* runs on.

Logging In

In most cases, your workstation will boot up to a graphical login screen. You will likely see the names of users you set up during the installation of your system, with a box for the username and another for the password. Remember that both the username and password are case-sensitive, so you must type both as they were created. You can always change the password at a later time (I'll tell you about it later in the chapter).

This graphical login screen is known as the *login manager*. Depending on the installation, it may appear different from system to system. The KDE login screen will look something like the one shown in Figure 4–1, which comes from a Mandrake Linux system. Login managers, like so many things on your system, can be configured to take on different looks and styles. As a result, the companies that provide Linux distributions will often customize them to suit their needs. What they will all have in common is a place for your login name, your password, and an option for selecting your desktop environment (KDE, GNOME, etc.).

Start by logging in with the *non-root* user you created when you installed the system. For session type, make sure you choose KDE. If this is your first time logging in, you may be presented with the KDE personalizer. I say "*may*" because some distributions will log you in to a default desktop with a given look and feel which you can then change to suit your needs and tastes, something we'll talk about in detail in Chapter 6.

Figure 4–1 A graphical login manager.

Quick Tip If you don't see the KDE personalizer after logging in, you should still take a few minutes to read through this section as it does introduce you to some basic concepts. You can always run the KDE personalizer by clicking the button in the bottom left hand corner of your screen, and selecting *"Run command."* Simply type `kpersonalizer` and press <Enter>. Note that SuSE 8.1 Pro does not include the kpersonalizer , but provides a *tour* which lets you set some of the same items. Even so, all of these settings can all be changed using the tools I will describe in Chapter 6. The kpersonalizer information only applies to first time logins.

When `kpersonalizer` runs, you'll first be asked for your country and language of choice (Figure 4-2). Aside from the obvious usefulness of the language setting, this sets some intelligent defaults for you based on that decision, for instance, currency and date format.

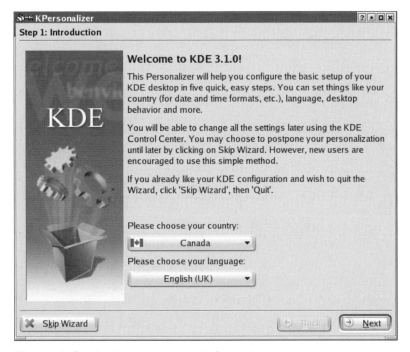

Figure 4–2   Setting your country information.

The next screen, *System Behavior*, is particularly interesting (Figure 4–3). If you are coming from the Windows world, you are used to double-clicking on desktop icons to make things happen. Not so in the Linux world. A single click on an icon activates your program. If you like the double-click, choose Windows for system behavior or stick with the single-click KDE default.

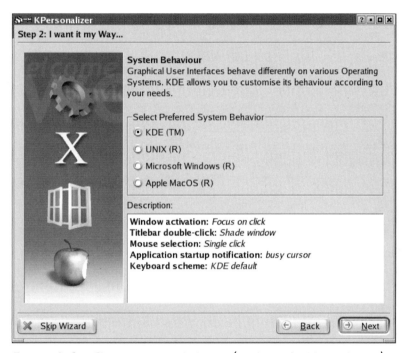

Figure 4–3   Changing system behavior (single vs. double-click, etc.).

Before we move on from here, I want to mention one other thing. Notice the Window activation item? This is sometimes referred to as *focus*. On a windowing system, it is possible to have many application windows on your screen at the same time. Sometimes they overlap. When you want to start using a particular window, you click on that window to bring it forward. That's *focus on click*. Aside from the KDE and Windows behaviors, you could also choose UNIX, which has an interesting method of focus. Simply moving your mouse cursor over the background window brings it forward. This is referred to as *focus follows mouse*. It takes some getting used to, but some people, particularly those with large monitors, may find it useful.

The next step brings up the *Eyecandy-O-Meter* (Figure 4–4). If you have a powerful, fast machine, you might want to just crank the slider to the maximum. What you will get are animated icons, sound themes, and special effects of various types. Click on the Show details button to find out just what you get for your processor and memory buck.

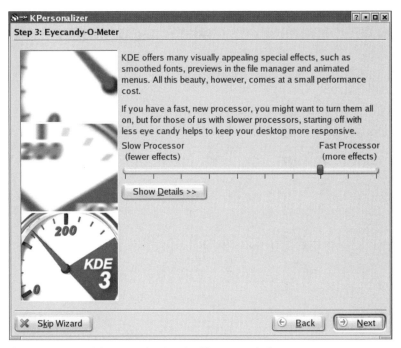

Figure 4–4   Adjusting the level of "eye candy."

Hot on the heels of this screen is even more eye candy—this time in the guise of a desktop theme (Figure 4–5). What kind of style would you like for your desktop? Pick one, click Next, and your desktop style will change automatically. If you don't like the choice, hit the Back button and try again. *For the time being, I would highly recommend that you pick the KDE classic theme.* That's because the look and feel of the windows I'm going to describe will be affected by the theme you choose. I will revisit this subject in the next chapter, at which point, you can go wild.

Finally, kpersonalizer offers to load up your panel with some default settings and icons. For now, just accept the default, click Next, and you are done setting up your desktop.

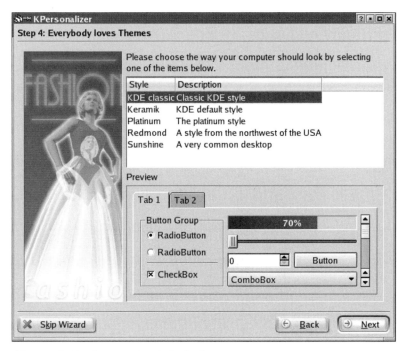

Figure 4–5   *Setting the default theme.*

Click Here! Click Here!

A quick note on clicking before we continue. Everything is pretty much launched with a single click of the *left mouse button*. As I mentioned above, you can change that to a double-click if you prefer, but I would suggest that you (for the moment, anyhow) try to get used to the single click. I think you will like it.

Clicking on the *right mouse button* almost anywhere will bring up a menu of available options.

The *middle mouse button* (if you have one or have configured your two-button mouse to emulate a three-button mouse) serves a number of purposes, based on the application. The best one, to me, is pasting text from one application to another.

Becoming One with the Desktop

The bar at the bottom of your screen is the panel, also called *Kicker*. Among other things, notice the large *K* icon in the bottom left-hand corner. This is the *Application Starter*, similar to the Start button on that other OS. Clicking the big K will bring up a menu of menus—a list of installed applications that you can run with a single click.

Speaking of running things, Kicker also has a taskbar embedded in it. When you start an application, you'll see it listed in the taskbar. This not only shows you what you have running on your desktop, it also provides a quick way to switch from process to process. Just click on the program in the taskbar. Alternatively, you can press <Alt+Tab> to switch from one running program to another. The taskbar can be configured to list all processes from all desktops, group similar processes together, or simply show you what is on your current virtual desktop.

Did he just say *virtual desktop*?

Yes . . . virtual desktop. This is one feature you are going to absolutely *love*! On the default installation, you'll also notice four little squares labeled (strangely enough) 1, 2, 3, and 4. This is your desktop switcher, allowing you to switch between any of the four virtual desktops with a mouse click. Think of it as having a computer monitor that is four times as large as you already have, with each desktop running different things. You can leave each one the way you want it without having to minimize things anytime you want to use them. It gets better; you can have four, five, six, or even more virtual desktops if you find that four aren't enough for you (Figure 4–6).

Figure 4–6   The desktop pager with six virutal desktops.

Another way to switch virtual desktops is by pressing <Ctrl+Tab>.

Kicker also has a number of icons to the right of the big K. To find out what each of these are, move your mouse over each one and pause. Context-sensitive bubble help, or "tooltips" will appear, showing you what each icon is for. Clicking on any of these icons will launch the program it represents. One you might want to take note of right now is the life-preserver icon (which you can also find by clicking the big K and looking for Help). This opens up your desktop documentation and help files.

Let's move to Kicker's far right. You might notice an embedded clock and some smaller icons: a clipboard, a calendar, or a speaker icon. These also represent programs—but running programs. These applications have been *swallowed* by the panel and can be called up with a click. That mini-icon area is called the *system tray* (Figure 4–7).

Figure 4–7   *System tray icons.*

Finally, notice the two little icons sitting together vertically. One looks like a lock and the other like a power button. On my desktop, the lock is blue and the power button is red. The lock button will lock your desktop and activate the screensaver. To unlock it, you move the mouse (or hit a key), after which you will be prompted for your password. The power button logs you out and returns the system to the login manager so that you or someone else can log in. I'll cover screensavers in the next chapter.

Your First Application

It's time to really get into this, nail down some terminology, and get you working with the system. Starting a program or opening up an application is as simple as clicking on an icon. Let's do that. In fact, let's open up *the* great KDE application, *Konqueror*.

You'll be using Konqueror a lot. This is the KDE file manager that lets you work with files and folders. Konqueror makes it easy to create folders (or directories, as they are known in the Linux world), copy, delete, and move other folders and files around by dragging and dropping from one to the other. Konqueror is also a Web browser from which you can surf the Internet, as well as a universal file viewer so you can view and organize your photo collection, preview documents, and much, much more.

Quick Tip   This is a good time to let you in on a *secret.* While you will find KDE under RedHat, Mandrake, SuSE, and others, the menus may vary somewhat. What this means is that things on your menu may not be in *exactly* the same place as on my menu. Menu organization is only important in that multimedia applications like the CD player will be under a menu that sounds like multimedia — it might say "*Enjoy music & video*") whereas a Web browser might be under the *Internet* menu or something that says "*Use the Internet.*"

What will be consistent is the command's name. For that
reason, I will be telling you how to call a program by name
throughout this book.

Down in your Kicker panel, notice the icon that looks like a folder with a little house in front of it. The tooltip that pops up when you hover your mouse
over it says *Home*. This will open Konqueror as a file manager in your home directory. Click it, and you should get something that looks like Figure 4–8.

On the left, Konqueror shows a tree view of your home directory. This is the
navigation panel. Pressing <F9> will hide (or bring forward) the navigation panel.
The tabs let you switch between a view of your home directory to bookmarks
for the Web, a history of places you've visited on the Internet, connected services (such as printers), ftp archives, and so on. On the right, the contents of the
current location are displayed. If this is a directory (like your home directory),
the various directories will appear as folder icons. Depending on how Konqueror
is configured, images in your folders may appear as little thumbnails. Would you

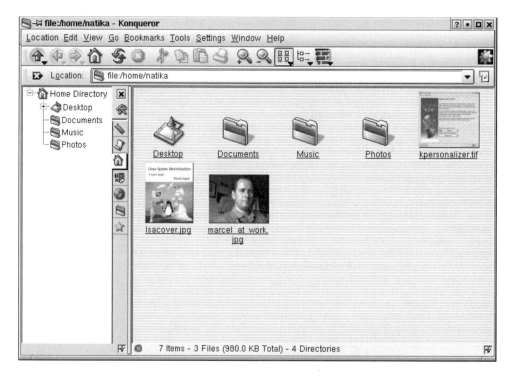

Figure 4–8   Introducing Konqueror, the all-purpose file manager and browser.

like to see the full-sized image? Just click on the thumbnail, and Konqueror will do the rest.

Konqueror is flexible, powerful, and definitely worth your time to get to know. In fact, it will likely become your most used desktop application. I'm going to give Konqueror the focus and consideration it deserves in the next chapter. For the moment, leave Konqueror where it is and read on as we discuss windows—and I don't mean the operating system.

Windows, Title Bars, and Menus, Oh My!

Each graphical program that runs on your desktop will have certain common characteristics. Have a look at the top of your Konqueror window, and you will see something like Figure 4–9.

Figure 4–9   Most windows will have a title bar, as well as a menu bar.

The Title Bar

The top bar on a running program is called the *title bar*. Depending on the application, it may display a program name, a document you are working on, a location on the Web, or a nice description explaining what you are running. Left-clicking on the title bar and dragging it with the mouse will move the program window around on your desktop.

Quick Tip Most modern desktops assume a fairly sizeable monitor running at least 1024x768, and a number of applications assume this to be a universal truth. This plays havoc when your monitor is smaller than this (say, 800x600) and the buttons you need to click are off screen. Clicking the title bar and dragging the window gets you only so far.

Don't despair. By pressing the <Alt> key and left–clicking on a window, you can drag it anywhere you wish, including beyond the boundaries of your desktop. This is particularly handy if you need to get at a hidden OK button.

Double-clicking on the title bar will *shade* your program—the application will appear to *roll up* like a window blind. Now move your mouse pointer to the title bar, and the application unrolls. Move off the application completely, and it rolls up again. Double-click on the title bar again, and the application will *unroll* and stay unrolled. Doing this with a number of running applications is an interesting phenomenon that takes some getting used to, kind of like someone reading your mind.

The title bar also has a number of small icons. Pause your mouse cursor over them, and a tooltip will inform you of their functions. Starting at the left-hand corner of the title bar, there are two icons of interest. The far left one brings up a small drop-down menu that makes it possible to move the program to another virtual desktop and to minimize or maximize the application (among other things).

You may also have a push-pin (or stick-pin) icon beside the menu icon— this makes a window *sticky*. Clicking it again makes it *unsticky*. Try this. Click on one of your other three virtual desktops. If you haven't already excitedly opened dozens of other programs on each one, you should find yourself with a nice, clean desktop. Now go back to your first virtual desktop. Click the stick-pin icon. Now jump back to virtual desktop two. Konqueror is there. Click on desktop number three, and it is there also. In fact, if you had 10 virtual desktops, Konqueror would be waiting for you on all of them.

Here's a cool bit of information, however. You are still running only *one* instance of Konqueror. It's just that it is available to you on every desktop. Finally, if you stuck the window on virtual desktop one and you unstuck it on virtual desktop three, it will stay on desktop three.

Before we move on to other things, we need to look at the buttons on the right-hand side of the title bar. You use the icon that has a *dot* in the center to minimize (or iconize) a window (remember that you can pause over the top with your mouse button to get the tooltip). The icon with a *square* in the center maximizes a window, causing it to take up every bit of space on your desktop except for Kicker's panel. Finally, the *X* does pretty much what you would expect it to. It closes a running application.

On to the Menu Bar

Directly below the title bar is the *menu bar*. The menu bar will generally have a number of labels (such as *File*, *Edit*, *View*, and so on), each grouping the various things you can do into some kind of sensible order.

Every program will have a different set of menu options, depending on the nature of the application. Clicking on a menu label will drop down a list of your options for that function (see Figure 4–10).

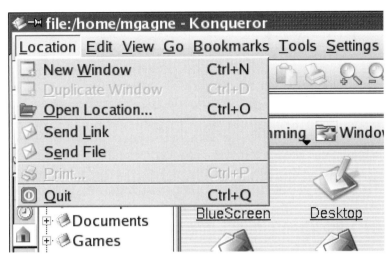

Figure 4–10   Drop-down menus.

Resizing Windows

The last thing you should know is that (for the most part) you aren't stuck with the default window size. By grabbing any of the corners of an application window, you can drag that corner and stretch the window to a size that is more comfortable for you. The same applies to the top, bottom, and sides of a program window.

As you position the cursor on a corner or a side, you'll see it change to a double arrow. Just drag the side or corner to where you want it, and you are done.

Command Central

Sometimes if you know the command, it is just as easy to type that command and tell the program to run without having to work your way through all those menus. On your old system, you would have clicked that Start button, selected Run, and typed something in, usually *setup* because that is when you tended to use the Run option. On your Linux system, you can do the same thing by clicking the big K and selecting the *Run command*. You can also simply hold down the <Alt> key and hit <F2> (Alt+F2). A nice dialogue box will appear, asking you to type the name of the program you want to run.

Are you wondering what those programs are called? Let me give you a hint.

Click on the big K, select the Multimedia menu, and start the CD player. Now look at the title bar at the top of the player. See that *Kscd*? That's the name of the program—almost. It's the name in mixed case. To run it, forget all those capital letters and just type the command in lower case—kscd is the name of the program that runs the KDE CD player.

To recap, pressing <Alt+F2>, typing kscd in the dialogue box, and hitting <Enter> is the same as going through the menus. Have a look at Figure 4–11 for an example.

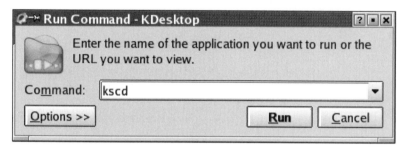

Figure 4–11   Running a command with <Alt+F2>.

A Polite Introduction to the Command Line

In your line of Kicker icons, there is something that looks like a screen with a shell in the lower right-hand corner. If you move your mouse over it and pause for a second, the bubble help will tell you that this is called *Konsole*. This is your command prompt. In Windows-land, you might have thought of it as the DOS prompt.

The reason there is a shell in front of the icon is because Konsole is your access to the Linux command line, known as the shell. There are many types of shells, each of which works similarly (e.g.: all allow you to run commands), but each may have different capabilities. The default on Linux is called bash, the *GNU Bourne-Again Shell*.

The shell is powerful, and learning about its capabilities will make you a wizard of the Linux world. Become one with the shell, and nothing can stop you. The shell is the land of the Linux systems guru and the administrator. For the most part, you can do just about anything you need to do by staying and working with the X window system and your KDE desktop. Still, from time to time, I will ask you to do something from the shell prompt. As time goes on, you too, will *feel the power* of the Linux shell.

Give me more! For those of you who get to the end of the chapters in this book and find yourselves wanting to know *more* about the shell, check out the appendix section.

Here's our polite introduction. Click the Konsole icon. The Konsole will appear with a Tip of the Day window in front of it (Figure 4–12). Early on in your Linux experience, you might want to leave these tips on. You can even walk through them by clicking on the Next button. When you've had enough of these tips, you can banish them by checking off the check box to Show on start and clicking Close. If you find yourself missing the tips later on, click Help on the menu bar and select Tip of the Day.

When you do click Close, you'll be left with an open Konsole and your cursor sitting beside a dollar sign prompt. This is the shell prompt. Whenever you find yourself at a shell prompt, the system is waiting for you to type in a command. Remember the CD player from earlier? You could type kscd here and have it start up just as easily. For now, type date at the shell prompt, then hit the <Enter> key.

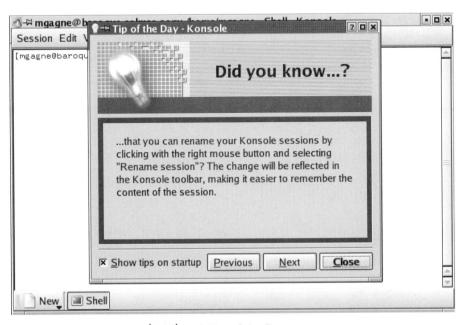

Figure 4–12   Konsole (shell) with Tip of the Day.

```
[marcel@mypc marcel]$ date
Tue Apr 8 10:37:22 EDT 2003
```

Aside from knowing the date and time that I wrote this paragraph, you'll also get your current date and time when you try it. That's what date is, a command that displays the date and time. You'll also find yourself back at the shell prompt as your system patiently awaits your next command. Type exit and press the <Enter> key.

The Konsole disappears. That's it. We'll use the shell again as we go through this book, but for now, your polite introduction to the shell ends here.

Changing Your Password

It is good security policy to change your password from time to time. Under your K menu, you'll find an option for changing your password (most likely under the Settings submenu). You can also run the command as in the CD player example above by using your <Alt+F2> run sequence and typing the command kdepasswd. A window will appear (Figure 4–13), asking for your current password.

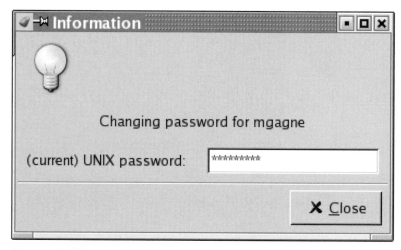

Figure 4–13   Using kdepasswd to change your password.

Notice that, like the login manager, your password is not visible. Instead, each key you press is echoed as an asterisk. When you have successfully entered your password, the system will ask you for a new password. Then you'll be asked for the password again, this time for confirmation. That's it. Be sure to remember your new password. You'll need it next time you log in.

Shell Out You can easily change your password from the command line as well. Just open a shell prompt and type the command "password" as in the example below:

```
passwd
[marcel@mysystem marcel]$ passwd
Changing password for user marcel.
(current) UNIX password:
New UNIX password:
Retype new UNIX password:
passwd: all authentication tokens updated suc-
cessfully.
```

Konquest of the Desktop

Now that you and your system have been *properly* introduced, it is time to do some exploring. In the next chapter, you are going to learn to wield Konqueror to navigate, work with, and otherwise unlock the mysteries of your Linux system. Ready? Then, let the Konquest begin.

chapter

5

Konquering
Your World

*Anyone who has ever had a system crash without a handy backup of
their files knows that nothing is more important than data. Other
than playing games (and even there), computers are about storing and
dealing with information. That's why getting the hang of working with
that data—moving, copying, renaming, and deleting it—is vitally important to getting comfortable in your Linux world.*

That means it is time to revisit your new old friend, Konqueror.

Files, Directories, and the Root of All Things

There's a saying in the Linux world that *"everything is a file"* (a comment attributed to Ken Thompson, the developer of UNIX). That includes directories. Directories are just files with files inside them. All these files and directories are organized into a hierarchical file system, starting from the root directory and branching out.

> *Note* Folders and directories are the same thing. The terms can be used interchangeably, but I will be calling them directories. If you are more comfortable thinking of them as folders, don't worry. Depending on the application, you'll see both terms used.

The root directory (referred to as *slash*, or /) is actually aptly named. If you consider your file system as a tree's root system spreading out below the surface, you start to get an idea of just what things look like.

Under the root directory, you'll find folders called usr, bin, etc, tmp, and so on. Open up Konqueror by clicking on the icon in your taskbar that has a house in front of a folder. This brings up Konqueror in file manager mode (remember that Konqueror is also a Web browser). If your navigation panel isn't up (Konqueror's left side panel), press <F9> to open it (Figure 5–1). To either the right or left of the navigation panel (this is all configurable, remember), you'll see a row of tabs. Click on the root directory tab, the one that looks like a small folder. *Here's a hint:* If you move your mouse over the tabs and pause, a tooltip will pop up to let you know you are in the right place. When the file system tree appears (over on the left side), click on the top folder, Root Directory, then look at the names of those folders.

These are all system directories, and they will contain all the programs that make your Linux system run, including documentation, devices, and device drivers. For the most part, you aren't going to be touching these files. Accidentally changing things around in this part of your system probably isn't a good thing, which is why everyone logs in with their own accounts.

One of the directories under the root is called home and inside that directory, you'll discover other directories, one for each login name on your system. These are the individual home directories and it is where you'll find your *personal* files and directories. If you want to store personal documents, music files, or pictures, this is the place. Once in Konqueror, you can jump to your home directory by clicking the house icon or clicking Go on the menu bar and selecting Home URL. This is your $HOME.

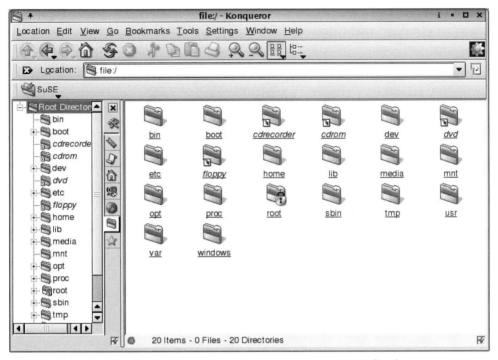

Figure 5–1   Konqueror's file manager view with navigation panel (left) open.

Quick Tip   My use of $HOME isn't just to be silly. The system can recognize some things based on environment variables, symbolic names that can refer to text, numbers, or even commands. In the DOS/Windows world, you had similars, for instance, the PATH in your AUTOEXEC.BAT file. $HOME is an environment variable assigned to every person who logs in. It represents a person's home directory. If you want to see all the environment variables assigned to your session, shell out and type the following command.

```
env
```

Try this. Over on the left side of the tree view, you'll see a little *plus sign* beside the home directory. Click on the plus sign, and the tree view will expand to show your own personal directory. Notice that the plus sign has become a minus sign. If you click it again, the directory view collapses. With the home directory expanded, click on your personal directory. You should see a few items appear in the right side view, including one icon labeled *Desktop*. For an example, see Figure 5–2. On the left side, /dev is expanded, and the right side view shows the same directory collapsed.

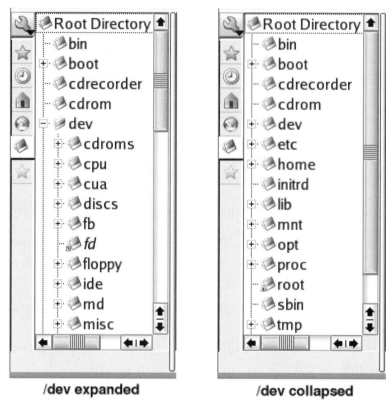

/dev expanded   **/dev collapsed**

Figure 5–2   Expanding and collapsing directories.

Before you do anything else, I want you to look down in your taskbar at the bottom of the screen. Do you see the desktop icon there, just to the right of the big K? It looks like a desktop blotter with a lamp above it . Move your mouse cursor over it, and the tooltip will display *Show Desktop*. Click it, and your desktop appears, free of windows. Click it again, and everything returns to normal.

Quick Tip If the Show Desktop icon isn't there, you can easily add it. Right-click on the big K, select Panel Menu | Add | Special Button | Desktop Access. The button will appear in your taskbar.

The reason I am having you do this is that I want you to take note of what icons are on your desktop. Now go back to your Konqueror session and click on the Desktop icon in the right (or main) window. All the icons on your desktop show up there. Now why is that, you ask? Because even those icons on your desktop are files or directories. Cool? Let's move on.

Shell Out Open a Konsole by clicking the terminal icon in your panel (the one with the shell). At the shell prompt, type `ls Desktop`. The ls command will list the contents of your Desktop directory. Compare what you see there with the icons currently on your graphical desktop. Do the names look familiar? When you are done, type `exit` to close the Konsole.

Directories (and subdirectories) will usually show up as folders, although this isn't a hard and fast rule because you can customize this. Nevertheless, some directories have different icons right from the start—the Desktop icon you just visited and the Trash can being two notables.

Wherever You Go . . .

To move from directory to directory, you can simply click on an icon, whether in the right tree view or in the left expanded view. You can also move the directory tree around by using your *cursor keys*. You'll see the highlight bar move from directory to directory. To see the contents in the main window, move to a folder and press <Enter>. To go up a level in the directory tree (rather than folder by folder), press <Alt+Up Arrow>. Substituting the down arrow for the up arrow will take you to the other directory.

There's another way, as well. If you look up at the menu bar, you'll see an up arrow, a left-pointing arrow, and a right-pointing arrow (Figure 5–3). Right next to that is an icon of a house. Clicking that house icon will always take you

Figure 5–3   *Konqueror's main navigation toolbar.*

back to your personal home directory. Clicking the up arrow will move you up the directory tree, and the left arrow will take you back to whatever directory you were last visiting.

The quickest way to navigate your file system (assuming you know the directory you want to be in) is simply to type it in the location bar. Clicking that little *X* on the black arrow to the left of the location bar (where it says "*Location*") will clear the field. That saves you having to select the text and erase it. From here, you can just type in whatever you want there, e.g., /home/marcel .

Navigating the Navigation Panel

We should spend a couple of minutes looking at that navigation panel (the left side panel you open and close with <F9>) because it is quite important. You've already seen how to use it to navigate your file system, but wait (as they say on television), there's more. Look at those tabs on the right side of the navigation panel. If you move your mouse over any of them, the tooltips will identify them. Click on them, and you'll switch to whatever view they offer. Click on them again, and the navigation panel will slam shut, leaving only the tabs behind and giving you more viewing space in the main Konqueror window.

Now, about those tabs . . . The first is a *bookmark tab*. When we talk about using Konqueror as a Web browser later in the book, you'll be using the bookmark feature a lot. For now, you should probably know that you can bookmark locations on disk. If you use a particular directory a lot (your music collection, for example), you'll want to bookmark that for easy access. You can also get to the bookmarks (or add them) by clicking Bookmarks on the menu bar.

After the bookmark tab, you'll see the *history tab*. Clicking it will show you a tree view listing various places on your disk (files and directories) or sites you've visited recently.

The tab with a house on it is a direct link to your personal home directory. Next to it is the KDE media player tab. You'll recognize it by the image of a little blue speaker with what appears to be music pouring out. We'll cover that later when we talk about multimedia. Below that is an icon with a globe of the Earth. That's the *network tab*. The network tab provides you with a quick link to the KDE download areas (FTP sites) and Web pages. For these to work, you must be connected to the Internet. This is another area that we will cover later in the book.

The second-to-last tab accesses your system's root directory, as discussed earlier in this chapter. That leaves only one tab, the *services tab*. This tab lets you zoom in on network services, such as printers or shared directories on other machines or your local CD-ROM device for playing audio tracks. Once again, this is something we will discuss later in the book. For the moment, I just wanted you to get a feel for what's there when you open Konqueror.

Enhancing Konqueror

Konqueror is an amazingly powerful tool, and some of its features may be lying dormant and unconfigured. When you ran kpersonalizer, you had the opportunity to select your favored level of eye candy. Keeping in mind that more toys means more demands on your system, some features that are fun but CPU-intensive may have been turned off if you selected anything other than "give me the works."

One of these features has to do with file tips. Try this. In an open Konqueror session, move your mouse over a file or directory and pause there. If you don't see a tooltip pop up describing the file type, its size, and other properties, I'm going to have you turn that feature on now.

Click Settings on Konqueror's menu bar and select Configure Konqueror. Konqueror's configuration dialog will appear (Figure 5–4).

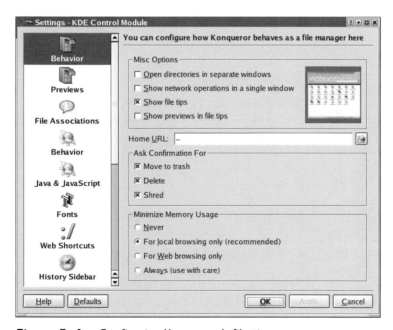

Figure 5–4   Configuring Konqueror's file tips.

To the left is a panel with the various setting groups that are available under Konqueror (e.g., File Associations, Fonts, etc). For the time being, click on Behavior (there are two behavior icons; the first is for the file system while the second is for the Web browser view – we want the first). Now, look to the right, under Misc Options. Check on the Show file tips option but leave the Show previews in file tips option off. Click Apply, then click OK to close the Settings dialog. We'll be using that file tips feature very shortly.

In just a moment, I'm going to tell you all about selecting, copying, and moving files. Before we move on, however, I should tell you about another really cool Konqueror trick that makes this whole copying and moving process a whole lot easier. Click on Window on the menu bar and select Split View Left/Right. Suddenly, Konqueror will have two main windows instead of just one (Figure 5–5).

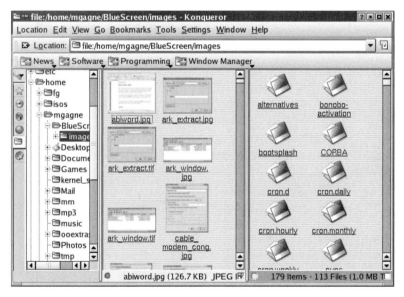

Figure 5–5   Konqueror with a two-panel split view.

The trick is in trying to remember which window you are working in at any given time. Look in the bottom left corner of one of your split windows. Do you see that little *green* light? It indicates the *active* window, and its pathname will be in the location bar just under the menu bar. Now click on the other window, and you'll see the green light jump to that window. You'll also see the location bar change to that location, which immediately makes you think, "Hey, I can just type in the pathname for the active window in the location bar, and my active window will take me there!" And you are right.

Uh, Roger, Copy That . . .

You can create, copy, move, rename, and delete files and directories by using Konqueror, but before you can do any of these things, you need to *select* a file or directory. Selecting files is something you will be doing a lot, so let's start with that. Place your mouse cursor just outside one of the icons of your choosing. Now drag the cursor across the icon and notice the dashed-line box you are creating as you drag the pointer. You'll know a file is selected because it becomes *highlighted*. Right-clicking also selects a file but in a somewhat different way, bringing up a menu dialog that will then ask you what you want to do with that file.

Don't forget your cursor keys either. Moving left, right, up, or down will highlight whatever file or directory you happen to be sitting on. You can then click on Edit in the menu bar (or press <Alt+E> to get to the edit menu) and decide what it is you want to do with the file. I'll talk about those decisions in a moment.

Sometimes, one just isn't enough—you need to *select multiple files*. The easiest way of all is with the mouse. Left-click to the top and left of the icon you want to start with, then drag your cursor across a series of icons. Notice again the dotted-line box that surrounds the files and directories you select. Perhaps you just want a file here and a file there. How do you pick and choose multiple files, you ask? Simply hold down the <Ctrl> key and drag with the mouse. Let's say that you have selected a group of four files, and you want one further down in your directory. Let go of the mouse button (but keep holding down the <Ctrl> key), position your mouse to the top and left of the next group of icons, and select away. As long as you continue to hold down the <Ctrl> key, you can pick up and select files here and there.

It is also possible to do all these things with the cursor keys by simply moving your cursor over the file you want to start with, holding down the <Shift> key, and moving the cursor to the left (or whatever direction you like). As you do this, you'll notice file after file being selected. Try it for yourself. For nonsequential selection, use the <Ctrl> key as you did with the mouse. Select (or deselect) the files by pressing the spacebar. When your cursor is sitting on the file you want, press the spacebar, and your files will be highlighted.

Finally, and probably quite important for the future, you can also select by extension. Let's say that you want to select all the files with an .mp3 or .doc extension in your directory. Click Edit on the menu bar, then click Select. A small window will pop up, asking you for an extension. If you wanted all the .mp3 files, you would enter *.mp3. The .mp3 extension will limit your selection to a certain type of file, whereas the asterisk says "give me everything" that matches.

Creating New Directories

If you aren't already running Konqueror, start it up now and make sure you are in your personal home directory. In the main Konqueror window, right-click on any blank area and look at the menu that pops up. Move your mouse pointer over the top item (Create New), and you'll see a secondary menu appear. The first item is Directory, as in "Create new directory." Click here, and the system will prompt you for a directory name. This can be pretty much anything you like. If this directory will house your music files, perhaps its name should be *Music*.

Just remember that you can create directories inside directories, and you can start organizing things in a way that makes sense. For instance, you might want to create directories called *Rock*, *Jazz*, *Hip Hop*, and *Classical* in your Music directory.

"I've Changed My Mind" or Renaming Files

You created a folder called *Classical*, and you really meant *Opera*. You could delete the folder or you could simply rename it. To rename a file or directory, select it and right-click to get the menu, then choose Rename. The name will be highlighted under the appropriate icon—just type the new name and press <Enter>. Alternatively, select it and choose Rename from the Edit menu in the menu bar. The easiest way of all is to press <F2> after you have selected the file or directory.

 Shell Out   Open a Konsole and type `ls` to see your directories. Renaming a file or directory from the shell is easy. Type `mv oldname newname` and press <Enter>. For instance, to change your Classical directory to Opera, you would type the following command:

```
mv Classical Opera
```

Copying Files and Directories (and Moving, Too!)

Ah! This is where you learn another great trick with Konqueror. An easy way to copy a file from one directory to another is to fire up two versions of Konqueror. In the first, you find the file (or files) you want to copy. In the second

Konqueror window, you locate the directory to which you want those files copied. Simply drag the file from one window into the other. A little menu will pop up, asking you whether you want to copy the file here or move it here (Figure 5–6).

Figure 5–6   *Confirmation when moving or copying files.*

An interesting question, isn't it? That's because copying and moving files is done in pretty much the same way. Both involve a copy. The difference is in what happens *after* the copy is done. In one case, you copy the file over and keep the original, thus giving you two copies of the same file but in different places. A move, on the other hand, copies the file and deletes the original from where it was.

One easy trick is to select the file you want, right-click to get the menu, then click on Copy. Now go into the directory where you would like this file to appear, right-click somewhere on a blank space of Konqueror's main window, and click Paste from the pop-up menu. You can also specify the Copy and Paste options from the menu bar under Edit.

 Shell Out The Linux command to copy is *cp*. If you wanted to copy a file called *big_report* to *notsobig_report*, you would type the following command:

```
cp big_report notsobig_report
```

Wait! What about Links?

If you're following along, you probably noticed that the pop-up menu for dragging and dropping a file offered a third option, Link Here. Links are a kind of copy that don't take up much space. In the world of that other OS, you probably thought of them as *shortcuts*. Links let you create a pseudo-copy of a file or directory that doesn't take up the space of the original file. If you wanted a copy of a particularly large file to exist in several places on the disk, it makes more sense to point to the original and let the system deal with the link as though it *were* the original. It's important to remember that deleting a link doesn't remove the original file, just the link.

Speaking of links, if you know the pathname to something, you can create a link in any directory at any time. You might remember that I said your desktop itself was a directory—in fact, you saw it in Konqueror when I had you navigating your personal home directory. Anyhow, by right-clicking in Konqueror's active window, you can choose Create New (like you did to create a directory) and select Link to Location (URL) from the menu.

A pop-up window will appear with the words *New Link to Location (URL)* and a blank box for you to enter a location. In this case, you have to know the name of the location that you are linking. For instance, your system comes with a number of sample wallpapers (which we will talk about in the next chapter). If for some reason I wanted to have a copy of one of these wallpapers in my home directory, I might link to it as Figure 5–7 shows. Enter the full pathname and press <Enter>. That's it.

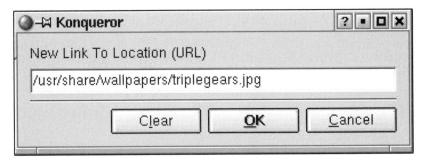

Figure 5–7 Creating an icon link to a URL.

When the icon shows up on your desktop, the full path to the file will be the name. If you would like to see something different, right-click on the link you just created and select Properties. A dialog box will appear with three tabs: General, which is the link name; Permissions, which represents security-related information; and URL, the path to the file itself (Figure 5–8). Once created, you probably shouldn't need to change the URL.

On the General tab, you should see an icon next to the name of the file you are linking to. You can change that icon by clicking on it and selecting a new one from the list that pops up (you'll find hundreds). Furthermore, you can change the name of the link you just created to something that makes more sense to you. When you first open the Properties dialog, the file name is already highlighted. Just type the new name and hit <Enter>.

The middle tab, Permissions, lets you change who gets access to a file or directory and what kind of access they get.

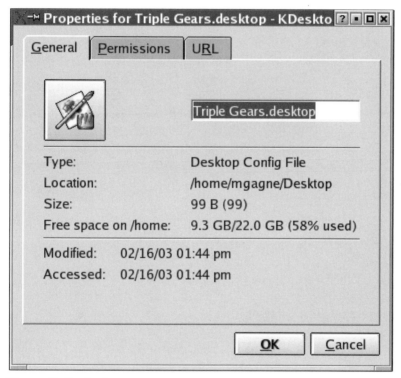

Figure 5–8   Desktop icon properties.

Which Brings Us to Permissions

This is your first look at Linux security, this time at the file (or directory) level. Under that Properties tab, you'll see a list of access permissions (Figure 5–9).

Figure 5–9 *File permissions in Properties dialog.*

This is how you would go about changing permissions. There is, however, another way to identify file permissions that doesn't involve opening up a properties dialog for every file. Remember those file tips I had you configure for Konqueror? Well, we are going to use those now.

Move your mouse pointer so that it hovers over any file. A file tip dialog will pop up (Figure 5–10), telling you the type of file, the size, the last modification date, and the permissions.

There are actually 10 columns describing permissions for a file. For the most part, you'll see either a hyphen or a d in the first column—this would represent a directory. The next nine columns are actually three sets of three columns. Those other nine characters (characters 2–10) indicate permissions for the user or owner of the file (first three), the group (second group of three), and others or everyone else (last three). If you look at an image and see -rw-rw-r--, you'll see that the user and group have read and write permissions. All others have *read-only* permission, the same permission everyone else has.

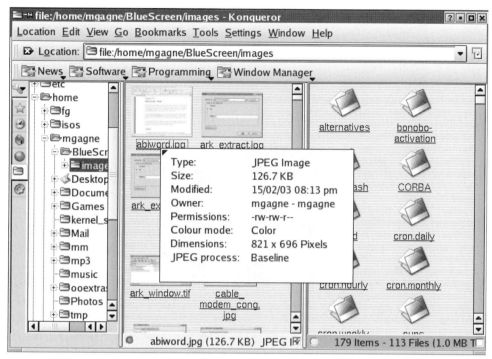

Figure 5–10   File tips displaying permissions in Konqueror.

 Shell Out Want to see the permissions at the shell prompt? Simply add `-l` to the `ls` command, like this:

```
ls -l directory_name
```

From time to time during your Linux experience, you will have to change permissions, sometimes to give someone else access to your directories or files or to make a script or program executable. By using the Permissions tab, you can select read, write, or execute permissions for the owner (yourself), the group you belong to, and everyone else by checking off the permissions in the appropriate check boxes.

Deleting Files and Directories

Every once in a while, some file or directory has outlived its usefulness. It is time to be ruthless and do a little cleaning up on the old file system.

As you've no doubt come to expect, there are several ways to get rid of an offending file or directory. The friendliest and safest method is to drag the file from Konqueror to the *trash can icon* on your desktop. For the novice, this is a safer method because items sent to the trash can be recovered—until you take out the trash, that is. Until that time, you can click on the trash can icon and (*you guessed it*) a Konqueror window will appear, showing you the items you have sent to the trash. These items can then be moved (or copied) back to wherever you need them. To remove files from the trash permanently, right-click on the trash can icon and click on Empty Trash Bin.

 Note Once you empty the trash bin, those files are gone forever.

I did say that there were other ways of deleting a file. From Konqueror, you can select a file or directory, right-click, and select Move to trash. Notice that there is another option on the menu labeled simply *Delete*. If you are absolutely sure that you don't want this file hanging around (even in the trash bin), select Delete from the menu or press <Shift+Delete>. The file will be gone for good.

 Note To really and truly delete something, *shred* it. You do this by selecting a file and pressing <Ctrl+Shift+Delete>. This writes random bits of garbage over the file before deleting it.

My World, My Way

I'm hoping that you are walking away from this chapter impressed with the power and flexibility of the tools you have at your disposal. Konqueror may well become your most important application by the time you are finished reading this book. I've barely touched on some of its capabilities. Never fear, you'll see more of Konqueror when you get to Chapter 11.

Before we move on to the next chapter, I have a special treat for the power users among you. You know who you are because you were getting excited every time I had you shell out. Click Window in Konqueror's menu bar and select Show Terminal Emulator. Just like that, a shell prompt opens up at the bottom of your Konqueror window (Figure 5–11).

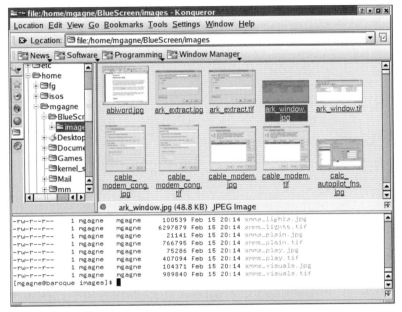

Figure 5–11   A command shell running inside Konqueror.

From there, you can type all your Linux commands. When you are done, simply type `exit`, and the window will close.

Making Your Home a Home

By now you're starting to feel like this isn't so difficult after all. In fact, it's probably starting to feel pretty familiar. After all, there are many similarities in desktop environments and working with KDE isn't like working in a totally alien environment. Well, it's time to make your new virtual home even more of a home. It is time to personalize your desktop experience.

In the next chapter, we'll talk about changing your background, adding icons, setting up a screensaver, and all those other things that help make your desktop yours and yours alone.

6

Customizing Your Desktop (or Making Your World Your Own)

After having taken the first steps into the Linux world, you are probably thinking, "Hey, this is pretty easy" and "I wonder what the fuss was all about." For what it's worth, I'm thinking the very same thing. Now that the fear of dealing with a new operating system is gone, it's time to get really comfortable.

In this chapter, I'm going to show you how to make your system truly your own. I'll show you how to change your background, your colors, your fonts, and anything else you'll need to create a desktop as individual as you are. Would you like some icons on your desktop? Perhaps some shortcuts to programs you use on a regular basis? No problem. I'll cover all those things, too.

I Am Sovereign of All I Survey . . .

As I've already mentioned, working in the Linux world is working in a *multi-user* world. What this means is that everyone who uses your computer can have his or her own unique environment. Any changes you make to your desktop while you are logged in as yourself will have no effect on little Sarah when she logs in to play her video games. If she happens to delete all the icons on her desktop or changes everything to a garish purple and pink, it won't affect you, either.

Let's start with something simple. The first thing most people want to change is their background. It's sort of like moving into a new house or apartment. The wallpaper (or paint) that someone else chose rarely fits into your idea of décor. Same goes for your computer's desktop. Let's get you something more to your liking.

Changing the Background

Start by right-clicking somewhere on the desktop. From the menu that appears, choose Configure Desktop. You'll get a configuration card (see Figure 6–1) with the words "You can customize the desktop here" on it (KDE 3.1 says "Change the appearance of the desktop" instead). On the left side of that card, there's an item called *Background*. Click on that, and you will be able to modify your background settings.

Over on the right side, a display shows you a preview of what your new desktop will look like. Directly beside that, on the left, is a box that gives you the opportunity to change your settings for all your virtual desktops or each individually. When you start feeling *particularly creative*, you can play around with creating a unique identity for every virtual desktop, but for now, leave the check box set for Common Background.

To change the background image, you must select the Wallpaper tab. Then make sure that the radio button Single Wallpaper is clicked on. Now select an image by clicking on the drop-down list, Wallpaper. These are the default system wallpapers, and you'll find that there are quite a few already installed. Scroll down the list, highlighting titles as you go, and notice that a preview of your new wallpaper appears in the small monitor image. To find images in something other than the default directory, click Browse, and a Konqueror-like file manager will pop up, allowing you to navigate the disk in search of your personal images. When that file dialog opens, make sure you click on the icon directly beside the drop-down navigation bar. It turns the image preview on and off. You'll definitely want it *on*.

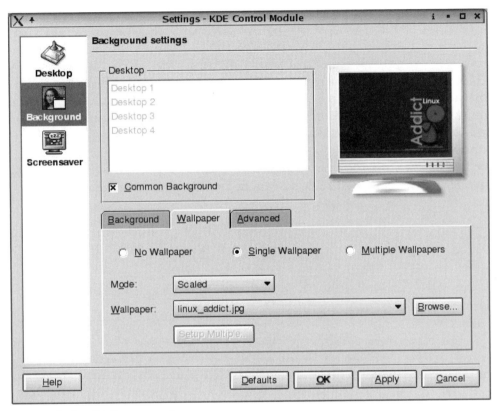

Figure 6–1   Wallpaper settings.

When you see something you like, click on either OK or Apply to make it official. The difference between the two is that OK will exit the configuration program, whereas Apply will change your background but leave the settings program running (in case you are feeling particularly indecisive).

Another setting you might have noticed on the Wallpaper tab is *Mode*. This tells the system how to treat the image you select. Some images are only small graphic *tiles*, designed to be copied over and over until they fill your screen. For these, you would change the mode to Tiled. If the image you are using is a bit small for your screen, you might consider Centered Maxpect, which will grow the image as much as possible while retaining the relative width and height. If you just want the image to fill your screen and you don't care what it looks like, go for Scaled. Play. Experiment. These are *your* walls.

It is also possible to configure multiple wallpapers. What this does is provide you with a means of picking several wallpapers that you can have automatically switch at whatever interval you decide on (the default is 60 minutes). Once you click on the Multiple Wallpapers radio button, the Setup Multiple button at the bottom will become active. Click here, and you'll be asked to select the time interval for the images to rotate and whether you want the rotation to be sequential or random. I happen to like random. Now click Add, and that Konqueror-like file manager will pop up so that you can select the images you want to use in the random rotation. Select as many or as few as you like, click OK to exit the various dialogs, and you are done.

Incidentally, you don't *have* to have a wallpaper. You can create a nice, plain background by going to the Wallpaper tab and clicking the No Wallpaper radio button. After that, you would select one or two colors from the Background tab. The Mode lets you select different ways of blending the colors.

Save My Screen, Please!

Okay, screensavers don't really do much screen saving these days. The idea, once upon a time, was to protect screens from phosphor burn-in. Old-style monochrome screens were particularly bad for this. In time, the letters from your menus (we were using text in those days) would burn in to the phosphor screen. Even when you turned off the monitor, you could still see the ghostly outline of your most popular application burned into the screen itself. As we moved to color screens and graphics, that changed somewhat but the problem continued to exist for some time, partly due to the static nature of the applications we were using.

Time passes, and some bright light somewhere got the idea that if you constantly changed the image on the screen, that type of burn-in would not be as likely. What better way to achieve this than to have some kind of clever animation kick in when the user walked away from the screen for a few minutes (or hours). Heck, it might even be fun to watch. The screensaver was born. Modern screens use scanning techniques that all but banished burn-in, but screensavers did not go away. Those addictive fish, toasters, penguins, snow, spaceships, etc., etc. have managed to keep us entertained, despite the march of technology. Let's face it, we are all hooked.

Depending on your distribution, your screensaver may or may not already be active by default. Getting to your screensaver setup involves the same first steps as changing your background. Right-click on a clear part of the desktop and choose Configure Desktop. The desktop configuration card will appear ("You can customize the desktop here"). On the left side of that card, there's an item called *Screensaver*. Click away.

Like the wallpaper manager before this, you get a nice little preview window over to the right that will give you an idea of what your screensaver will look like (Figure 6–2). The first thing you will want to do is click the "Enable screensaver" check box, assuming, of course, that it isn't already on (the message on KDE 3.1 says "Start screen saver automatically"). Now pick a screensaver from the list and watch the results on the preview screen. To see the real thing in action, click the Test button. To go back to the configuration screen, press any key. Some screensavers can be modified, which is why you also have a Setup button. For instance, the *Rock* screensaver, which simulates flying through space, lets you change the number of rocks (or asteroids) flying toward you and whether your spaceship moves or rotates through the mess.

Before you click OK, you may want to change the default time before your screensaver kicks in. Mine is set for five minutes. In an office environment (or

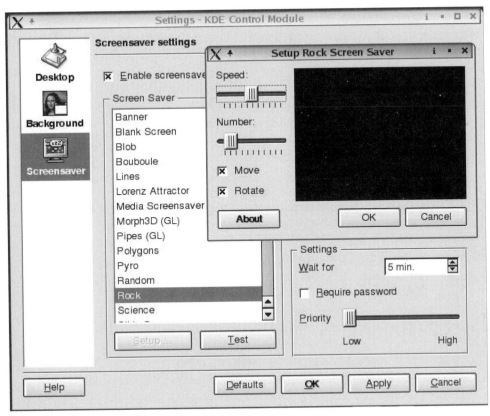

Figure 6–2   Selecting a screensaver.

a busy household), you will probably want to password-protect your screen when you walk away. To do this, click on Require password. When the screen-saver starts, you will need to enter your login password to get back to your work. Always remember that your password is case-sensitive.

Moving Things Around

If you haven't already done this, click on an icon (hold the click) and drag it to some other spot on the desktop. Easy, isn't it? When you log out from your KDE session later on, make sure that you click Save session for future logins so that any changes you make here will follow you into the next session.

The taskbar is something else you may want to move. Just drag the panel and drop it to one of the four positions on the desktop (top, bottom, left, or right side). The location, by the way, can also be changed by right-clicking on the taskbar, selecting Preferences (or Configure Panel), and choosing the location of the panel. On the card that appears (Figure 6–3), you can select the location, the size of the panel and its icons, and the length that you are willing to allow the panel on your desktop.

Semantics Technically, the taskbar is that portion of the *panel* that shows your open programs, letting you quickly click from one to the other. That said, you may find that people speak of the taskbar and the panel interchangeably.

On that customization card, you can lock in on some taskbar-specific con-figurations. For instance, by default, your taskbar will *show all programs* you have open on your desktop, regardless of which virtual desktop you opened them on. Some people like this feature but I am not one of them. This is some-thing I check off because I want to see only the programs on the virtual desk-top I am currently running on. Remember, these settings are a personal thing.

The Show window list button option provides a small popup right next to the taskbar. This popup shows a quick list of all windows on all desktops; handy if, like me, you turned off the first option. Group similar tasks is another very personal option. Let's say that you opened up three Konsoles. If you have this option set, only one task group will show up in the taskbar—a small black arrow on the task will let you know that there are more like that. If you click on the Konsole task (in the taskbar), you'll see all three.

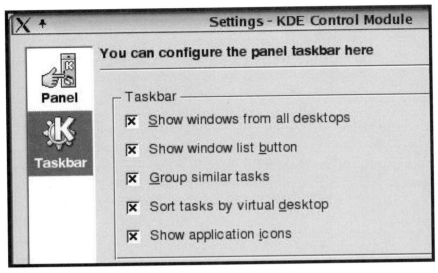

Figure 6–3   Panel and taskbar settings.

The last two items aren't particularly exciting but I will quickly mention them. The first lets you sort tasks by virtual desktop, and the other shows tiny icons next to the task name.

Is That a Theme or a Motif?

Not a musical theme, but a desktop theme. A theme is a collection of buttons, decorations, colors, backgrounds, and so on, preselected and packaged to give your desktop a finished and coherent look. Some themes even incorporate sounds (for startup, shutdown, opening and closing program windows, etc.) into the whole package. It can be a lot of fun.

Then we have *styles*, which are sort of like themes but not as all-encompassing. Styles tend to concentrate on window decorations and behavior, as well as *widgets*. Widgets are things like radio buttons, check boxes, combo boxes (drop-down lists), sliders, tabs, and so on.

All right, I know you want to get to it and change your theme a time or two, but first I'm going to tell you something rather important. Most (if not all) of the things I've shown you so far on customizing your desktop can be done through the *KDE Control Center*. You'll find it by clicking on the big K and looking for Control Center. If you are having trouble locating it, remember that you can bring it up by pressing <Alt+F2> and typing in `kcontrol`, its program name.

Quick Tip You may recall a friendly little warning I gave you earlier. Different Linux distributions will arrange the menus in different ways. You may also find a *Preferences* menu (or it may also be called *Look and Feel*) in your K menu. As you will hear again and again, *there's more than one way to do it.*

Incidentally, when you bring up a submenu from the main (big K) menu, notice the dashed line under that menu. This is a *"tear-off"* line. Clicking here on a submenu will detach it and let you have constant access to it from your desktop. This is extremely handy when you are using the same functions over and over again (like when you are playing with themes and colors). When you are through with the submenu, simply close it by clicking the *x* in the corner.

As soon as the KDE Control Center loads up, it displays some capsule information about the system, its hostname, and the version of Linux running on it. Over on the left side, an index page covers a number of items that can be either viewed or modified on the system. I say either because some of what you see here is just information and cannot be changed. One of the modifiable items is Look and Feel. Click the plus sign beside it, and you'll get a list of options for changing your desktop environment's look and feel (Figure 6–4).

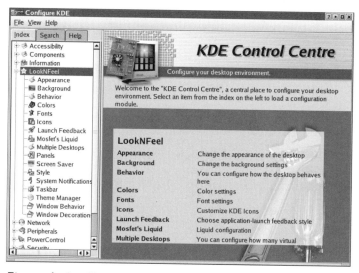

Figure 6–4 Changing the look and feel in KDE's control panel.

Almost everything you could possibly ever want to do to alter your desktop experience is here. Change the background, colors, fonts, icons, screensaver . . . you name it. It is all here! That includes your themes and styles. Go ahead. Click on Style and select a style from the Widget Style list. As you click, the preview window will show you how it affects the overall look. If you just want to see it in action but you don't want to commit yet, click Apply. When you know you can live with the changes, click OK.

Let's look at a couple of those Look and Feel changes and how they affect what you do and how you work.

Window Decorations

This is also your opportunity to undo something I had you change back in Chapter 4. When you ran kpersonalizer, I had you select the KDE Classic style so that we could all be on the same page (so to speak) in terms of what you see in your title bar. With the introduction of KDE 3.1, the default theme is called *Keramik*, a slick, modern-looking theme that changes a number of things related to your desktop experience. Figures 6–5 through 6–7 show the KDE2 (Classic), ModSystem, and Keramik window decorations, respectively.

If you would like to use something different, you can make that change now. Just remember that things may look a little different than what I show you in the book from here on in. With that little disclaimer in place, you may now express your individuality.

Figure 6–5   KDE 2 Classic window decoration.

Figure 6–6   ModSystem window decoration.

Figure 6–7   Keramik (KDE 3.1 default) window decoration.

Themes and Styles

Themes and styles are essentially collections of look and feel changes. A style is a collection of definitions affecting primarily widgets (buttons, tabs, etc., see Figure 6–8).

A theme, on the other hand, might encompass changes in window decorations, wallpaper, colors, and icons to create a cohesive, integrated desktop experience, whereas a change in window decoration would affect only the window decoration itself.

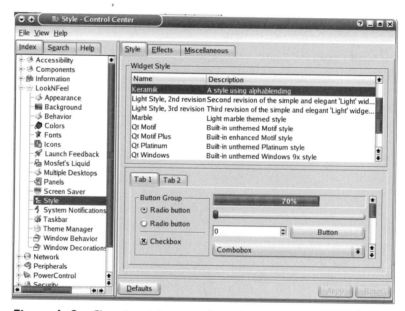

Figure 6–8   Changing styles are reflected in the KDE Control Center.

The theme manager (Figure 6–9) is similar. Under the Installer tab, it lists the installed themes and provides a preview window. The Contents tab is interesting, in that you can limit what changes the theme manager will apply to your system. For instance (and I know this will sound like sacrilege to some), I hate sound themes—honestly, I can't stand having little tunes play each time I start a program or minimize a window. That's why I personally uncheck the Sound effects check box.

The fashion slaves among you will quickly grow tired of the themes and styles your system comes with—there are quite a few but not nearly enough for those surfing the edges of what's hot today. That's why you should keep this little Web site in mind:

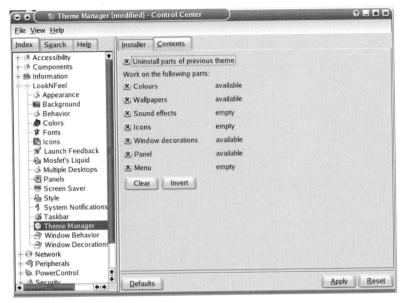

Figure 6–9   Theme manager options in the Control Center.

```
http://www.kde-look.org
```

This site has tons of themes, styles, alternative wallpapers, and icons— enough to keep you busy for a long, long time. Now I know we haven't talked about getting on the Net yet; we still have a few things to cover. If you just can't wait, you could jump over to Chapter 9, "Connecting to the Internet." Just make sure you come back here. You wouldn't want to miss anything.

Adding Icons and Shortcuts to Your Desktop

I covered this topic somewhat in the last chapter, but it is time to look at this in detail. While working with Konqueror, you might recall that you had a directory called *Desktop* and that this directory actually *was* your desktop. If you wanted to get a file onto your desktop, you could just drag and drop (copy or link) a file there. A good reason for doing this is that it puts things you use on a regular basis (a business spreadsheet perhaps or a contact list) right where you can quickly get to them.

The single most useful icon you will want to add to your desktop is a link to a program on your system, something you might have called a *shortcut* under your old OS. Maybe you need to have your word processor or your CD player handy. Whatever it is, you would like it there in front of you.

The second most useful link is a Uniform Resource Locator (URL) to a regularly visited Web site. We already looked at creating a Link to Location in the last chapter because a URL can point to a file just as easily as a Web site. Instead of the path to a file, simply type in the URL to your favorite site. I will cover surfing the Net in greater detail later in this book. Let's continue by adding a program to your desktop.

What you need to understand is that you won't really be putting the program there but rather a link to it. Right-click on the desktop and move your mouse cursor over Create New, then select Link to Application. The dialog box or card that opens has four tabs. The first, *General*, lets you choose a name for the program. Notice that the words *Link to Application* are highlighted. You can just type a name that makes sense to you here. To the left of the name is a square with a gearlike icon. Clicking this square brings up a large collection of icons from which you can select whatever happens to take your fancy (Figure 6–10).

Figure 6–10 Selecting an icon for your new shortcut.

Once you have chosen an icon, skip over to the third tab, *Execute*. This is where you enter the program's real name. For example, if you wanted a link to the calculator, you would enter `/usr/bin/kcalc`. Another way to get there is to click the Browse button and navigate your way to the application. The *Permissions* tab lets you decide whether others can see, modify, or execute the icon (remember that it is possible to create these links in other directories, including public directories). If you are creating an icon for your personal home directory, you can pretty much ignore this.

When you are happy with your changes, click OK. Your new program link (which you can launch with a single click) should appear on your desktop.

 Shell Out To create a shortcut icon for a command, you first have to know what the command is and where it is. To be honest, a command or program (such as the KDE calculator, kcalc) could be almost anywhere on the disk. For the most part, programs tend to be in one of the "bin" directories, `/bin`, `/usr/bin`, or `/usr/local/bin`. You can also use the whereis command to tell you exactly. For instance, in order to know where the `kcalc` program is, I would do the following at the Konsole shell prompt (the "$" sign).

```
[mgagne@mysystem mgagne]$ whereis kcalc

kcalc: /usr/bin/kcalc /usr/lib/kcalc.la
/usr/lib/kcalc.so
```

As you can see, there are other files associated with the kcalc program, but the actual executable kcalc (the one to use) is in `/usr/bin`.

Miscellaneous Changes

Now that I have shown you how to find all these things, I'm going to let you explore the Look and Feel menu on your own. Check out the Fonts dialog if you would like different desktop fonts than what is set by default. You might find it interesting to note that there are different icon sets available than the ones you currently see. Click Icons and go wild. If you do change the icons, just *be aware* that those I describe when pointing to the panel or to various applications may look a little different than what you now see.

Let me give you one final *treat* before I close this chapter. Still working from the KDE control center, look for Keyboard Shortcuts (under either Look and Feel or Accessibility), and you'll discover lots of interesting keyboard short-cuts to do things such as switching from one application to the other, switching from one desktop to the other, opening and closing windows, getting help, taking a desktop screenshot (in case you want to share your fashion sense with others), and so on. A minor word of warning, though—you may have to scroll down through the list to see everything.

7

Installing
New Packages

The average Linux distribution CD comes with several gigabytes of software. SuSE, for one, delivers several CDs in a boxed set with enough software to keep you busy for weeks, maybe months. I'll tell you how to install that software, easily and without fuss. Despite all that your distribution has to offer, sooner or later you will find yourself visiting various Internet sites, looking for new and updated software. Where will you find this stuff, and will installing be the same as getting it from your CDs?

Before we get into finding, building, and installing software, I'd like to address a little myth. You have no doubt heard that installing software on Linux is difficult and that it is inferior to what you are used to in the Windows world. Nothing could be further from the truth. In fact, software installation under Linux is actually quite superior to what you are leaving behind in your old OS.

Security Note When you install software and software packages, you must often do so as the root, or administrative user. As root, you are all powerful. Linux tends to be more secure and much safer than your old OS, but that doesn't mean disasters can't strike. Know where your software comes from and take the time to understand what it does. When you compile software (which I will cover later in this chapter), it might even be a good idea to get into the habit of building as a non-root user, then switching to root for the installation portion. Don't worry—I'll explain.

Linux and Security

When it comes to installing software, security is something we should talk about. I've already said that you should know where your software is coming from, but that is only part of the consideration. That's why I'm going to clear up some bad press Linux gets when it comes to installing software.

In the Windows world, it is frighteningly easy to infect your PC with a virus or a worm. All you have to do is click on an email attachment, and you could be in trouble. With some email packages under Windows, it does the clicking for you and by being so helpful, once again, you could be in trouble. You won't find many Linux packages provided as simple executables (.EXE files and so on). *Security is the reason*. To install most packages, you also need root privileges. Again, for security reasons. Linux demands that you be conscious of the fact that you might be doing something that could hurt your system. If an email attachment wants to install itself into the system, it will have to consult the root user first.

Package managers, such as `rpm` (the RPM Package Manager) or Debian's `dselect` and `apt-get`, perform checks to make sure that certain dependencies are met or that software doesn't accidentally overwrite other software. Those dependency checks take many things into consideration, such as what software already exists and how the new package will coexist. Many of you are probably familiar with what has been called *DLL hell*, where one piece of software just goes ahead and overwrites some other piece of code. It may even have happened to you. Blindly installing without these checks can be disastrous. At best, the result can be an unstable machine—at worst, it can be unusable.

Installing software under Linux may take a step or two, but it is for your own good.

Searching for Common Ground

Every major Linux vendor wants to make the Linux experience as wonderful as possible, particularly when it comes in installing software packages. Consequently, almost everyone has a software installation tool that they have tweaked to make the user experience as simple as possible, a tool that deals with package dependencies easily.

SuSE provides YaST2. Mandrake has RpmDrake (or the command-line `urpmi`). Lindows has its Click-N-Run service. As you can see, there are many alternatives. In this chapter, however, I'm going to try to be release-*agnostic* and cover those tools that should be in almost any distribution.

Let's start this exploration with KDE's own package manager, *kpackage*.

Note In the initial release of Red Hat 8.0, kpackage was not compiled into the kdeadmin package (of which kpackage is part). If you are working with this release and kdeadmin has not yet been updated by the time this book is released, there is still a way. When you find a package you want (while surfing with Konqueror), click the one you want to install and click Open when Konqueror asks whether you want to open using Install Packages.

Kpackage

KDE's package tool, kpackage, uses a graphical interface to allow for easy installation or removal of packages. When you first start up kpackage (which you can quickly call by pressing <Alt+F2> and typing `kpackage`), you'll get a two-pane display with the installed packages on the left and an information window on the right. Click on an installed package (such as *tar* in Figure 7–1), and you'll get to know all about that package in the right-hand window's Properties tab.

Click on the File List tab, and you'll get a listing of every file that makes up this package and where these files live on your system. This is actually a great way to get to know the packages installed on your system, and I would highly recommend walking through the list and getting a feel for what comprises your Linux system.

Notice as well that all of the packages in that tree view to the left are in a category hierarchy, based on what kind of package they are.

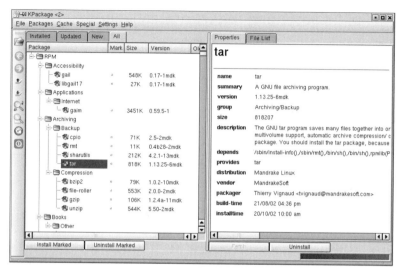

Figure 7–1   Kpackage, the KDE package manager.

To remove (or uninstall) a package, just click on the Uninstall button at the bottom of the screen (Figure 7–2). A warning screen will appear, listing the package (or packages) you are looking to uninstall. If this is really what you want to do (and by the way, *I do not recommend that you uninstall* tar), click Uninstall. A report of the uninstall process will appear in the right-hand side information window.

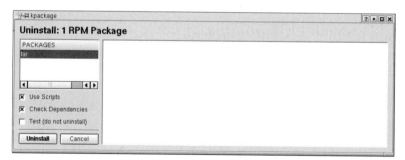

Figure 7–2   Using kpackage to uninstall software.

Installing Packages

To install a package, we first need to identify one, and there are many ways of doing this. Using Konqueror, I surfed over to http://www.rpmfind.net and searched for a package. In this case, I chose the bzflag package (a cool

3D networked tank game). I typed *bzflag* in the search field, then I found in the list of packages a release that was compiled for Mandrake (which I happened to be running at the time), and I clicked on the file. Konqueror recognizes this as an RPM package and offers to bring up Kpackage, the installation tool (Figure 7–3). You can also right-click on the package, click Open with from the menu, and select or type *kpackage*.

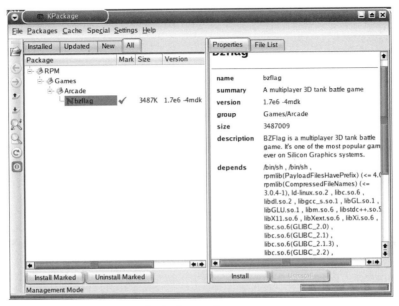

Figure 7–3   Installing the bzflag tank game.

Quick Tip You'll see many different types of packages in these listings. Pay particular attention to the last two suffixes in the package name, for example, `.i386.rpm`. This implies a package built for the Intel (x86) architecture. A `.i586.rpm` would indicate a package that will not work on anything less than a Pentium architecture (no 486 for you). Another you may see is `.alpha.rpm`. This one represents the Power PC architecture. If you see `.src.rpm`, this represents a source package. It is nonbinary and would have to be built on your system before you could use it.

I click Open, and the system downloads the software and presents me with a window listing that package. After clicking Install, the options presented are Upgrade, Replace Files, Replace Packages, Check Dependencies, and Test (doesn't actually do an installation). You can safely accept the default options, which are to upgrade, replacing old packages as well as checking dependencies. When you are ready to do the install, select your package (listed to the left) and click Install. You will now be asked for the root password (Figure 7–4). Enter it and press <Enter>.

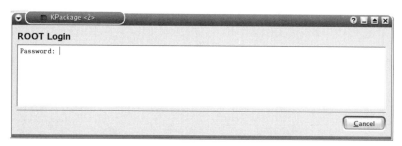

Figure 7–4   Package installations must be cleared by root.

After a few seconds, the package installation will complete, and kpackage will display the status of the new package, along with its description.

Quick Tip There's another way to install using kpackage, and this is particularly good if you are installing more than one piece of software (or if you are a big fan of drag-and-drop computing). After finding a package with Konqueror, simply drag the rpm package onto a running kpackage and follow the steps.

When dependencies are an issue (you may see a list of unsatisfied dependencies in the Properties tab of the install screen), just drag the missing packages into the kpackage window, mark each package by clicking on the dot in the Mark column (a green checkmark will appear), then click Install Marked to do them all as a batch. In Figure 7–5, I installed GnomeMeeting (similar to NetMeeting) to demonstrate this method.

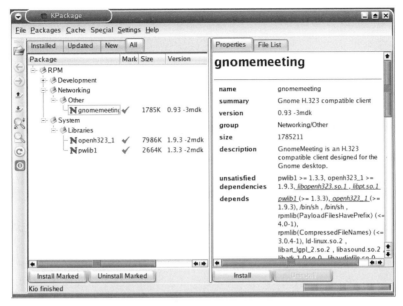

Figure 7–5   Installing multiple interdependent packages.

RPMs, the Shell Way

Would you like a very fast and easy way to install RPM packages? You may find this hard to believe, but at times, opening up a shell and typing commands can be much faster than going through all those graphical steps. I'll show you how it is done in this *extended Shell Out session*. Let's pretend that you have just downloaded some great package, and now the RPM file for it is sitting in one of your directories. Using a hypothetical package of my invention, let's install that package with command-line rpm.

```
cd /directory_where/package_lives
rpm -ivh ftl-transport-2.1-1.i386.rpm
```

The only thing you need to be aware of here is that package installation needs to be done as the root user. The command that does all the work is called rpm. The flags that I am passing to it tell rpm to install the package (the -i flag), to be verbose (the -v flag), and to print out little hash marks while it does its work (the -h flag). Note that you do not have to have a dash before each letter option (-i -v -h)—you can combine them instead (-ivh).

```
# rpm -ivh ftl-travel-2.1-1.i386.rpm
ftl-travel
##################################################
```

If you want to know everything that is happening, drop the -h flag and add two more v's. The results are pretty wordy, but you do get to see what is happening during the various stages of the installation, as well as what files are being installed and where.

 Note Commands in the Linux world are case-sensitive. The hypothetical command `makecoffee` would be different than `MakeCoffee`. The same is true for command-line parameters such as in the RPM example above; options and flags such as `-U` mean different things than `-u`.

Upgrading an existing package is just as easy. As part of the process, older versions of files will be replaced, and the package's default configuration files may be moved or renamed to preserve the originals (you will usually see appropriate messages if this occurs). Upgrading is more or less the same as installing except that you use the -U flag on the command line instead of the -i flag.

```
rpm -Uvh matter_transporter-1.2-1.i386.rpm
```

To erase a package, use the -e flag, instead.

```
rpm -e matter_transporter
```

Notice that when I delete the package, I don't add the release number extensions (the -2.1-1.i386.rpm type of suffix).

A full-blown Linux installation will have a lot of packages installed. If you are curious, you can list every single package by typing the following command.

```
rpm -qa | sort | more
```

That shell command is actually three in one. The rpm -qa portion tells rpm to *query* the RPM database and list *all* the packages. The bar that you see is called the *pipe* symbol. It literally means to pipe the output of the first command into the second command. The second command in this case is sort. After the packages have been listed and sorted, we pipe that output one more time into the more command. In other words, show me a screen full of information, then pause before showing me more. To see the next page, press the space bar. To quit the listing, type the letter q by itself.

RPM can tell you a lot about the packages you have installed. To find out what version of the fileutils package you have on the system and what it is, use the -q flag along with the -i flag.

```
$ rpm -qi fileutils
Name        : fileutils              Relocations: (not relocateable)
Version     : 4.1.11                     Vendor: MandrakeSoft
Release     : 5mdk                   Build Date: Wed 28 Aug 2002
08:39:42 AM EDT
Install date: Sun 20 Oct 2002 10:00:04 AM EDT     Build Host: ke.mandrake-
soft.com
Group       : File tools             Source RPM: fileutils-4.1.11-
5mdk.src.rpm
Size        : 2344533                   License: GPL
Packager    : Thierry Vignaud <tvignaud@mandrakesoft.com>
URL         : ftp://alpha.gnu.org/gnu/fetish/
Summary     : The GNU versions of common file management utilities
Description :
The fileutils package includes a number of GNU versions of common and
popular file management utilities.  Fileutils includes the following
tools: chgrp (changes a file's group ownership), chown (changes a
file's ownership), chmod (changes a file's permissions), cp (copies
files), dd (copies and converts files), df (shows a filesystem's disk
usage), dir (gives a brief directory listing), dircolors (the setup
program for the color version of the ls command), du (shows disk
usage), install (copies files and sets permissions), ln (creates file
links), ls (lists directory contents), mkdir (creates directories),
mkfifo (creates FIFOs or named pipes), mknod (creates special files),
mv (renames files), rm (removes/deletes files), rmdir (removes empty
directories), sync (synchronizes memory and disk), touch (changes file
timestamps), and vdir (provides long directory listings).
```

Using -l instead of -i will list all the files in the package. You can even do a sort of reverse file listing by asking rpm to look in its database to identify what package a particular file belongs to. To find out what package a file belongs to,

use the -f flag. For example, in my /sbin directory, there is a file called
sysctl. If I want to know where this file came from and what package it be-
longed to, I use this command:

```
rpm -qf /sbin/sysctl
procps-2.0.7-14mdk
```

To discover all the things the rpm command can do for you, type man rpm,
and you will be able to read the manual page related to that command. As you
can see, it really isn't all that complicated to work from the command line. If you
prefer the graphical tools, then by all means use them. But don't be afraid of
using the shell when you have the opportunity.

Look, Use the Source . . .

Once you've downloaded that new software, you'll no doubt be anxious to
take things out for a spin. The truth is that there is an *amazing* amount of software available for Linux. If trying out new things is exciting for you, I can pretty much guarantee that you won't get bored anytime soon.

Much of this software is available as source—not surprising because the
GPL license (under which much of the Linux software out there is distributed)
requires that you distribute source along with the programs. There are also
open source projects that have no relation to the GNU projects that employ the
license as a means of copyright. Then there are other open source projects that
use BSD-style licensing, artistic licensing, postcard licensing, and many others; all distribute their programs in source format.

At first glance, this may appear to be nothing but a *nuisance*, yet source
makes software *portable*. The number of platforms on which a single package
can be compiled tends to be much higher because the applications can be built
using your system at your operating system level with your libraries. It means
that if you are running VendorX 8.1, you don't need to go looking for the VendorX 8.1 package.

Here's another reason. It takes developers time to provide packages compiled and ready to run on multiple platforms—time they may not have, particularly if they are doing this without pay. Consequently, developers sometimes
have source code available that is much more recent than the precompiled

packages they offer. Why? Because they haven't found the time to build the packages for all those platforms. Here's a plus side you may not have considered: If at some point you decide that you want to try your hand at programming, open source means that *you too* can get into the game.

Note As crazy as it may sound, building from source is not all that complicated, and many of the steps required are common across most source distributions. At first it may sound difficult, but no more so than any of the myriad things you've learned how to do with your computer over the years. I admit that compiling from source isn't as straightforward as downloading an RPM package and installing it, but it does open up *thousands* of possibilities.

Here's an added bonus—if you can build one software package, you can pretty much build them all.

The Extract and Build Five-Step

The vast majority of source packages can be built using what I call the *extract and build five-step*. I suppose that step one could also involve the downloading of the software, but I'll pretend you've already found and downloaded something, a hypothetical little package called *ftl-travel*, and you are now anxious to take it for a ride. I'll give you the five steps, then I will discuss them in more detail.

```
tar -xzvf ftl-travel-2.1.tar.gz
cd ftl-travel-2.1
./configure
make
su -c "make install"
```

Easy, isn't it? Now you can just type `ftl-travel` and be on your way. Now that you've seen a source package installation, let me give you some details.

Step 1: Unpacking the Archive

Most program sources are distributed as *tarballs*, meaning that they have been stored using the tar archiving command. In the name above (`ftl-travel-2.1.tar.gz`) the `ftl-travel` part of it is the name of the program itself. The `2.1` represents the version number of the package, and the `tar.gz` tells us that this package is archived using the tar command and compressed using the `gzip` command.

You can, therefore, extract the archive with the command:

```
tar -xzvf ftl-travel-2.1.tar.gz
```

The `x` means extract. The `z` tells the tar command to use the `gunzip` command to extract. The `v` says that tar should show us a list of the files it is extracting—in other words, be verbose. Finally, the `f` identifies the file itself, the one you just downloaded.

Sometimes the extension `.tar.gz` will be shortened to `.tgz`. There are a few other extensions in use out there. For instance, the package may have a `.tar.Z` extension instead, meaning that the file has been compressed using the compress command. To extract the source from this tarball, you first uncompress the file using the uncompress command. Then you continue with your tar extract:

```
uncompress ftl-travel-2.1.tar.Z
tar -xvf ftp-travel-2.1.tar
```

To make life even easier, you could also just shorten the whole thing to:

```
tar -xZvf filename.tar.Z
```

Every once in a while (if the package is very large), the extension will be `.bz2`, otherwise known as a *bzip2 archive*. To open this one, you perform essentially the same steps you did with compress. Use the command:

```
bunzip2 ftl-drive-1.01.tar.bz2
```

to uncompress the file, then extract using the standard `tar` command.

Steps 2–5: Building Your Programs

Once you have extracted the program source from the tar archive, change directory to the software's distribution directory. That's step 2. Using my current ftl-travel example, type `cd ftl-travel-2.1`. From there, I build and install my software, like this.

```
./configure
make
su -c "make install"
```

The `./configure` step builds what is called a `Makefile`. The `Makefile` is used by the next command, `make`. In building the `Makefile`, the `configure` step collects information about your system and determines what needs to be compiled or recompiled in order to build your software. This brings us to the next step, which is to type `make`. You'll see a lot of information going by on your screen as programs are compiled and linked. Usually (after a successful compile), you follow the make command by typing `su -c "make install"`. This will copy the software into the directories defined in the `Makefile`.

Quick Tip The reason that I have you type `su -c "make install"` is because the final step of an installation usually needs to be done by the root user. Because we don't want to be running as root on a regular basis (for security reasons), the `su -c` step lets us quickly jump into root user mode for one command (where you will be prompted for the root password) and just as quickly jump back out.

A number of programmers also provide a `make uninstall` option, should you decide that you do not want to keep the program around.

Note If you are an open source programmer (or plan to be one) and you want to make people happy, *always* provide an uninstall option.

README, Please!

If you are like me, you tend to want to just install and run that software, which is partly why I jumped ahead a bit and skipped a very important step. You generally do not have to do this because 95% of installs are the same, but . . . just before you go ahead with your final three steps, you should consider pausing in the source directory and typing *ls* to list the files in the directory. What you would see are numerous files, something like this:

```
CHANGES     README Makefile      Makefile.in   configure
INSTALL     ftl-travel.h         ftl-travel.c  engine.c    config.h
```

The first thing you want to do is read any README and INSTALL files. The next step is almost always going to be the `./configure` step I mentioned as part of my extract and build the five-step, but there may be details you want to know about in those files. There may also be some prerequisites that you should know about or some personal options that you may want to set. It takes only a few minutes, and it may be extremely useful.

Getting Your Hands On Software

Way back when, at the beginning of this chapter, I mentioned that there was plenty of software available for your Linux system. Finding it isn't difficult and there are many ways to start your search. One way is to join a Linux User Group or chat with other Linux enthusiasts or users. That's a sure fire way of getting your hands on the latest, greatest, and coolest software.

Another way is to visit some of the more popular Linux software repositories. These include search engines for both packaged software (RPMs) and source (tarred and gzipped files). My favorites in this arena are Rpmfind and TuxFinder (I'll list all of these in the resources section). Take a moment as well to visit the monster archive at ibiblio.org.

You might also want to look at the project and review sites. My favorites in this group are Freshmeat, Sourceforge, and Linux TUCOWS.

Finally, if you are strictly looking for fun and games, check out Chapter 18 for a list dedicated to *downtime*.

At this rate, you'll never run out of software to try out!

Resources

Freshmeat

http://www.freshmeat.net

Ibiblio.org

http://www.ibiblio.org

Rpmfind

http://www.rpmfind.net

SourceForge

http://www.sourceforge.net

TUCOWS Linux

http://linux.tucows.com

TuxFinder

http://www.tuxfinder.org

chapter

8

Working
with Devices

Ah, hardware ... "I hate hardware!"

Part of the personal computer experience seems destined to be an eter-
nal battle in getting your current system to talk to the latest and
greatest devices. There's always a new, hyper-fantastic, 3D video card;
mind-blowing stereo sound system; or hair-trigger game controller out
there. Then there are more mundane things, such as modems, scanners, and printers. Getting all these devices to work with your system
is something that has caused us all grief over time, regardless of what
operating system we were running.

We are used to assuming that anything works with Windows, but
even that isn't true. From time to time, even Windows users must visit
hardware vendors' Web sites to download a driver. I personally spent
several hours looking for and downloading an accelerated video driver
for my little niece's Windows computer so she could run a Barbie ice-
skating program (she is my niece—I couldn't really let her down).

In this chapter, I'm going to give you the tools you need to deal with common issues and give you some tips on avoiding problems in the first place.

Yes, It Runs with Linux!

Device support under Linux is excellent. No, really. The sheer number of things that will work "out of the box" without you having to search for and install drivers is impressive and, quite frankly, beats your old OS. That doesn't mean all is rosy, however. Let me be *brutally* honest here. Some devices have been written to work with Windows and only Windows . . . or so it seems. One of the great things about this open source world is that developers are constantly working to write drivers to make it possible to run that faster-than-light communications card.

That said, if you haven't already bought that new gadget, there are a couple of things that you should do. For starters, if you are in the store looking at that new printer, pull the salesperson aside and *ask* whether it runs with Linux. If the person doesn't know (which is sometimes a problem but less so as time goes on), take a few minutes to check out the excellent Hardware HOWTO document. You can always find the latest version by surfing on over to the LDP's Linux Hardware Compatibility HOWTO page:

```
http://www.tldp.org/HOWTO/Hardware-HOWTO/index.html
```

If you don't find what you are looking for there, check out the hardware compatibility guide on your Linux vendor's site.

 Quick Tip Red Hat's hardware compatibility guide is worth the visit, regardless of what version of Linux you are running. The URL follows. However, keep in mind that things do change on Web sites. If you don't find it there, just go to the main Red Hat site at `http://www.redhat.com` and look for *hardware*.

```
http://hardware.redhat.com/hcl/
```

Here's a hint. Once there, use the Quick Search option for a fast keyword search.

Although Linux is Linux, different releases of different vendors' products may be at different levels of development. Consequently, at one time or another, Red Hat may have slightly more extensive support for hardware than the others, and a month later SuSE may have the widest range of support.

As Linux gains in popularity, you'll find that hardware vendors are increasingly interested in tapping into this ever-growing market. I've had the experience of being on site, adding hardware to a customer's system (Ethernet cards come immediately to mind), and finding that the system did not have the drivers. I quickly visited the Ethernet card manufacturer's Web site and found precompiled drivers ready and waiting for me.

Plug and Play

For the most part, adding a device to a Linux system is simply a matter of plugging it in. If you don't want to configure it manually, a reboot will force hardware detection, and the device should be recognized by the system and configured. USB devices tend to be even easier because of their hot-plug nature. In other words, you don't need to reboot the system in order to have a USB device recognized, and you can unplug it while the system is running.

Getting a device recognized is only part of it, though. Just because your system knows about the device doesn't necessarily mean that it is configured for your applications.

Going back to the driver issue, you may still have to install a driver, as you sometimes had to do in the Windows world. I wouldn't be fair to you if I simply ignored this little tidbit, so I won't.

Getting Familiar with Your Hardware

Meeting new people isn't always easy. Sociologists tell us that there is a complex interplay that takes place whenever we meet someone new, much of it subconscious. Although it is possible to meet someone and instantly like him or her, it is more likely that you become comfortable enough to develop a friendship only after having been around a person for some time—in other words, after you've gotten to know a person better.

Now, what the heck does this have to do with hardware and your Linux system?

Well, it's like this . . . For most, the computer we use is a black (or beige) box with a few things plugged into it and some magic happening inside that makes it possible to surf the Internet. Anything that falls outside the small subset of applications we use makes us uneasy. That's why the notion of trying something new may be intimidating. The best way to get over that is to become comfortable with what you have.

The KDE Control Center (Figure 8–1) is the perfect place to start for getting to know what makes up your system. You'll find it by clicking on the big K and looking for Control Center or by clicking on the Kicker panel. If you are having trouble locating it, remember that you can bring it up by pressing <Alt+F2> and typing in `kcontrol`, its program name.

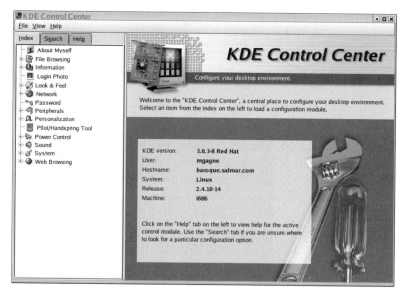

Figure 8–1   The KDE Control Center.

As soon as the KDE Control Center loads up, it displays some capsule information about the system, its hostname, and the version of Linux running on it. Over on the left side, an index page covers a number of items that can be either viewed or modified on the system. I say *either* because some of what you see here is just information and cannot be changed. This tends to be true as far as your devices are concerned. Let's start with a quick overview.

In the category list, you'll see an Information heading with a plus sign beside it. Click on that plus sign, and your hardware's hidden side will start to appear. Would you like to know just how fast your processor really is? Click on Processor in the category list. You might be surprised. How about memory? Just click on Memory, and you'll know where every bit of RAM and swap is allocated. For a look at your X window configuration, click X-Server. There is a lot to it, isn't there? Why don't you take a few minutes to explore this hardware landscape? When you are ready to continue, I'll spend a little time on some specific areas, starting with PCI devices.

Quick Tip In later KDE releases, the *Information* list was broken out into its own program called the *KDE Info Center* (command name `kinfocenter`). If you don't have an information heading in your list, try calling up `kinfocenter` instead.

PCI Devices

Adding a PCI device definitely requires a reboot because we are talking about internal devices. These are cards that fit in the slots inside your computer. When you reboot the machine, Linux should be able to scan for these cards and identify them without any problem. When you click on PCI in the Control Center Information category, you'll get a detailed list of every device known to the system (see Figure 8–2).

Shell Out You can also run the command `/sbin/lspci` for a more succinct list.

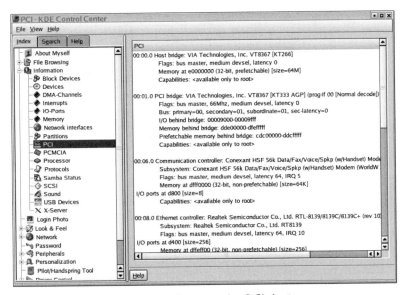

Figure 8–2 Using Control Center to list PCI devices.

If the Linux kernel has the appropriate device drivers available as modules, they will be loaded automatically, and nothing else needs to be done to make the device available. The reason that this information is useful has to do with those times when you do not have a driver handy or directly available. Being able to get the details on the troublesome device in this way is the first step toward getting it working.

A classic example of this is the *Winmodem*, so called because it was designed to work specifically with Windows. If you have one of these modems and it was not automatically configured by the system, never fear. I'll talk about Winmodems in more detail later in the chapter. For the moment, let's talk USB.

USB Devices

The whole idea behind USB was eventually to replace all those different connectors on the back of a computer. That includes serial ports, parallel ports, and mouse and keyboard connectors. The acronym stands for *Universal Serial Bus*. To get a list of USB devices, click on the USB Devices information category. On any USB system, there will be at least one USB hub and whatever devices are attached. If you look at Figure 8–3, you'll see a generic webcam and an Epson scanner connected to my system.

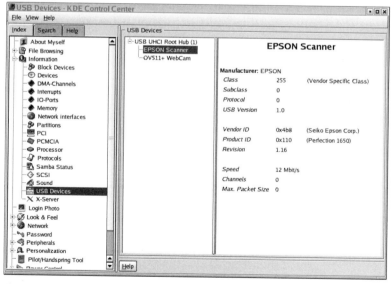

Figure 8–3 Control Center USB device list.

The sheer number of USB devices available is phenomenal, to say the least, and the list is growing. Many of these devices use a standard set of drivers, which means that a number of things can literally be plugged in and used—no need to mess with loading drivers because it is all being done for you.

You noticed the word *many* in that last sentence, right? Keeping track of what works (*and what doesn't*) and providing access to drivers that aren't included in current distributions is the *raison d'être* of the *Linux USB Device Overview* Web site. If you find yourself looking at a new webcam and you aren't sure whether it is supported under Linux, look there first.

```
http://www.qbik.ch/usb/devices/
```

The site is organized into sections, depending on the device type (audio, video, mass storage, etc.). Each device is assigned a status identifying just how well a device is supported, from *works perfectly* to *works somewhat* to *don't bother*.

Printers and Printing

This might seem like a silly thing to mention, particularly if your printer was automatically detected, configured, and tested at boot time. Nevertheless, there are things that you might want to do with your printer, and we should probably cover some of these now. Furthermore, *printing is one of the most important functions* a personal computer can perform. It's good to get it right. On that note, I'm going to spend a little bit of time talking about printers and printing. *Trust me*, it's going to be lots of fun.

Printing under Linux works on the basis of *print queues*. At its simplest, this means that whenever you send something to the printer, it is queued in a directory where it awaits its turn at the printer. This de-queuing is known as *spooling*. Consequently, the process that sends the print jobs from the queue to the printer is called the *spooler*. That spooler can be one of a small handful of programs, all of which are transparent to you when you print from applications. Here's a quick roundup of the more popular spoolers.

CUPS, the Common Unix Printing System, is designed to be a platform-independent printing system that works across a great number of UNIX flavors, including Linux. CUPS uses the Internet Printing Protocol (IPP), a next-generation printing system designed to allow the printing of any job to any printer, anywhere. At this point, CUPS certainly looks like the spooler of the future. Most modern Linux distributions include CUPS, and KDE will use it transparently.

The second most likely spooler you will run into is LPD, the classic UNIX spooler. LPD has been around for a long, long time and continues to be distributed with pretty much every Linux out there.

Whether it is CUPS or LPD, KDE handles printing beautifully. Adding, configuring, or removing a printer is done through the KDE Control Center. After kcontrol has been activated, click on System (in the left side category window) and select Printing Manager (for KDE 3.1, click on Peripherals, then Printers).

We'll start by adding a printer. Because adding hardware, like adding software, is an administrative function, start by clicking the Administrator button at the bottom of the Printing Manager window. A window will pop up, asking you for the root password (Figure 8–4).

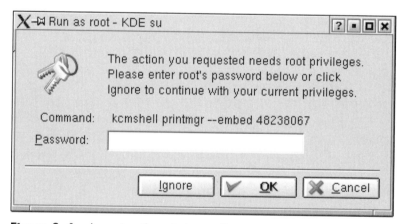

Figure 8–4   Accessing the printer configuration requires the root password.

When you have entered the password, you'll be looking at the same interface, but things will be a little different. For starters, the window to the right is now surrounded by a *red border*. Furthermore, some of the icons have gone from being grayed out to being active. If the toolbar and icons are not visible, right-click in the printer list window (at the top of the printer configuration window). A pop-up menu will appear (Figure 8–5), from which you should select View Toolbar or View Menu Toolbar. Both have the same menu options but are presented somewhat differently. One of those is the Add printer/class icon. Clicking that icon brings up the KDE Add Printer wizard (see Figure 8–6).

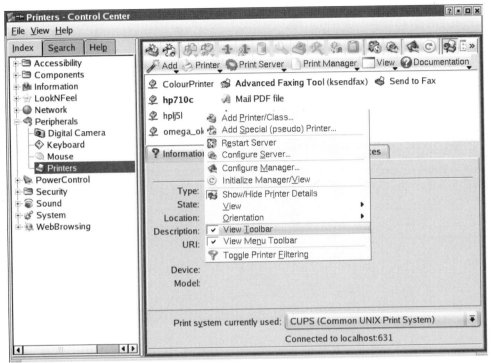

Figure 8–5   Toolbar menu options in the KDE printer configuration manager.

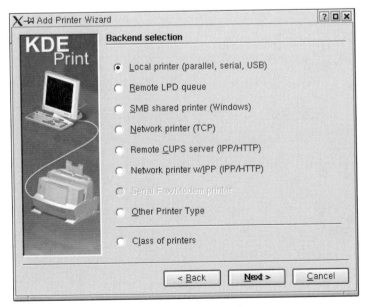

Figure 8–6   The KDE Add Printer wizard.

Click Next through the welcome screen, and you can select the type of printer, whether it is connected directly to your PC with a parallel or USB cable or via the network in some way. Network-connected printers could be good old LPD printers, Microsoft Windows-connected and -shared printers (SMB), CUPS, HP JetDirect, IPP, or others. Click on the one you are looking to connect and click Next. In my example, I was hooking up an HP Deskjet 710C.

When you click Next after selecting your connection, you'll face different choices, based on whether the printer is local or on the network. For a local printer, your choices are parallel port, serial port, or some kind of USB connection.

After clicking Next, the wizard will load its printer database. Select your vendor and model from the list (Figure 8–7) and click Next.

This brings us to the Printer Test screen. The information regarding your new printer will be displayed, and you'll have the option of sending a test page to the printer. I *strongly recommend* that you do print a test page before moving on.

At this point, you can also click the Settings button and personalize certain defaults, for instance, the default page size (U.S. letter, A4, etc.), margins, print quality, or (in the case of a color inkjet like mine) how ink cartridges are ac-

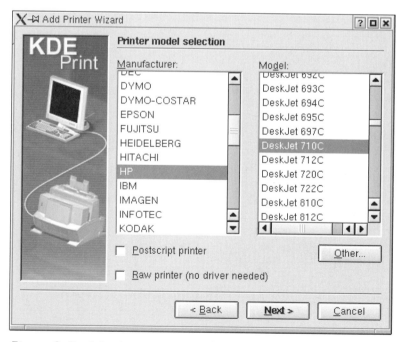

Figure 8–7   Selecting a printer vendor and model.

cessed and used. If everything looks as you expect it to on your test page, click Next one more time. You'll be looking at the banner selection screen. Simply put, would you like a banner page before or after your print job has completed? Unless you are in an office with many people trying to keep their jobs straight, you probably don't want to waste the extra paper. Luckily, no banners of any kind is the default.

Click Next and you'll be looking at the Printer quota settings (Figure 8–8). You might be asking what the heck a printer quota is and why you should care. Once again, if this is your home printer, you can just click Next and completely ignore this. In some office environments, it may be practical (or necessary) to limit the number of jobs any single user can print to a printer in a given time period. The time period can be per hour, per day, or per week—even per minute. The size of job can be based on the number of pages or the amount of data sent.

Click Next, and it is time for the User access settings where you can decide who can and can't use your printer. You can either specify a list of *Denied users* where everyone can use your printer except those listed or a list of *Allowed users* where only those listed can use the printer. It is at times like this that Linux reminds you it is a *multiuser* system.

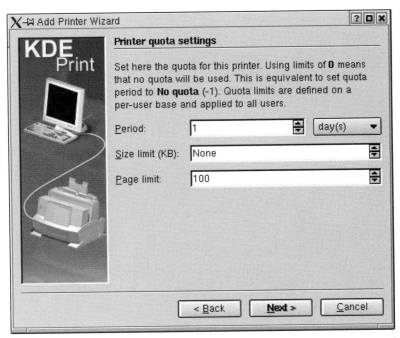

Figure 8–8   You can add restrictions on printer use.

After making all these decisions, we come to the General information, or summary screen. Enter a name for this printer (a one-word name is best), followed by a location and a description. In reality, the only thing you need to enter is a name for the printer. Click Next, and you'll have a final opportunity to review the choices you've made up to this point. At this point or at any point before now, you can still click Back and make different choices. If you are happy, click Finish, and you are done. Congratulations, you've added and configured a printer.

Let's have a closer look at the Printing Manager (Figure 8–9). Take a moment to move your mouse slowly over the various icons at the top and take note of the tooltips. You can do a lot in terms of printer modification and administration here. If you are looking to share your Linux printer with Windows workstations in the office (or home), you can even export the driver for use. Notice the tabs, as well—Information, Jobs, Properties, and Instances.

Information is just that, basic information about your printer, such as its name, location, and so on. Under the Jobs tab, you can see all the jobs currently waiting in your print queue.

Let me tell you about a great way to work with printers, monitor print jobs, and so on. For quick access to your printing subsystem, right-click on the application launcher (the big K), select Panel Menu | Add | Special Button, and click on Print System. A *new icon* will appear in your Kicker panel. Click on

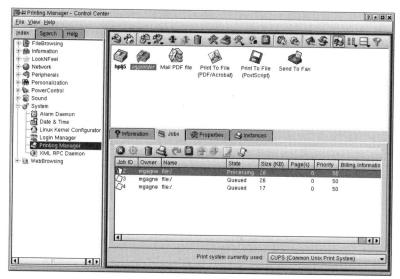

Figure 8–9   The Control Center Printing Manager provides all the information you need.

that icon, and all your printers will appear in a pop-up list (along with quick access to other print system tools). Click on the appropriate printer icon, and a
window will appear with a list of jobs waiting to be printed (Figure 8–10).

From the jobs list, you can delete jobs, change the order in which they print,
or redirect them to another printer if yours is particularly busy. Using the *Properties* tab, you can change some of the characteristics that you assigned to your
printer when you configured it, such as quotas, banner pages, and so on (just
make sure you are in Administrator mode).

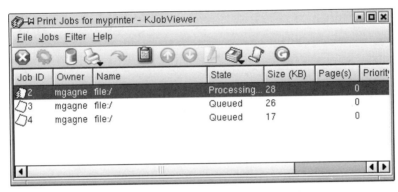

Figure 8–10   Checking on queued print jobs.

That brings us to *Instances*. Each printer you create will have at least one
instance, the default instance. The idea behind this is that you can create multiple instances of the same printer. Let's pretend that we are talking about a
color printer and that you often switch between a high-quality color mode (for
photographs) to a lower quality draft mode when you want to conserve that
expensive colored ink. Just add another instance of the same printer but with
different characteristics.

Now that you have added a printer (or printers), configured it, and given
yourself supreme power over all print functions, it is time to print something.
Luckily, this is the easiest part of all. Whenever you print from any KDE application (Kmail, Konqueror, and so on), you'll be presented with a common
printer dialog (Figure 8–11).

From that window, you can select the printer of your choice or click Properties and change the number of copies, the paper size, and a number of other
settings associated with that particular printer and that particular job. If you
want to see those details up front, click on the Expand button for a somewhat

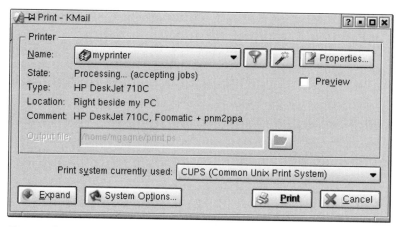

Figure 8–11   KDE print dialog.

more *panoramic* view. Finally, you can even start from here to add yet another printer. Notice that little icon to the left of the Properties button, the one that looks a bit like a magic wand. Clicking this fires up the Add Printer wizard.

Yes, we've come back around to where we started.

Modems versus Winmodems

Way back when, in the introductory chapter, I mentioned Winmodems as one of the few minuses of running Linux. You'll recall that a Winmodem is a modem designed to work only with Windows. They are sometimes referred to as *software* or *controllerless* modems and tend to be less expensive than controller-based modems.

If you are running a Winmodem, all is not lost. The Linux community is nothing if not resourceful. Even when manufacturers are slow to notice Linux users, the same isn't true the other way around. As more and more people run Linux, this becomes less and less of a problem. In time, hardware manufacturers may be building for Linux first and Windows second. In the meantime, check out the *Linmodems.Org* Web site at `http://www.linmodems.org` and you should be up and running shortly.

So just how do you transform a Winmodem into a Linmodem? Well, let me give you an example.

Among the more common Winmodems out there are those based on the *Conexant* chipset; these are starting to be very well supported. For the latest driver, just head on over to Marc Boucher's page at `http://www.mbsi.ca/cnxtlindrv/`. Not only can you get source drivers, but precompiled packages are available for a number of popular Linux distributions.

Identifying the Winmodem is your first step. You can use the KDE Control Center to get a listing of your PCI hardware, where you will get a lot of detail. You can also *shell out* and use the `lspci` command for a quick list of all the PCI devices found on your system. Here's what it looks like.

```
$ lspci
00:00.0 Host bridge: VIA Technologies, Inc. VT8367 [KT266]
00:01.0 PCI bridge: VIA Technologies, Inc. VT8367 [KT266 AGP]
00:06.0 Communication controller: Conexant HSF 56k
Data/Fax/Voice/Spkp    (w/Handset) Modem (WorldW SmartDAA) (rev 01)
00:08.0 Ethernet controller: Realtek Semiconductor Co., Ltd. RTL-
8139/8139C (rev 10)
00:11.0 ISA bridge: VIA Technologies, Inc. VT8233 PCI to ISA Bridge
00:11.1 IDE interface: VIA Technologies, Inc. Bus Master IDE (rev 06)
00:11.2 USB Controller: VIA Technologies, Inc. USB (rev 18)
00:11.5 Multimedia audio controller: VIA Technologies, Inc. VT8233
AC97    Audio Controller (rev 10)
01:00.0 VGA compatible controller: nVidia Corporation NV11
[GeForce2 MX DDR] (rev b2)
```

In some cases, you will find precompiled driver packages. These are the RPMs, as we discussed earlier. Some are specific to your release, and others will be generic. In the case of my Conexant-based Winmodem, I downloaded the RPM package and installed it.

As per the instructions that followed the RPM install, I typed the following command:

```
/usr/sbin/hsfconfig
```

A short dialog followed, asking me for the country (Canada, in my case), after which the program compiled and installed my driver for me. It even linked the newly created device, `/dev/ttySHSF0`, to `/dev/modem`. I was ready to use my modem without a care.

Shell Out From the shell prompt, I can verify the location of my modem with this command:

```
$ ls -l /dev/modem
```

The system then responds with this information:

```
lr-xr-xr-x    1    root    root    8 Sep    9
11:23    /dev/modem  -> /dev/ttySHSF0
```

The Winmodem/Linmodem Roundup

Clearly, none of this whole Winmodem problem applies if you are using an *external* modem or happen to be among the lucky ones using a cable modem connection or high-speed DSL access from your local phone company. For others out there, it can be a bit more complicated. I've already given you the address of the Conexant Web site, and I will give you more right here.

Remember, *many of these modems* can be made into useful and productive members of Linux society with a visit to the right Web site. On that note, here's my roundup.

Conexant Modems (HCF and HSF)

http://www.mbsi.ca/cnxtlindrv/

Smart Link Modems

http://www.smlink.com/download/Linux/

Lucent Modems

http://www.physcip.uni-stuttgart.de/heby/ltmodem/

PCTel Modems

http://linmodems.technion.ac.il/pctel-linux/

What? More Devices?

We've covered a lot of ground here, but we are by no means finished. Those things we attach to our PCs aren't much good if we don't put them in context with the tools we use them for. Those tools tend to require a somewhat more in-depth examination. For instance, burning CDs isn't just about creating collections of your favorite songs. People use them for backups, as well, or to make collections of digital photos for sharing with the family.

The same is true of scanners. These gizmos are incredibly handy devices for the home or office. Aside from converting nondigital pictures to place on your Web site, you can use your scanner as a photocopier and as a way to send faxes when the pages require your signature (you can fax from a word processor, after all).

We'll cover all those things in the chapters to come.

Resources

Linux Hardware Compatibility HOWTO

http://www.tldp.org/HOWTO/Hardware-HOWTO/index.html

Hardware Compatibility List at Red Hat

http://hardware.redhat.com

Linmodems.org (Winmodems under Linux)

http://www.linmodem.org

LinuxPrinting.org (Linux Printer Database)

http://www.linuxprinting.org

Linux USB Device Overview

http://www.qbik.ch/usb/devices/

chapter
9

Connecting
to the Internet

I'm going to start this chapter with a little Networking 101. It will be fun—really. For those of you who already know everything about TCP/IP and how IP networks operate, you can skip ahead a few paragraphs.

Communication over the Internet takes place using something called the TCP/IP protocol suite. TCP/IP actually stands for Transmission Control Protocol/Internet Protocol, and it is the basic underlying means by which all this magic communication takes place. Everything you do on the Net, whether it is surfing your favorite sites, sending and receiving emails, chatting via some instant messaging client, or listening to an audio broadcast—all these things ride on TCP/IP's virtual back.

TCP/IP is often referred to as a *protocol suite*, a collection of protocols that speak the same language. Essentially, this comes down to the transmission and reception of IP packets. Those packets have to get from place to place, and that means they need to know how to get there. IP packets do this in exactly the same way that you get from your house to someone else's house. They have a home address from which they go to a remote address.

Each and every computer connected to the Internet has a unique address called an *IP address*, four numbers separated by dots (i.e., 192.168.22.55). Some systems that are always online (banks, Web sites, companies, etc.) will have a *static* address. Dial-up connections for home users tend to be shared—when you aren't connected, someone else may be using the same address—which is referred to as a *dynamic* IP address.

You may be wondering how a symbolic Web site address such as `www.marcelgagne.com` translates to the dotted foursome I mentioned above, and that would be an excellent question.

Think of the real world again. We don't think of our friends as "136 Mulberry Tree Lane" or "1575 Natika Court," but rather by their names. To find out where our friends live, we check the phone book (or ask them). The same holds true in the digital world, but that phone book is called a *domain name server* (DNS). When I type a symbolic (i.e., human-readable) address into my Web browser, it contacts a DNS (assigned by my Internet Service Provider [ISP]) and asks for the IP address. With that IP address, my packets almost know how to get to their destinations.

Almost?

To reach an address in the real world, you get out of your driveway and enter some road to which all other roads are connected. If you drive long enough, presumably you get to Rome (having often been told that *all roads lead to Rome*). Before you can get to Rome, you enter your default route, namely, the street in front of your house. The same principle exists in the virtual world. For your IP packages (an email to your mother, for instance) to get to its destination, it must take a particular route, called a *default route*. This will be the IP address of a device that knows all the other routes. Your ISP will provide that route.

That concludes Networking 101. Not particularly complicated, is it?

Before You Begin

Connecting to the Internet is one if those things you setup once, then forget about. Still, you do need to get some information from your ISP up front. The basics are as follows:

- Your user name and password
- The phone number your modem will be dialing to connect
- The IP address of the DNS (name servers - described above)
- The IP address of your SMTP and POP3 email hosts
- The IP address of your news server (optional)

All of this information likely came with your contract when you first signed up with your ISP. Armed with this information, you are ready to begin.

Getting on the Net

As I write this, there are three very popular methods of connecting to the Internet, notwithstanding your own connection at the office. These are cable modem, DSL service from the phone company, or good old-fashioned dial-up modem. The first two are usually referred to as *high-speed* or *broadband* connections, and dial-up access is usually made fun of.

With all the press and hype about high-speed service, you would think that this is all people run. Think again. As I write this, the vast majority of people in North America are still connecting through a dial-up connection. Make no mistake—as Mark Twain might have remarked, the rumors of dial-up access's demise are greatly exaggerated. You may be among the majority who are still using dial-up; I'll cover that in detail.

Before we get started, make sure that you have all the information provided by your ISP. At bare minimum, this information will consist of a username, a password, and a number to connect to. You will likely also be given a default route, a DNS address (possibly two), and the addresses of your mail server (we'll get to that in Chapter 10). If you are ready, let's begin.

Connecting to the Net with a Modem

Most ISPs provide dial-up access through the Point-to-Point Protocol, or PPP. The KDE program that gets you connected to the Internet with a modem is called kppp. On a standard KDE setup, you'll find it under Kicker's big K by choosing the Internet menu, then clicking Internet Dialer. On Mandrake, look under Networking, then Remote Access; and Red Hat has it under Extras and Internet. You can always just start the application with the command kppp & from an X window terminal session or by using your old friend, the <Alt+F2> combo—once again, just type kppp.

Tip You may have noticed in the paragraph above that I added an ampersand (&) to the end of the kppp command. When you start a command from a shell prompt, it normally runs in the foreground. What this means is that you can't start another process at the shell until the current one finishes (you could, of course, open up another shell). The ampersand tells the shell to put the process in the background so that you can run other things.

When KDE's Internet connection tool comes up for the first time (Figure 9–1), there isn't much to see because nothing has been configured. You'll see a blank Connect to list, as well as blank user name and password fields.

To get started, click the Setup button. This will take you to the KPPP Con-figuration screen.

I realize that the Accounts tab is the first, but I want to talk about the Device tab for a moment. I covered devices back in Chapter 8, specifically the issue of modems, and it is particularly relevant here. If you click on that tab, you'll notice that the modem device is set to /dev/modem, which is a symbolic link to the actual port for the modem. That might be /dev/ttyS0, but it could be many other things, as well.

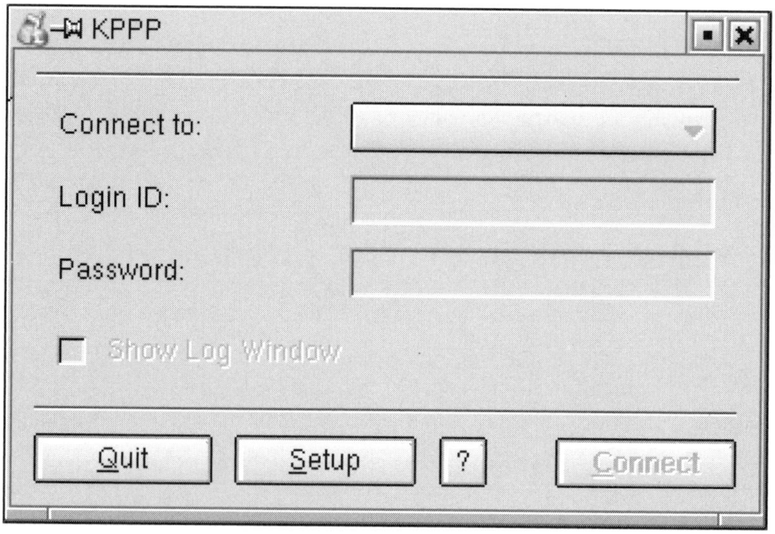

Figure 9–1 First time with KPPP.

If you find yourself having problems here when you dial out, it may be that the link wasn't set properly. Never fear, click on the drop-down list, and you will see a number of potential devices. After choosing a device, click on the Modem tab and choose Query Modem. If kppp successfully sees your modem, you should see something similar to Figure 9–2.

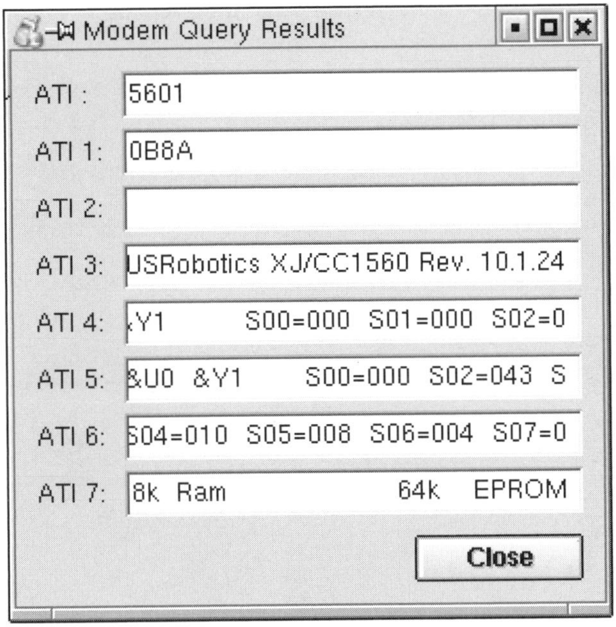

Figure 9–2   Modem query results.

Let's get back to the Accounts tab now. As you can probably infer from this screen, it is possible to configure and maintain several dial-up accounts from here. Most people will probably use just one, but you can also use it to set up multiple profiles of the same account. If you happen to be a road warrior or globe trotter with a notebook, you can create profiles for the various cities you visit.

From the Account setup window, click New to create a new account. Skip by the Wizard option (which tends to be for European sites) and choose the Dialog Setup instead. You'll be asked for a connection name, a phone number for your ISP, and the authentication type (see Figure 9–3). This defaults to PAP authentication (which most ISPs today use). If your ISP still has you go through some kind of authentication script (known as an *expect/send dialog*), choose Script-based from the list.

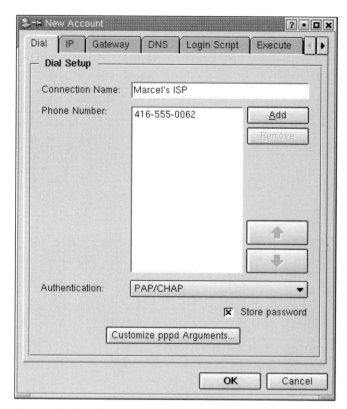

Figure 9–3 New account setup.

Notice that you have some additional tabs on the menu. The IP tab enables you manually to enter the IP address provided by your ISP. Because most dial-up accounts use dynamic addresses, that is the default selection, and you probably don't have to change anything there. The same goes for the next tab, the Gateway tab. This is usually set for you as you connect. Once again, you can override this setting by providing a static gateway address if your ISP provides it.

The last tab is one you will probably need to worry about—the DNS tab. In all likelihood, you will want to configure an address here as indicated by your ISP. Click the Manual button. Enter the DNS address you were given into the DNS IP Address field, then click Add. If you have a second address, enter it in the same way.

Of course, the most work you may have to do comes under the Login Script tab, where you may have to provide your dial-up configuration with the appropriate dialog for a connection. This is also something your ISP should have supplied you with.

When you click OK, you'll find yourself back at the configuration screen. Click OK one final time and you return to the initial Kppp window, with one difference. In the Connect to connection list, your new connection should be visible (see Figure 9–4). Enter your login name and password, click Connect, and you are on your way.

Before I move on, notice the Show Log Window check box. If you find that you are having problems connecting, checking this box will show you a login script window as the connection takes place. This can help you debug any problems you might have with the connection.

Cable Modems and High-Speed DSL

For the most part, if you installed your Linux system with the cable modem connected, this is probably already working, and you have nothing left to do. If, however, you are already up and running and you are just now getting a cable

Figure 9–4   First time out with GAIM.

modem, it is probably time for a few pointers. Quite frankly, these days (with a modern Linux distribution), there isn't much to it.

To begin with, cable modems aren't modems in the classic sense. The so-called modem is connected to your cable TV service on one side and to an Ethernet card inside your PC on the other. High-speed access through your phone company's DSL service is similar, in that they will provide you with an external, modemlike device (in many cases, it is really a router) that also connects to an Ethernet card.

The Ethernet card (which should be automatically detected by your system) gets an IP address from the cable modem via the Dynamic Host Configuration Protocol (DHCP). Although this address may appear permanent, in that it rarely (if ever) changes, it is nevertheless dynamic, because your actual Ethernet card gets its address whenever it connects.

The process of getting your system configured varies a little bit from distribution to distribution but only cosmetically. When you install your new Ethernet card (for access through the cable modem), it will be autodetected by the system on reboot. As part of that process, the system will ask you whether you want to configure the card. The answer is yes, of course. Next, the system will ask whether you want to supply an IP address or have it autoconfigure via DHCP. With a cable modem, as with DSL, auto-configuring is what you want.

Now that I've told you how incredibly *easy* it is to do this, I'm going to mention that there are many different providers of high-speed cable and DSL access. What this means is that if your system doesn't autorecognize and configure your connection, you may need to do one of these things. For cable modems, the answers vary, but start by checking out the Cable Modem HOWTO at `http://www.tldp.org` for details on your particular geographic location.

If you are on a phone company DSL service, look on your distribution disks for the `rp-pppoe` package (PPP Over Ethernet) and install it. You can also get the package from Roaring Penguin at `http://www.roaringpenguin.com/pppoe/`, but you probably have it on your CDs. Make sure that you check there first.

Once the package is installed, open a shell (Konsole) and switch to the root user. Do this by typing "`su - root`" at the shell prompt. You'll be asked for the root password. Once you have entered it, type this command:

```
adsl-setup
```

This is basically a fill-in-the-blanks session. Your phone company will have assigned you a username and password, along with some connection information, and will have provided you with this. Answer all of the questions (the information is case-sensitive, so be careful entering it). When you have answered everything, type the following at your shell prompt:

```
adsl-start
```

That's it. You have no doubt guessed that there is also an `adsl-stop` command, as well as `adsl-status` (which, among other things, will tell you your IP address). If you install the RPM package from your distribution, `adsl-start` will run automatically when you reboot your system, so you don't need to worry about it each time.

Okay, I'm Connected. Now What?

Good question. For starters, you have everything the Internet has to offer. You can surf the Web (which I'll cover in Chapter 11), send email (Chapter 10), and find and download software, music, and video. The Internet is a vast cornucopia of news, information, conversation, sights, sounds, and a thousand other things. When looking at all these things, it is easy to forget that it really all comes down one thing—*communication*.

The Internet was born on communication; email specifically was the tool that drove its development into the globe-spanning network that it is today. That's why I'm going to devote the entire next chapter to electronic mail.

These days, however, a new kind of communication has evolved—call it "mini-email." The one-liner. The short and sweet message. The *instant message*. The Net-connected society has grown to love those quick, always-on means of sending each other information. My own parents (who live in another province) send me a daily one-line weather report via their Jabber instant messaging client. If you are coming from the Windows world, there's a good chance you already have one of these accounts, either with Yahoo!, AOL, MSN, or Jabber.

What is Jabber?

Glad you asked. The best way for me to answer that is to tell you about a great instant messaging client that very likely came with your distribution. It is called *GAIM*.

Instant Messaging with GAIM

To start GAIM, look under your Internet (or Networking) menu. The actual command name is `gaim`, in case you would rather start it from the shell or via the <Alt+F2> run program dialog.

The first time you start up GAIM (Figure 9–4), you'll get a simple window with text fields for Screen Name and Password. The Screen Name field will have the words <New User> entered, letting you know that you don't have any accounts set up. Obviously, before we start using instant messaging through GAIM, we are going to need at least one account. You could use pretty much any instant messaging account you already have (Yahoo!, MSN, etc.) but I did promise to explain Jabber, so for now, we'll start from scratch.

Look below the text fields and you'll see six buttons labeled *Quit, Accounts, Signon, About, Options,* and *Plugins*. By default, GAIM is ready to accept an ICQ account, but it can also talk to AOL's instant messaging client, to Yahoo!'s client, to Microsoft's MSN client, and to others. It does this through the use of *plugins*, making GAIM one of the most flexible instant messaging clients around. One of these protocols is the open *source* and open *protocol* Jabber.

Why Use Jabber?

There are several reasons aside from the two I just mentioned (open source and open protocol). The Jabber *protocol* doesn't belong to any one in particular, so there is no company driving its destiny (although there are companies using Jabber). Jabber uses a decentralized approach, so the system is more robust. In fact, anyone can run a Jabber server if he or she wants to. This is a boon to companies that may want to run a *private, secure* instant messaging network.

You can also create your own account name instead of having an account assigned to you. For these reasons and more, in this little tour of plugins and account setup, I will show you how to create a Jabber account. On that note, let's continue.

Selecting a Plugin

To use Jabber as one of your protocols, you may need to load its plugin, which isn't activated by default. This is very easy to do. Click the Plugins button.

Tip At this writing, a new version of GAIM was just nearing release. While most things worked in exactly the same way, a few cosmetic differences were added. Furthermore, the need for selecting a protocol plugin was being removed. Since you may find yourself using either version of GAIM, I will still cover the topic of plugins.

The GAIM Plugins window appears. Click on Load, then select a protocol from the pop-up list. In the case of Jabber, you would click on `libjabber.so` and click OK. You would follow the same steps to load the Yahoo! protocol (`libyahoo.so`) or the MSN chat protocol (`libmsn.so`). Once you have loaded the Jabber plugin (or any other that takes your fancy), click Close (Figure 9–5).

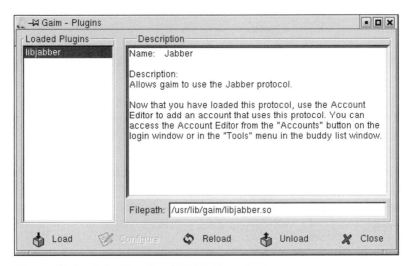

Figure 9–5   Selecting the GAIM Jabber plugin.

When the plugin window disappears, click the Accounts button. The Account Editor window will appear (Figure 9–6). At this stage of the game, there is nothing in it.

Figure 9–6   Time to add instant messaging accounts in GAIM's account editor.

Click Add, and the Modify Account window will appear. Halfway down that window, you should see a drop-down list labeled *Protocol*. By default, it says AIM/ICQ. Click on it, select Jabber, and watch as the window changes to reflect the requirements of setting up a Jabber account (Figure 9–7).

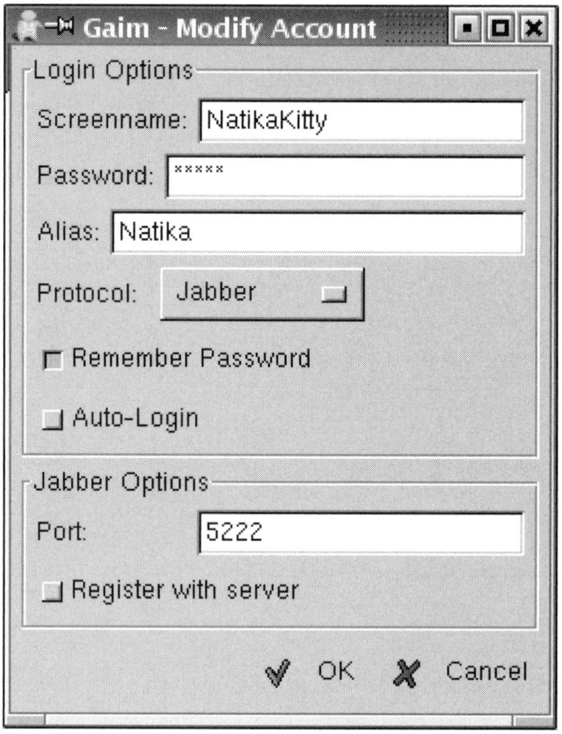

Figure 9–7   Creating a Jabber account.

Enter your Screenname, Password, and Alias, then click on the Register with server radio button. If you would like your GAIM client to log in to Jabber automatically every time you start up the client, click on the Auto-Login radio button, as well. When you are happy with your changes, click OK. Your Account Editor window will show your new account (Figure 9–8).

You can either sign on here (by clicking the Sign On/Off button) or click Close and sign on from the main GAIM window. With your first time in, you'll get a welcome message from the Jabber.org server. You can close this window or visit the site (as indicated in the message) for additional information.

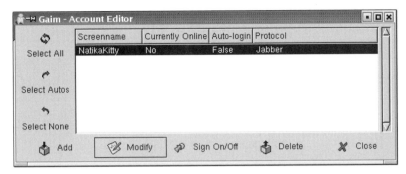

Figure 9–8   The account editor reflects the newly created account.

Now that you have your very own Jabber instant messaging account, you need some people to talk to. There are online chats that you can join by clicking File on the menu bar and selecting Join A Chat. You can also use the keyboard shortcut by pressing <Ctrl+C> instead. You can add friends to your Buddy List by selecting Add A Buddy from the menu. Your friends will have to give you their screen names, of course.

After you have added your buddies to the list, they will get messages letting them know that you want to add them. When they see the pop-up (Figure 9–9), they will click Accept, at which point, you can begin conversations with them.

This accepting of buddies has to happen at both sides of the connection. They accept you, after which you accept them. Think of it as saying "*I do*" but to a more casual, dare I say, *virtual* relationship.

Figure 9–9   Accept your new buddy?

Once all this accepting has taken place, your buddies will appear in your buddy list (Figure 9–10). The icons beside their names in your buddy list will indicate whether your friends are on.

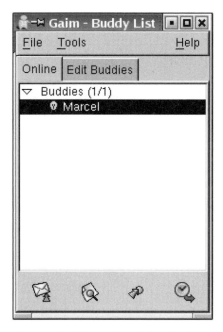

Figure 9–10   A lonely buddy list.

If they are, double-click on their names and start chatting (Figure 9–11). It is that easy.

What about My Windows Friends?

One of the really great things about this particular chat client is that it supports so many different protocols up front. You don't need a separate client for Jabber and one for Yahoo! and another for MSN and . . . well, you get the idea. The second nice thing is that the GAIM team also make a Windows version of the program. For that very reason, you may want to point your friends who are running Windows over to the GAIM Web site (`gaim.sourceforge.net`) so they, too can cut the clutter and take advantage of this great little piece of software.

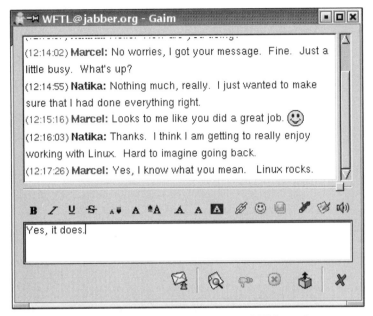

Figure 9-11 Chatting with friend in the GAIM window.

Resources

GAIM Instant Messaging
http://gaim.sourceforge.net

Jabber Software Foundation
http://www.jabber.org

JabberStudio (for a list of other client programs)
http://www.jabberstudio.org/project/?cat=5

Linux Documentation Project
http://www.tldp.org

Roaring Penguin's PPPOE Page
http://www.roaringpenguin.com/pppoe/

chapter
10
Electronic Mail

These days, it seems that when we think about the Internet, we think about Web browsers first. To those of us who have been on the Net for more years than we care to admit, that always seems a bit strange. The chief medium of information exchange on the Internet has always been electronic mail, or email. Although the perception has changed, email is probably still the number one application in the connected world.

For a powerful, graphical email client, you need look no further than your KDE desktop. Its email package is called Kmail, and I'm going to tell you all about it. Keep reading, though. In just a few keystrokes, I'll have you sending and receiving mail like a Linux pro.

I'm also going to talk about an alternative package called Evolution. Those of you who are coming from that other OS and who might be pining for the look and feel (and the integration) of Outlook are going to be pleasantly surprised.

Be Prepared . . .

Before we start, you will need to have some information handy. This includes your email username and password, as well as the SMTP and POP3 server addresses for sending and receiving your email. All of this information will be provided for you by your Internet service provider (ISP).

Kmail

On a default installation of the KDE desktop, you'll find an icon for Kmail already sitting in your Kicker panel. The icon has an envelope leaning against an orange *E*. You can also get to it by clicking the big K, looking into the Internet submenu, and selecting Kmail from there.

Shell Out If you wish to start Kmail from the shell, just type its command, `kmail &`, at the shell prompt. Alternatively, you can press <Alt+F2> and type the command there.

The very first time you use Kmail, it will create a directory called *Mail* in your personal home directory. A dialog box will pop up, asking you to confirm this. Click OK. Kmail will then create some default mail folders for you. These are inbox, outbox, sent-mail, trash, and drafts. You should then see a window similar to the one in Figure 10–1.

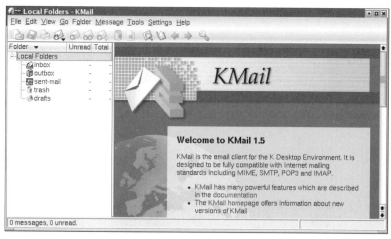

Figure 10–1   Kmail as it appears the first time.

Notice the folders listed down the left side. On the right is the main window where you'll read your messages. Before we can actually do anything in terms of sending and receiving email, we need to tell Kmail a little bit about ourselves.

Click on Settings on the menu bar and choose Configure Kmail. Immediately after, you will have to go through a little question-and-answer session. The window to the left contains a handful of sections (Figure 10–2). They are Identity (highlighted by default), Network, Appearance, Composer, Security, and Miscellaneous.

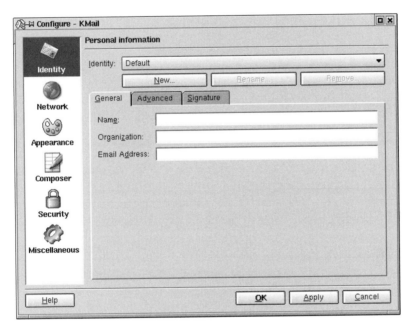

Figure 10–2   Kmail settings configuration.

Notice that there is a drop-down list next to the label that says *Identity*. That's because Kmail lets you set up multiple identities. This is handy if you use different signatures or return addresses for work and home. For the moment, we'll deal with your default identity.

The layout for email identities is a little different on KDE 3.0 versus 3.1. In 3.0, the tabs are on the screen with the current identity in a drop-down list (Figure 10–2). In KDE 3.1, identities, including the default, are listed alone on the screen. Click Modify first to bring up the tab dialog.

On the General tab, start by entering your name (or what you like to be known as) in the Name: field. If this is your home account, you can probably skip the Organization field if you wish (I've been known to enter silly things here, such as "Dis-Organization"). Then enter your email address.

When you are done here, switch to the Advanced tab and enter your Reply to address (if it is different than your email address). Finally, if you would like a signature to be automatically added when you send mail, click on the Signature tab and enter the information there. Note that you will have to click the Enable signature check box, after which you can enter what you would like to have appear at the end of your emails. Note that there is also a drop-down list so that you can specify a text file with your signature or a program (or script) that automatically generates some kind of (no doubt clever) text dynamically.

The Importance of Being Networked

Now that Kmail knows who you are and what kind of wittiness you like to provide at the end of your communication, you are no doubt anxious to send and receive some mail. For that you need a little network configuration. Click on the Network icon in the Configure Kmail dialog sidebar, and you'll wind up with two tabbed windows on the right-hand side— one for Sending and one for Receiving. Because the Sending tab is selected by default, let's start with that one.

You can actually specify different transports here, as well as different hosts to use for outgoing mail. You are probably already aware that your Linux system isn't your run-of-the-mill operating system. Depending on your distribution's default install, it is quite capable of acting as its own mail server. In fact, notice that there is already one outgoing account setup, that being *Sendmail*. This is your system's default mail transport, and depending on your network or your ISP, you may simply be able to leave that as it is. Unfortunately, that isn't likely. Most ISPs I know of that service home users *don't allow* sendmail traffic from their clients to pass through their servers. If you are sending mail, they would prefer that you use their servers. What this means is that you have to click Remove and get rid of the default outgoing account. Now click Add to create a new account. The dialog box shown in Figure 10–3 will appear, asking you to specify a Transport.

Choose SMTP. This will bring up the Add Transport dialog, where you will specify a name for this connection (this is just a name that means something to you, such as "My ISP"), the mail Host (which your ISP or office will provide), and a Port number. Although technically your ISP could run an SMTP host on something other than port 25 (the default), this will likely

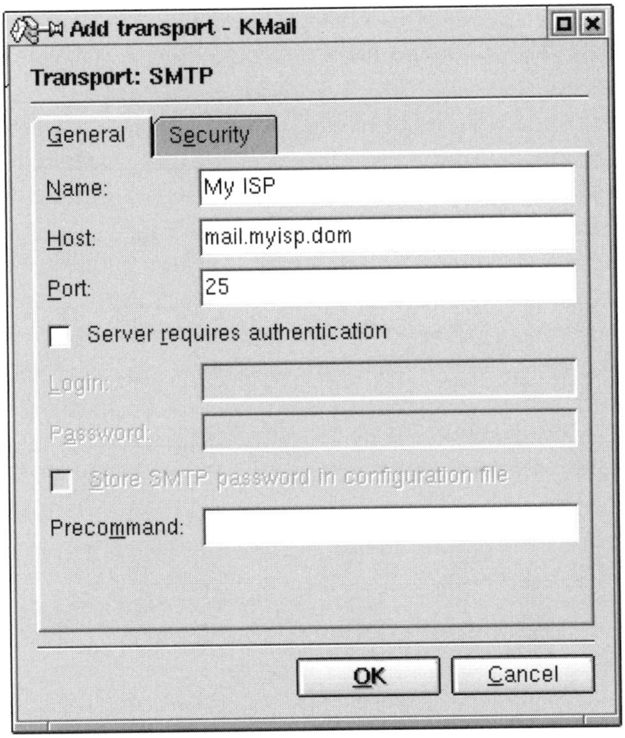

Figure 10–3   *SMTP server configuration.*

never happen. Accept the default of 25, click OK, and you are ready to send. That means we are halfway there.

Click on the Receiving tab to prepare Kmail for your incoming mail, then click on the Add button on the right. A small box will appear, asking you for the type of account you want to set up. Your choices are Local Mailbox, POP3, IMAP, and Maildir Mailbox. Most ISPs are still using POP3 as the default mail delivery protocol but this is something you should make sure of. If you are setting your PC up in an office environment, you are likely going to use either IMAP or POP3. When you are happy with your choice, click OK, and you should be presented with the dialog box shown in Figure 10–4.

The Add Account dialog window will appear, and this is where you configure your account. Please note that you can configure a number of different accounts, and all of them can be accessed through Kmail (just as you could configure many identities).

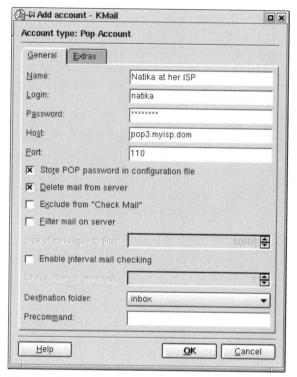

Figure 10–4 Configuring a POP3 mail account.

Start by filling in the Name: field. Once again, this is just a name that makes sense to you, so it can be anything you like. The Login, Password, and Host information will be provided by your ISP or system administrator. As with the SMTP port 25 discussions earlier, although it is *possible* that your ISP could use something other than port 110 for POP3 (or 143 for IMAP), I can pretty much *guarantee* that it won't happen. You can safely leave those settings as the default.

Before you go clicking OK in all this excitement, there are a couple of other options you should consider. Notice the check box on the window that says *Store POP password in configuration file*. Unless you want to be asked for your password each and every time you check your mail, it is probably a good idea to set that here. You probably also want to make sure that you *Delete mail from server* when you pick up mail.

The last thing I want to point out is near the bottom of the window, the Destination folder. Most people will want to have their new mail arrive in their inboxes. But for those of you who are going to configure multiple accounts and identities (there's a joke there somewhere), this is where you will specify different folders for each of those accounts and personalities—uh, I mean *identities*.

Click OK when you are done with the account information, then click Apply, then OK to leave the configuration settings.

That is all there is to it. If you are connected to your ISP or through your company LAN, you can start sending and receiving mail. For those who configured an IMAP account, you'll notice a folder with that account's name in your folder list. When you click on the plus sign beside the folder, Kmail will connect to your IMAP server and show you the rest of your folders.

Let's Communicate!

Sending messages is easy. Click on the New Message icon—it's the first one at the top left, just below the File menu. If you like the idea of keyboard shortcuts, press <Ctrl+N>, and you'll achieve the same result. The Kmail composer window (Figure 10–5) will appear, and you can start typing your message.

I'm working on the premise that you have all sent email at some point; I'll let you take it from there. Fill in whom the message is going to and the subject of your message, then start writing. When you are ready to send the message, click the Send Message icon (directly under the Message menu on the Kmail composer menu bar). For the keyboard wizards out there, try <Ctrl+Enter>.

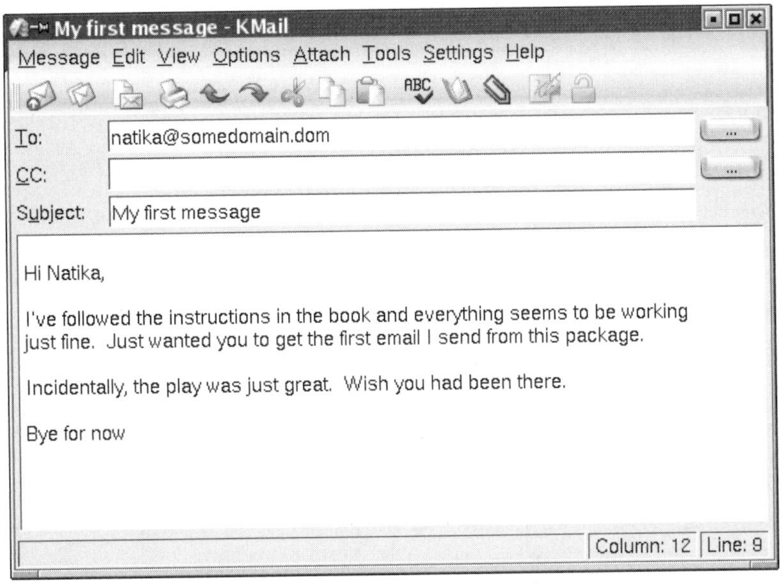

Figure 10–5 Writing an email in the composer window.

Receiving Mail

To pick up your mail, click File on the menu bar and select Check mail. You can also use a <Ctrl+L> keyboard shortcut or the Check Mail In icon (Figure 10–6). It is usually fourth from the left in the icon bar.

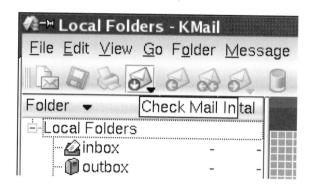

Figure 10–6   Checking for mail with a click.

Your Little Black Book

The ladies and gentlemen reading this book have by now wondered when I was going to talk about address books. After all, email implies some kind of socializing, whether it be email or personal. When composing an email message (as in Figure 10–5), notice the button with the ellipsis at the end (. . .)—clicking these buttons will bring up the address book, from which you can select whom you would like the message to go out to.

The only problem is that you probably don't have anything in the address book at this moment. Assuming you are starting from scratch, look in the icon bar at the top of either Kmail's main window or the composer window. You should see a little icon that looks like a book. You can also get to the address book by clicking on File on the menu bar and selecting Address Book. When KDE's address book opens up, click on File and select New Contact or click the icon directly beneath the file menu. The keyboard wizards can press <Ctrl+N>. You will see the dialog box shown in Figure 10–7.

When the Entry Editor appears, add whatever information is appropriate for the contact. The person's name and his or her email address are sufficient if these are all you need. When you are done entering information, click OK. You can add as many names as you want in one sitting but when you are ready

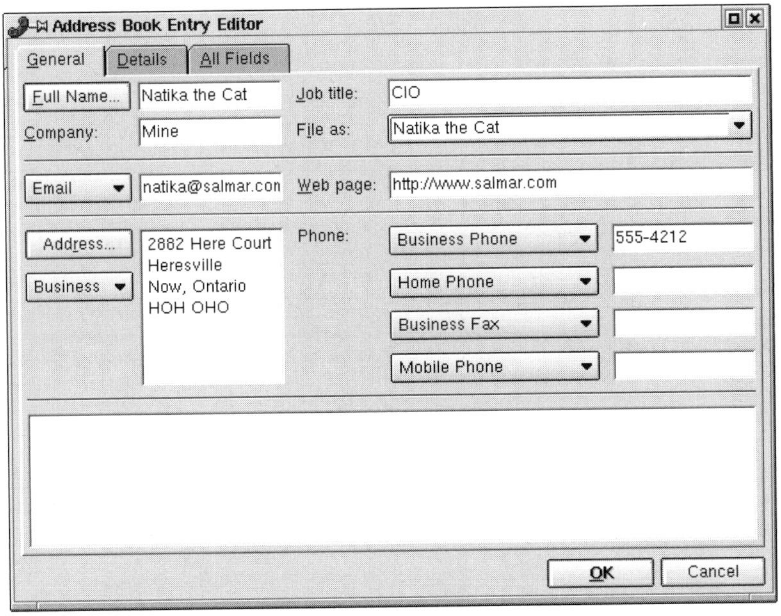

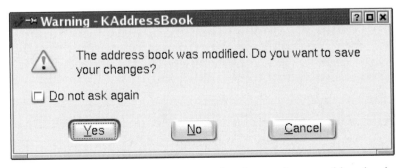

Figure 10–7   New contact address book information.

to close, you should click that little diskette icon to save your work. If you don't, a warning will appear, suggesting that you do so, as shown in Figure 10–8.

Another way to add names to your address book (and by far the *easiest*) is to take the address from a message that has been sent to you. While you are viewing someone's email to you, right-click on the email address in the From field. A small pop-up menu will appear. Click Add to Address Book, and you are done.

Figure 10–8   Making sure you save the changes in your address book.

Attached to You . . .

As you sit there writing your letter to your old high-school friend, it occurs to you that it might be fun to include a recent picture of yourself. After all, you haven't seen each other in 20 years. To attach a file, click on the paper clip icon directly below the menu bar. If you have a Konqueror file manager window open, you can also drag an icon from Konqueror into your composer window. In fact, if you have an icon on your desktop, you can drag that into your composer as well, and the images (or documents) will be automatically attached.

If you prefer the menu bar, click on Attach and select Attach File. The Attach File dialog window appears, giving you the opportunity to navigate your directories to find the appropriate file. Directly to the left of the navigation bar, there's an icon that lets you turn the preview mode on and off. This is handy when you are trying to find the right picture to attach. Figure 10–9 shows this dialog in use.

Figure 10–9   Browsing for an email attachment.

Once you have attached a file, it will show up in a separate attachments pane in your composer window. From there you can select those attachments and change your mind. Right-click on the attachment and select Remove.

Send Now or Later

People who aren't online all the time may find that it makes more sense to queue messages, rather then to send them immediately. When the time is more convenient (or you are online), you can send all queued messages. To do this, write your message as always. When you are ready, click Message on the menu bar and select Queue; the messages will be transferred to your outbox folder. You can also click the icon directly to the right of Kmail's Send icon (on the default KDE theme, it looks like a stack of pages). To actually *send* the messages, dial up to your ISP, click File on the menu bar, and select Send Queued. Note that this menu option will be grayed out if there are no messages in your outbox.

Convenient timing affects more than just when you are online; it also affects when you can finish an email message you happen to be working on. Let's say that you are composing a rather long message to Aunt Sybil, who lives in Australia. After about an hour of typing, you realize that you are supposed to be at your brother's wedding. Looking at your watch, you note that you only have 10 minutes to get to the wedding, and Aunt Sybil's email will certainly take another hour. Because you've already done all this work and you don't want to risk losing it, consider saving your email in your drafts folder.

From the composer window, click Message on the menu bar and select Save in Drafts Folder. When you are ready to resume your email (after the wedding, of course), click on the drafts folder and double-click on your email in process.

Evolution

What's hard for some people moving to Linux is saying goodbye to certain familiar applications. One of the most commonly used email packages in the Windows world is Outlook and its cousin, Outlook Express. Those users will feel right at home on their new Linux desktops when they fire up *Evolution*. A look at Figure 10–10 will no doubt seem extremely familiar. In fact, Evolution looks and feels like Outlook but with some very important improvements.

Once again, it is likely that you will find Evolution on your distribution CD. Another way to get a copy is to head over to http://www.ximian.com, the site of the Evolution authors.

Upon starting Evolution for the first time, you will be presented with the Evolution Setup Assistant to take you through the various preparatory steps. After clicking Next through the introductory window, you'll be asked for your default identity. This is where you enter your full name and email address, along with other options, such as a default signature (Figure 10–11).

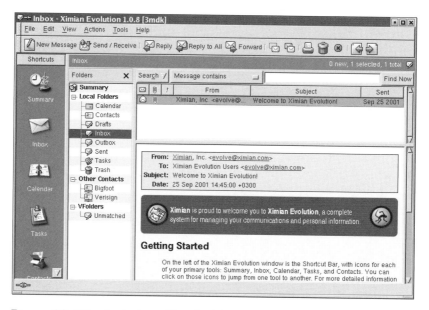

Figure 10–10   Evolution will make Microsoft Outlook users feel right at home.

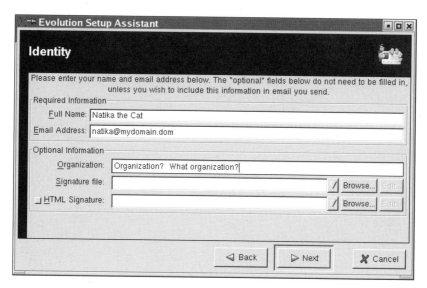

Figure 10–11   Evolution's Setup Assistant.

When you are done, click Next, and it will be time to enter information for receiving mail. You start by selecting a Server Type. For most users, this will be POP or IMAP (as with Kmail earlier). Enter the host name of the POP3 or IMAP host (as provided by your ISP), as well as your user name. If you don't want to enter your password each and every time Evolution checks for mail, you should click the "*Remember this password*" check box. When you click Next, you'll have the opportunity to decide whether Evolution checks for mail automatically (the default is to check every 10 minutes). Don't set this unless you are always connected. Click Next again, and you will be able to configure your outgoing mail.

The default Server Type for sending is SMTP, and that is almost certainly what you will need. Enter the hostname as provided by your ISP (or system administrator), and click Next. The Account Management screen follows with your new email account listed as it will be displayed in Evolution. You could change this to be a name rather than an email address if you prefer. If this is your initial setup, leave the button labeled *Make this my default account* checked on, and click Next.

You are almost done. The final step is to select your time zone. Select an area on the map (preferably near to where you live) to narrow down your search. The map will zoom in to the area you clicked, allowing you to fine-tune your selection (Figure 10–12). Make your final selection (you can use the drop-down box to aid in your selection), click Next again, then Finish, and you are done.

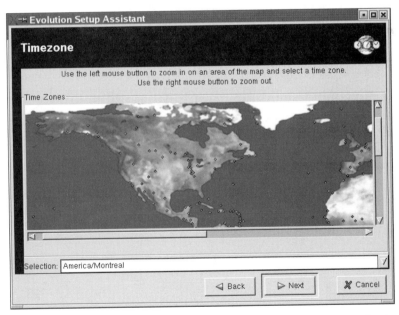

Figure 10–12   Evolution's Setup Assistant zooms in to help in selecting your time zone.

Evolution starts up with a *summary* screen (Figure 10–13), showing you the weather for an area of your choice, your Tasks and Appointments lists for the day, as well as a summary of what is in your inbox and your outbox. Like the Outlook package in Windows, a set of icons runs down the left-hand side-bar, giving you access to your Calendar, Tasks, Contacts, and email.

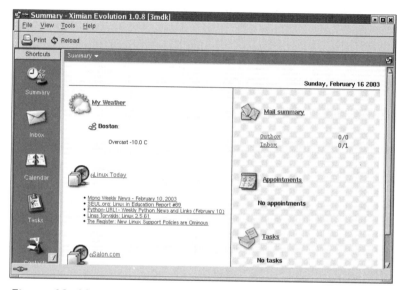

Figure 10–13   Evolution's summary screen.

Sending and Receiving Mail

To send a message, start by clicking on the Inbox icon (under the Shortcuts sidebar), then click the New Message button just below the menu bar (you can also click File on the menu bar and select New Message from there). Evolution's compose window will appear (Figure 10–14).

As with Kmail, this is pretty standard stuff. Fill in the person's email address in the To: field, enter a Subject, and type your message. When you have completed your message, click the Send button on the compose window (or click File on the compose window's menu bar, then select Send).

To pick up your email, make sure once again that you have the Inbox button selected, then click the Send/Receive button at the top of Evolution's main window (or click Actions on the menu bar and select Send/Receive).

The first time you pick up your mail, Evolution will pause and ask you for the password (Figure 10–15). You have an interesting choice to make here. Beside the words *Remember this password* is a radio button that lets you lock in

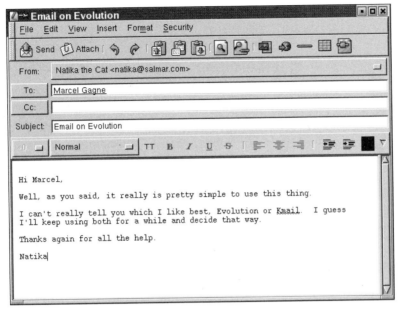

Figure 10–14   Sending a message with Evolution—the compose window.

the information. If you choose not to record your password with Evolution, you will have to enter your password each time you check for mail.

Like Microsoft Outlook, Evolution is an integrated contact management, email, and scheduling system all in one. Aside from basic email functionality, you can also plan your day, set alarms, keep a contact list, and more.

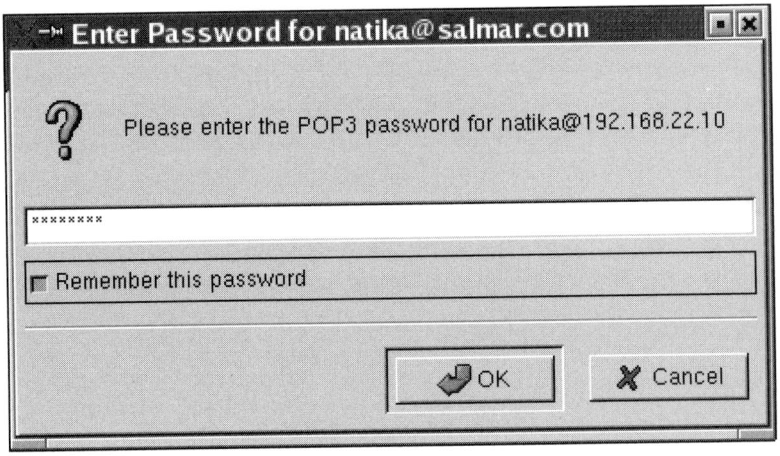

Figure 10–15   Remember the password?

What to Use?

As to whether you use Kmail or Evolution (or some of the other options I'll mention in a moment), this is something you will have to experiment with in order to decide. Personal preference is a huge factor here. I, for one, do not particularly enjoy integrated clients such as Evolution. I want my email package to be an email package only (for scheduling, I may decide to use another tool). Others can't imagine using anything other than Evolution for reasons that are exactly opposite to the one I mentioned. It's your system and your choice. The best way to discover what you want is to try things out.

Other Options

In this chapter, I've paid a lot of attention to Kmail and introduced you to Evolution. By no means should you look at these as your only options. If you are used to working with Netscape (or Mozilla) mail in the Windows world, these very options are available with Linux, and they work exactly the same.

Graphical clients aren't the only things available, either. Some people find that they prefer to work with text-only clients. After all, email is primarily about writing and reading words, and less about attached files. The average Linux distribution installs a handful of very nice, text-only email clients. Notable among these are *mutt* (http://www.mutt.org) and *pine* (http://www.washington.edu/pine/). In both cases, check your distribution CDs first before you download.

As you might have noticed, I mentioned Netscape and Mozilla. On that note, it's time to turn the page. In the next chapter, we'll look at what is probably today's most popular Internet application, the Web browser.

Resources

Kmail Homepage
http://kmail.kde.org

Ximian Evolution
http://www.ximian.com/products/evolution

11

Surfing the Net
(Just Browsing?)

When it comes to Web browsers on the desktop, Linux users are faced with an embarrassment of riches. The classic favorite, Netscape Navigator, is still here and mirrors its Windows counterpart. The same can be said for Mozilla (http://www.mozilla.org), Netscape's powerful cousin. For those who may not be aware of the history (or the connection), in 1998, Netscape released its source code under an open source license, and eager developers accepted the challenge. Mozilla was born. A few short years later, things are very different. The current incarnation of Netscape is based on Mozilla and not the other way around. Chances are that Mozilla is part of your distribution and is most likely installed by default.

I should tell you that I do tend to move back and forth between browsers. In fact, I tend to be a two-browser guy, flipping back and forth between Mozilla and KDE's own browser, Konqueror. Besides being a great browser, Konqueror is also a powerful file manager (as you discovered earlier in the book). If you are running KDE, you won't need to download Konqueror. It's part of the whole KDE environment.

Konqueror

To start surfing the Net with Konqueror, you'll need to connect to the Internet—it's a good thing we covered that in Chapter 9. Starting Konqueror as a browser is the same as starting Konqueror any other way. Most distributions, however, have an icon either on the desktop or on Kicker itself to start up Konqueror as a browser. The difference is that in the browser configuration, you can set a home page (more on that later).

Konqueror does pretty much anything you expect from a graphical Web browser and some things you don't. You can go forward and back, save bookmarks (click Bookmarks in the menu bar), download files, or print pages. Because I am assuming that you have all used a browser before, I'll concentrate on the things that I think you will want to know. To start surfing the Net, this is all you have to do. Fire up Konqueror, enter your favorite Web site's URL into the Location: bar window, and press <Enter>. In a few seconds, your Web site's page should appear.

 Quick Tip   Notice the black arrow with an x through it, to the immediate left of the Location label. Clicking this will automatically clear the Location field. No need to select or backspace over the last URL.

Page Home for Me . . .

Setting your home page is easy. Simply visit the site of your choice, drag the Konqueror browser window to the size you want, then click Window in the menu bar and select Save View Profile | Web Browsing. This brings up the Profile Management dialog (Figure 11–1), where you can save this as your default Konqueror Web view.

Notice the two check boxes at the bottom. Make sure you click them both if you want to preserve the size of browser window that you specified along with the link to your home page. Click Save, and you are done. Next time you fire up the Konqueror browser, you'll head straight to your home page.

You might wonder what the point of creating a profile just to set your home page might be. Profiles are interesting because you can create custom Konqueror views for yourself as desktop icons. When you start any other browser, you have one home page. Sure, you could put links on your desktop that go to a specific site simply by right-clicking on the desktop, choosing Create New,

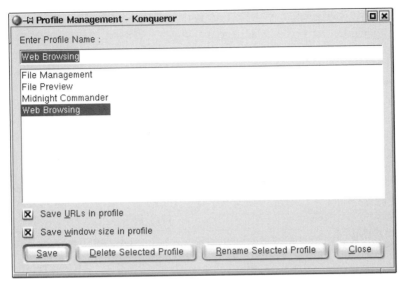

Figure 11–1   Saving your Konqueror browsing profile.

and selecting Link to Location (URL). But what if you wanted one browser to be a certain window size, as well? What if on some sites you wanted the navigation panel on and others off? Profiles let you do this.

Here's how it works. Start by creating a new profile. You do this by clicking Window on the menu bar and selecting Configure View Profiles. Enter a name where it says Enter Profile Name, then click on Save. Now click on Window one more time, select Load View Profile, and select the profile you just created. Surf over to the site of your choice, size the windows as you would like them to be, open (or don't) a navigation panel, and so on. When you are happy with your new *starting point*, click Window and click on Save View Profile YourProfileName.

Almost there. The last thing we need is a desktop icon that automagically loads this profile. The easiest way to do this is to click on the big K, open the Internet menu, and find Konqueror. Click and drag the Konqueror icon onto the desktop. You'll be asked whether you want to Copy, Move, or Link the program. Choose Copy. Now right-click on the new icon and select Properties. As before, you can choose an icon that suits you, and you probably want to pick a name for the newly created icon. The real work here is done on the Execute tab (Figure 11–2). Notice that under Command, it says *kfmclient openProfile webbrowsing*. That represents the default profile. You want to replace the word *webbrowsing* with whatever you called your profile. A word of caution: If you used spaces in your profile name (I created one called My Daily News), you will need to surround the profile name with quotes. For example:

```
kfmclient openProfile "My Daily News"
```

Click OK to save your icon, and you are done.

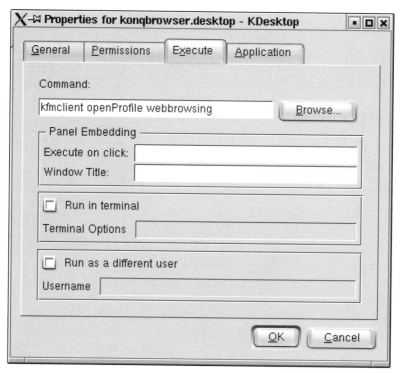

Figure 11–2   Creating a new browsing profile.

Cool Konqueror Tricks

I am going to show you a few things to try with Konqueror that you may find quite handy. As you read the next couple of pages, you will learn some great tricks, shortcuts, and otherwise fun things to do with your KDE browser.

Split Views

Remember all the things that you learned when using Konqueror as a file manager? Those things still apply. For instance, you might remember that you could split your Konqueror window to provide you with multiple views. Let's say that you wanted to look at two Websites simultaneously, with the top half of the browser displaying one site and the bottom half displaying another. Try this. Open Konqueror and surf over to the site of your choice. Now click on Window in the menu bar and choose Split View (either top/bottom or left/right). You should have two copies of the same site open in two separate views. You can close either view by clicking on Window, then clicking on Remove Active View.

As when you used Konqueror as a file manager, the active window will have a little *green light* on in the bottom left-hand corner. Click that bar on either window to switch from one to the other. You can now enter a new address into the Location field to open a new Web site.

Super-Speedy Searches

Ah, shameless alliteration . . . Let's say that you wanted to search on Linux media players in Google. Normally, you would enter `http://www.google.com`, wait for the site to load, type in *Linux media players*, and click to start the search. With Konqueror, a number of quick search shortcuts have been defined that make searching feel so much easier. To search Google for our media players, you could simply type the following in the Location field.

```
gg: Linux media players
```

Konqueror automagically feeds the search terms to Google. You can do a rapid-fire search of the Google *Usenet groups'* archive, as well. Pretend that you are having problems with an FTL3D VR card for your system.

```
ggg: FTL3D VR card setup Linux
```

There are other great shortcuts. For instance, typing `fm:` will let you search the Freshmeat software archives, and `rf:  package_name` will search RPMfind.net for RPMs of your favorite software. Here's a list of others you may want to try:

```
av:        Use the AltaVista search engine
hb:        Search HotBot
ly:        Search Lycos
sf:        Look through SourceForge
wi:        Perform a WhatIs query
```

You can check all these out for yourself by clicking on Configure Konqueror in the menu bar under Settings. Then choose Enhanced Browsing from the sidebar on the left, and you will get a nice long list of these shortcuts. One of my favorite shortcuts of all time is the *online dictionary* search. Using the `dict:` shortcut, Konqueror will search through the *Merriam-Webster Dictionary*, and the `ths:` shortcut will look things up in the online thesaurus.

    ths: thesaurus

You know, there really is no synonym for *thesaurus*.

 Quick Tip You can add your own Web search shortcut. When looking through the shortcuts under Enhanced Browsing, select one, click Modify, and follow the example to create your own.

Go for the Big Screen

Nothing beats looking at the virtual world through a big screen. As much as I would like to, I can't increase the size of your monitor, but I can help you with the next best thing. When you are busy surfing the Internet and you want as much screen as possible, why not try Konqueror's full-screen mode?

At any time while you are viewing a page, you can click Window on the menu bar and select Full-Screen Mode. The title bar will disappear, as will Kicker and all other border decorations. When the switch happens, pay attention to the icon bar (just below the menu bar). A *new icon* appears to the right of all the others. Clicking on that icon will return your Konqueror session to normal. You can also quickly toggle back and forth by pressing <Ctrl+Shift+F>.

Yum . . . Cookies

Not that kind of cookie. Cookies are simply small text files transmitted to your browser (or system) when you visit a Web site. The original idea behind cookies was that a server would give you a cookie as a marker to indicate where you had previously visited. That cookie might store a username and password to access a particular Web site or other information related to your visit, such as an online shopping cart. When you next visit the site, the server would ask your browser whether it had served you any cookies, and your browser would reply by sending the cookies from before. In this way, the Web site would recognize you when you next visited, and certain useful defaults would be set up for you. Cookies can be very good.

The problem with cookies is that they can also be shared within larger domains, such as advertising rings. Using these shared cookies, advertisers can build a profile of your likes and dislikes, tailoring and targeting advertising to you specifically. Many people object to this method of building user profiles and consider the use of cookies to be quite unethical, an invasion of privacy. The dilemma then is to find a way to accept the cookies you want and reject the others. Konqueror lets you do just that.

Click on Settings, then select Configure Konqueror. From the side panel, click on Cookies. Under the Policy tab, make sure that you have cookies enabled with the check box. Then, using the check box below that, select Ask for confirmation before accepting cookies (Figure 11–3).

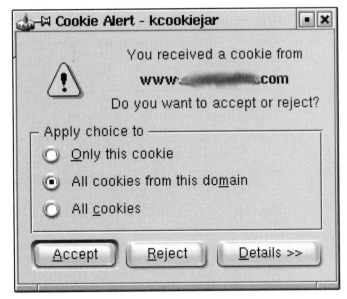

Figure 11–3   Do you accept or reject this cookie?

The first time a site offers you a cookie, a dialog box will appear, asking you whether you want to accept or reject that cookie. Best of all, it asks you whether you want to reject them now or always. Choose All cookies from this domain before you click Reject, and that ad site will never store another cookie on your computer.

Ban the Pop-Ups Forever!

Honestly, I can't think of a single person who likes to visit a Web site, only to have that site throw up annoying pop-up window ads. Konqueror lets you turn off this *feature* that certain sites provide. Once again, click Settings | Configure Konqueror, and choose Konqueror Browser from the sidebar. Select the JavaScript tab and click whichever radio button suits your taste (Figure 11–4).

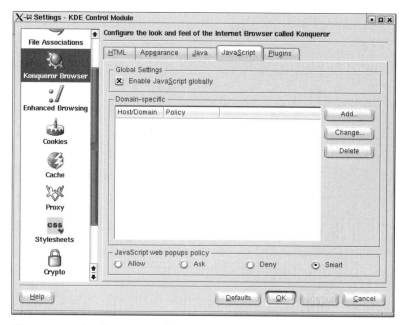

Figure 11–4   Configuring Konqueror to ban pop-up ads.

I've found that Smart is indeed pretty smart and that it generally takes care of deciding whether to allow pop-ups. You can also decide to have Konqueror ask you each and every time a site tries to open a pop-up, or you can simply Deny everything.

Keeping Tabs on the Web

As of KDE 3.1, Konqueror sports a great feature called *tabbed browsing* (Figure 11–5). Here's how it works.

Sometimes when you are viewing Web sites, you want to keep a particular site open while moving to another place on the Web. Normally, you would

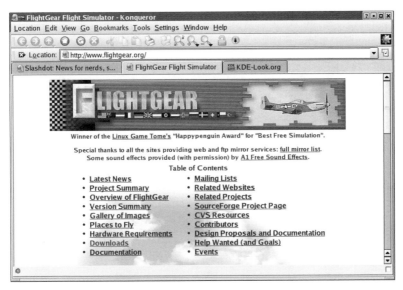

Figure 11–5   Konqueror does tabbed browsing.

click File and select New Window. This is fine, except that if you keep doing this, you'll wind up with however many versions of a browser open on your desktop. Switching from one to the other involves doing a little digital juggling. Tabs make it possible to bring a nice, clean air of sanity to what could otherwise become a very cluttered taskbar (or desktop).

To open new tabs, click Window on the menu bar and select New Tab or simply press <Ctrl+Shift+N>. You can also open a new tab from a link in the current Web page by right-clicking on that link, then selecting Open in New Tab. Have a look at Figure 11–5 to see Konqueror's tabs in action.

Mozilla

To this day, I find myself switching back and forth between Mozilla (Figure 11–6) and Konqueror. The features I've mentioned for Konqueror make it an amazingly useful browser—in some ways, it is more like the Swiss Army knife of browsers. Mozilla, on the other hand, has the Netscape Navigator look and feel that I've grown accustomed to over the years in a much more mature and *flexible* package. It includes an email package and IRC client, is ideal for reading newsgroups, and comes with an HTML editor.

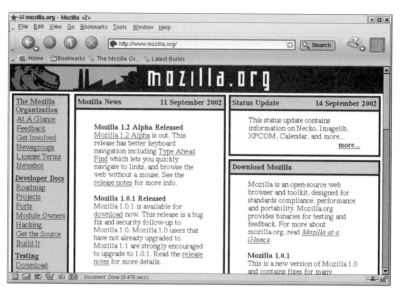

Figure 11–6   Mozilla, an excellent browser.

To start Mozilla, click on Kicker's big K, select Internet, and choose Mozilla from the list. If Mozilla isn't installed, you can get the package at `http://www.mozilla.org` or simply get it off your distribution CDs. If you do head to the Mozilla Web site, it probably makes sense to choose a stable release unless you are feeling particularly adventurous and want to experiment with the leading edge. Just remember that it can be wobbly on the edge.

Working from Home

When you first start Mozilla, it will take you to its home, the Mozilla welcome page. Getting to a Web site and navigating Mozilla is much the same as it is in any other browser you have used, particularly if you were using Netscape (or Mozilla) with your old OS. All you do is type the URL of the Web site you want to visit into the location bar, and away you go. If you would like to start each time on a personal home page, this is easily done.

Click on Edit in Mozilla's menu bar and select Preferences. The Preferences window opens up with a left-hand Category panel, from which you select what part of Mozilla you want to modify. By default, it opens up to the Navigator category—Navigator is the browser part of Mozilla (Figure 11–7). Over on the right side, there are three radio buttons. Clicking the top button will start Mozilla on a blank page, and clicking in the middle will let you specify a home page. The third radio button will tell Mozilla always to start up on the last page visited. Now looking below, you'll see a field for entering the URL of your desired home page—enter the URL there. When you are done, click OK.

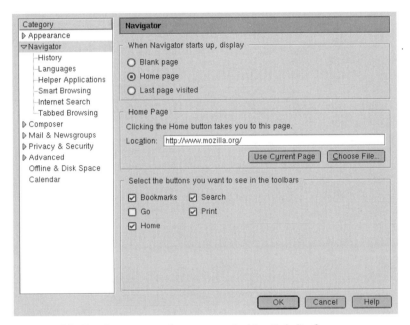

Figure 11–7   Setting your home page in Mozilla's Preferences menu.

Mozilla Does Tabs, Too

Before I tell you how tabs work in Mozilla, it seems only fair that I should tell you that Mozilla had tabbed browsing before Konqueror did (particularly because I gave Konqueror first billing). The concept behind tabbed browsing in Mozilla is the same, but the keystrokes are a little different.

Start by visiting a site of your choice. Now click on File, select New, and choose Navigator Tab from the drop-down menu. You can also use the <Ctrl+T> keyboard shortcut to do the same thing. Notice that Mozilla now identifies your sites with tabs just below the location bar (Figure 11–8). Add a third or a fourth if you like. Switching from site to site is now just a matter of clicking the tabs on your single copy of Mozilla.

While in tab mode (as shown in Figure 11–8), you can right-click on a tab to bring up the tab menu. From there you can close or reload the current tab (or all tabs) and even open new tabs. Another way to close the active tab is to click on the X at the end of the tab list.

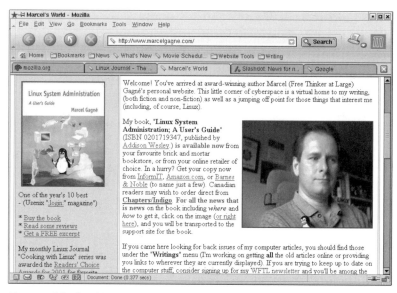

Figure 11–8   Mozilla showing off its tabs.

Still Don't Like Pop-Up Ads?

I have to mention this again because it is one of the things that make some of these Linux browsers so wonderful—the ability to stop unwanted pop-up window ads. Like Konqueror before, Mozilla lets you do this easily.

Start by bringing up the Preferences menu again (click Edit on the menu bar and choose Preferences). From the category list (Figure 11–9), choose Advanced and open the submenu (by clicking the little arrow directly to the left of the word *Advanced*). From that submenu, choose Scripts & Windows. The check box for Open unrequested windows is on. Check it off, then click OK to close the Preferences menu.

Controlling Cookies

Mozilla is also very versatile in its handling of cookies. Before you excitedly turn off all cookies, do remember that they can be useful, particularly with on-line services such as banks and e-commerce sites. That said, you may very much want to curb cookie traffic as much as possible.

From the Preferences menu, open up the Privacy & Security category submenu (Figure 11–10).

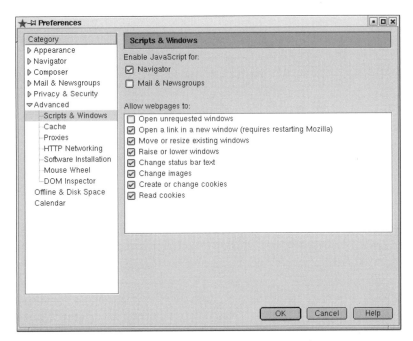

Figure 11–9   Configuring Mozilla to stop pop-up ads.

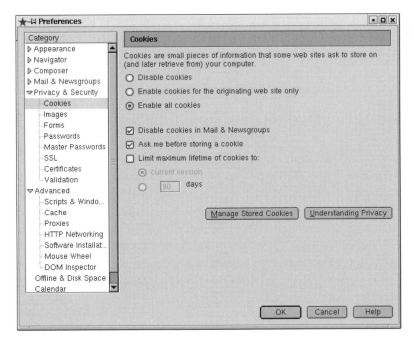

Figure 11–10   Back to Mozilla's Preferences menu to configure cookie policies.

Unless you really want to refuse all cookies, leave the Enable all cookies radio button checked on. Then make sure that you have radio button labeled *Ask me before storing a cookie* checked on. Click OK, and resume your surfing. When you visit a site that tries to set or modify a cookie, an alert will pop up, alerting you to the cookie and asking you how to proceed. If you decide to reject a cookie and you never want to see another cookie from that site, check *Remember this decision* before clicking No.

The Mozilla Sidebar

You have already seen the sidebar because it is open by default when you use Mozilla for the first time. The sidebar is a quick way to get to your information, be it bookmarks, active searches, and so on. You can quickly activate the sidebar by pressing <F9> or by clicking View on the menu bar, then selecting Show/Hide | Sidebar. The sidebar will appear (or disappear).

The sidebar makes Net searches easy. At the top of the sidebar, you'll see a search field. Just type your search keywords in the location bar and press <Enter>. By default, Mozilla will pass your search terms to Netscape's search engine. You can modify this default by going into the Preferences menu and choosing Internet Search under the Navigator category.

The sidebar is customizable, as well. While the sidebar is open, click on the Tabs drop-down list, select Customize Sidebar (Figure 11–11), and you can add, remove, or change the order of things as they appear.

Wrapping up

I started this chapter by telling you that Linux has many browsers available. On the GNOME side, we have *Galeon*, which is based on Mozilla's rendering engine. If you installed support for both the KDE and GNOME desktops, you should have it already installed. Galeon can be downloaded from `http://galeon.sourceforge.net`.

Another browser worth a look is *Opera*, an excellent, very fast, lightweight graphical browser that is distributed using an interesting model. The freeware version of the browser serves up small banner ads in the upper part of the browser as you use it; you can also purchase an ad-free version. To take Opera for a spin, you will have to head to the Opera Web site at `http://www.opera.com` and pick up a copy.

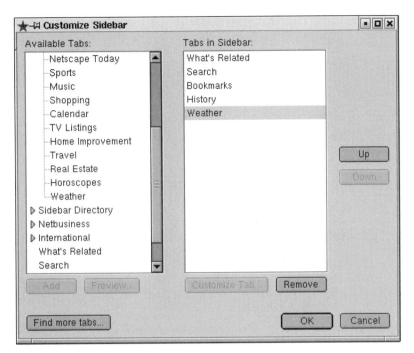

Figure 11–11   Customizing the Mozilla sidebar.

We can't stop there. Most Linux distributions include several browsers, in-cluding some text-only browsers such as *lynx* and *links*. If these aren't already installed on your system, they are very likely on your distribution CDs.

Shell Out When you feel like seeing the World Wide Web without its clutter of images, why not give lynx or links a try? Just open a Konsole shell and try the following:

```
lynx http://www.marcelgagne.com/

links http://www.marcelgagne.com/
```

You may be amazed at the speed and performance of nonflashy Web.

Resources

Galeon, the GNOME Web Browser

     http://galeon.sourceforge.net

Konqueror Web Site

     http://www.konqueror.org

Links Text Web Browser

     http://atrey.karlin.mff.cuni.cz/~clock/twibright/links/

Lynx Browser

     http://lynx.isc.org

Mozilla

     http://www.mozilla.org

Opera

     http://www.opera.com

12

Keeping Up to Date

Nothing is ever perfect. Even when things are first released and all seems well, it takes only the passage of time to turn up errors of some sort. A typical Linux distribution can contain hundreds of packages and potentially thousands of files. Although great care is taken to make sure things are as perfect as they can be, with those numbers, errors sometimes happen. Updates aren't always about errors, either. Sometimes package updates reflect enhancements to the current software.

The nice thing about problems with your Linux system is that those problems don't tend to hang around for a long time. Thousands of programmers worldwide are involved in developing and maintaining the Linux kernel and the associated packages that make up what we call a distribution. When something goes wrong or a security bug surfaces, it is fixed and released to the community. Getting and applying these updates to your system is something that you should be doing on a regular basis.

These updates and patches may be free, but there are other considerations. Specifically, you'll find that when you are doing system updates, your network connection is definitely an issue. A given update may include multiple packages, and some of these packages may be quite large. A slow modem connection may be too little for a major update. You could still perform the update, but you may be online for hours.

Mandrake Update

It's quite easy to install updates to your Mandrake system. This is done through *DrakConf* (Mandrake Control Center), the all-in-one system administration tool that comes included with your Mandrake distribution. This interface lets you add users, configure your system, set up a firewall . . . pretty much anything related to administering your system. It is also the means by which you can do an online update of the latest patches and security fixes.

DrakConf is usually listed in your Mandrake K-menu under Configuration (you may see the KDE Control Center there as well). You can also run it from a shell (command name: `drakconf`) or via the <Alt+F2> command launcher. Because this program requires administrative privileges to do its work, you will be asked for the *root* password.

When the Mandrake Control Center appears, click on Software Management in the left sidebar menu.

You'll have four choices here; to install software (you can use this as an alternative to kpackage, which we discussed in Chapter 7), to remove software, to update the packages on your system, or to maintain the package sources. To update the packages on your system, choose Mandrake Update. If you have never used this service before, Mandrake Update will provide you with a list of download mirrors to choose from. Choose one that is close to you geographically. This will tend to provide you with faster downloads.

Mandrake Update will then return a list of packages that have been updated. Clicking on a package in that list will give you a description of the package and why it is being updated (Figure 12–1).

Beside each package is a check box. To select a package for update, click on the box, and it will be replaced with a checkmark. Should any conflict arise or should some package require another before it can be installed, Mandrake Update will inform you. If you aren't sure what to pick and choose, simply select them all.

When you are ready, click Install, and Mandrake Update will start downloading the packages in turn. When the download is complete, those packages will then be installed.

Red Hat up2date

Red Hat also provides an easy interface for keeping your system up to date, and it is actually called *up2date*. This program is the front end to Red Hat's Red Hat Network, a premium service that nevertheless offers a *free demo* service.

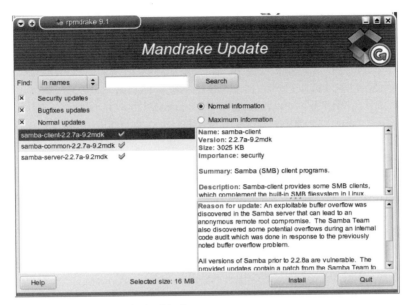

Figure 12–1   Mandrake Update.

In this case, the demo is no less functional than the full product, and you can use it to keep your system patched and up to date without spending any extra money. Getting started with the program takes a few more steps than Mandrake Update—to use up2date, you need to register with the Red Hat Network. The registration dialog is launched automatically if you are starting up2date for the first time.

The limitation of the demo service becomes evident during busy periods, at which times your up2date client will politely inform you that network load is too high to allow nonpaying customers to use the service. I've found that waiting until after business hours to perform updates is usually a satisfactory solution. For pricing and premium services on the Red Hat Network, visit `http://rhn.redhat.com`.

Running up2date

You'll find up2date under the System Tools submenu (under the big K) but it may be listed as Red Hat Network instead. Optionally, you may start up2date from the shell or by using your <Alt+F2> command quickstart and typing `up2date`. Because this program requires administrator privileges to do its work, you'll be asked to provide the root password.

If this is your first time using the service, the *Red Hat Network Configuration* dialog will automatically launch. Take a moment to fill out the form—you'll need to provide a username, password, and email address (*you don't have to use your own login id or password—in fact, you should create a completely different user*). When you click Forward, you'll get another, more detailed registration screen, but everything there is optional. You may, if you wish, just click Forward past this point. Finally, as part of registration, the program will suggest a profile name for your system. You are free to accept it or to select something new. With this information, your profile (including a list of packages installed on your system) will be created.

You need to go through this registration process only once. When up2date starts the next time, you'll only get a little welcome message. Just click Next and you'll be asked to confirm what "channel" you are subscribed to—in other words, what release of the Red Hat system you are running. You should just be able to click Next past this point.

The available packages for update may consist of two passes. The first are packages flagged to skip (usually the kernel, but this is configurable), and the second is a list of all available packages. Check off the packages you would like to install as part of your update (if you aren't sure, just check the Select all packages button, shown in Figure 12–2). When you have made your selection and clicked Next to continue, package dependencies will be checked (if you need additional packages installed, up2date will alert you), and the download will begin.

As packages are downloaded, a progress bar will indicate a percentage of completion for both the current package and the whole download. When all packages are downloaded, you will click Next again to install them.

SuSE's Online Update

SuSE follows a similar approach to Mandrake in that its package update tool is accessed through its all-in-one system administration interface, YaST2 (Yet Another Setup Tool 2). YaST2's program name is simply `yast2`. You can run it from a shell or by using your KDE quick launcher <Alt+F2>. Once again, the requirement for administrative privileges means you will be asked for *root's* password.

When the YaST Control Center appears, double-click on the Online Update icon. Another YaST2 screen will appear, this one offering you a choice of either an automatic or a manual update scheme. The manual update will show you all of the packages for which there is an update, allowing you to pick and choose between them. Unless you are completely confident with your system

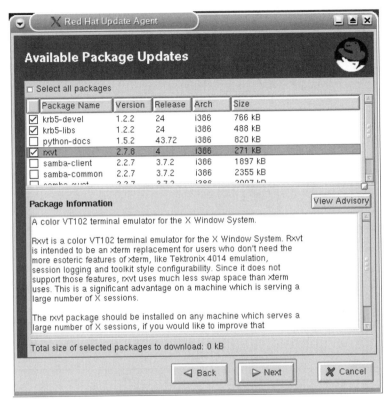

Figure 12–2   Fetching packages with Red Hat's up2date.

and what packages you want updated, it is probably best to choose the Automatic Update setting (do this by clicking the radio button).

When you have done so, click Next and YaST2 will initialize a network connection to search for package updates. When the update list returns, you'll have the opportunity to review the suggested updates and patches, as well as descriptions of what each patch does (Figure 12–3). To begin the update, click Accept.

Once all patches have been downloaded and installed, SuSE's update tool will write out the modified system configurations.

As packages are downloaded, a progress bar will indicate a percentage of completion for both the current package and the whole download. When all packages are downloaded, you will click Next again to install them.

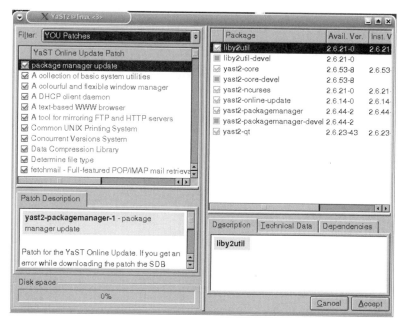

Figure 12–3   SuSE's online update system.

Ximian's Red Carpet

One of the great strengths of Ximian Red Carpet is the broad range of distributions it supports (Debian, Mandrake, Red Hat, SuSE, and others). Furthermore, the interface is consistent across all of these different platforms. Get used to Red Carpet on one system, and you'll find it just as easy on another.

Like the other options I've discussed, Red Carpet takes care of making sure that any dependencies necessary to install a package are met and taken care of—automagically. Best of all, Ximian offers this service free of charge. It also offers a premium service that gives you access to dedicated servers with much faster access. As part of its premium service, Ximian occasionally offers additional bonuses, such as free versions of commercial software. Whichever way you choose to go (free or premium service), you can get started by downloading the client appropriate for your system from the Ximian Red Carpet Web site:

```
http://www.ximian.com/products/redcarpet/
```

Ximian has a number of other products, including the email and calendaring package called *Evolution* (which I covered in Chapter 10). Ximian also produces its own version of the GNOME desktop called the *Ximian desktop*. When you visit Ximian's site to download Red Carpet, you'll get a message telling you that the best way to install Red Carpet is by installing the Ximian desktop. You can choose to do this if you like, but it is not necessary. Red Carpet works perfectly with KDE.

Download the Red Carpet RPM, then install it with kpackage, or download it and install it by opening a shell window and typing the following (keep in mind that the version number of the package will vary based on your system type and Ximian's own release cycle):

```
rpm -Uvh red-carpet-1.3.1-1.ximian.i386.rpm
```

To run Red Carpet, open a shell (or use your <Alt+F2> program launcher) and type red-carpet. Because Red Carpet needs administrative privileges to run, you'll be asked for the root password. The first time you run the program, it will ask you whether you are behind a firewall and whether you need to use a proxy to connect. Most people can safely ignore this screen and click OK to continue. That is pretty much it—no lengthy form to fill out.

Red Carpet works on the principle of *channels* that you subscribe to. When you first start the program, click on the Unsubscribed Channels icon on the left (Figure 12–4). Choose those areas that you wish to keep up, then click the Subscribe button for that channel.

Figure 12–4   Ximian's Red Carpet.

You can select individual packages or click Edit on the menu bar and click Select all to choose every package.

Ximian's Red Carpet is an excellent service. There are only a couple of drawbacks that I have seen. For starters, Red Carpet is usually a little behind in terms of providing client programs for the latest and greatest distributions. If Red Hat or Mandrake comes out with a new distribution, you might have to wait two or three weeks before Ximian provides a client. The second drawback is that Red Carpet tends to be GNOME-centric. This isn't surprising, given that Ximian is a major supporter and developer of the GNOME project.

The Not-So-Final Word on Updates

Regardless of your distribution, it is important to remember that your Linux system is the product of the hard work and dedication of people from every part of the world. There are Linux companies out there and large corporations contributing to the development and maintenance of the programs that make up your system, but in the end, Linux *really is* a community effort. Some people earn a living developing Linux software. Others do it for the good of the community. Still others do it just for fun.

Because this community exists, the quest to keep your system running as close to perfectly as is humanly possible is happening on many fronts. Keeping up to date with the latest and greatest package (for whatever reason) means you aren't limited strictly to your distribution's vendor.

Check out some of the Linux links on my own Web site at `www.marcel-gagne.com`. Subscribe to a Linux magazine. There are some great publications out there, including *Linux Journal*, *Linux Format* (a U.K. publication), *Linux Magazine* (of which there is a U.S. version and an unrelated U.K. version), to name just a few. All of these magazines offer their own Web sites with online articles and discussions pertinent to Linux.

Do you think you might have you discovered a bug? Report it. Click Help on the menu bar of almost any KDE application, and you'll see something labeled *Report Bug . . .* Click that menu item, and you'll see a window similar to that shown in Figure 12–5.

As with any community, there is also a social component. As with many groups of enthusiasts from model railroaders to gardeners, the Linux community gets together to discuss its area of interest. So join a local Linux User Group (LUG) and subscribe to the mailing list, even if you can't go to meetings. Check out the *Groups of Linux Users Everywhere* or *Linux.org* for help in finding out where and when your local group meets (see the Resources section at

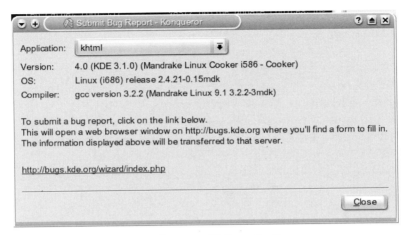

Figure 12–5 Reporting a bug in a KDE application.

the end of the chapter for links). If something important surfaces that you should know about, somebody is sure to mention it.

In short, get involved.

Resources

Groups of Linux Users Everywhere

http://www.ssc.com:8080/glue/

Linux.org's List of LUGs

http://www.linux.org/groups/index.html

Mandrake Errata

http://www.mandrakelinux.com/en/errata.php3

Red Hat Network Errata

http://www.redhat.com/apps/support/errata/

SuSE Security Updates (U.S. Site)

http://www.suse.com/us/private/support/security/index.html

Ximian's Red Carpet

http://www.ximian.com/products/redcarpet

13

Word Processors (It Was a Dark and Stormy Night...)

Sorry, but at some point, I just had to use that famous opening from Edward George Bulwer-Lytton's "Paul Clifford" (written in 1830). Those famous words "It was a dark and stormy night" were made even more famous (infamous?) by Charles M. Schulz's Snoopy, that barnstorming, literary beagle. It just seems fitting considering this chapter's topic—word processors.

Word processors run the gamut in terms of complexity, from simple programs that aren't much more than text editors to full-blown desktop publishing systems. Users coming from the Microsoft world are most likely to use OpenOffice Writer, part of the OpenOffice.org suite.

OpenOffice.org is actually the free sibling of the commercial StarOffice suite. When Sun Microsystems decided to open the source to StarOffice, it became another boon for the open source community, not to mention the average user. OpenOffice became the free version of this powerful word processor, spreadsheet, and presentation graphics package, and StarOffice became the corporate choice. Both of these are full-featured office suites, and users familiar with Microsoft Office will feel right at home with the similarities.

You might well be wondering what differences exist between these two sibling suites. The great difference is the price. For anyone with a reasonably fast Internet connection (or a helpful friend), OpenOffice is *free*. StarOffice, on the other hand, will cost you something for the boxed set. Included with StarOffice is documentation and support, as well as additional fonts and clip art. That said, you'll find that it is still *far less expensive* than the Windows alternative.

If you are following along and using the KDE desktop, you probably also have *KWord* at your disposal. Then, as I hinted, there are the others. We'll talk about a few of them at the end of this chapter.

Trivia Time It may interest you to know that this book was written using OpenOffice.org 1.0.1 (and 1.0.2), as well as its commercial cousin, StarOffice 6.0.

OpenOffice.org Writer

Start Writer by clicking on the big K, scrolling up to the OpenOffice.org menu (in some distributions, check under the Office menu), and clicking on OpenOffice.org Writer. The first time you start Writer, the Address Data Source AutoPilot dialog box will appear. The applications in OpenOffice.org can access information in your Netscape or Mozilla address book from an external LDAP server or from a number of other data sources, such as a database file. This information can then be used when you are creating mailing labels or distribution lists. If you don't have anything set up, don't worry. Simply click Cancel, and you are done.

Shell Out To run OpenOffice.org Writer from the command line (or via your <Alt+F2> shortcut), use the command `oowriter` (think OpenOffice.org Writer). Please note that some distributions may still use `swriter` (the StarOffice version of the command).

OpenOffice.org Writer starts up with a blank page, ready for you to release that inner creative genius. At the top of the screen, you'll find a menu bar where commands are organized based on their categories, including the friendly-sounding Help submenu (more on that shortly).

You should also see a selection box open on the screen for Paragraph Styles (see Figure 13–1). This lets you quickly access and apply styles such as headings, text boxes, and so on to your paragraphs. The *Stylist* floats above your document at all times for rapid access. I'll tell you more about the Stylist later. For now, click the *x* in the corner to close it. You can always turn it on at a later time by pressing <F11> or clicking Format on the menu bar and selecting Stylist.

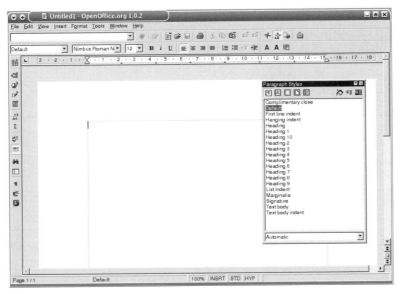

Figure 13–1 OpenOffice.org Writer on startup.

Write Now!

At this point, Writer is open, the Stylist is gone, and you are looking at a blank screen. Let's write something. As any writer will tell you, nothing is more *intimidating* than a blank page. Because I opened this chapter with a reference to the famous phrase, *It was a dark and stormy night*, why don't we continue along that theme? That phrase is often pointed to as an example of bad writing, but the phrase in itself is only so bad. The paragraph that follows is even worse. Type this into your blank Writer page, as shown in Figure 13–2.

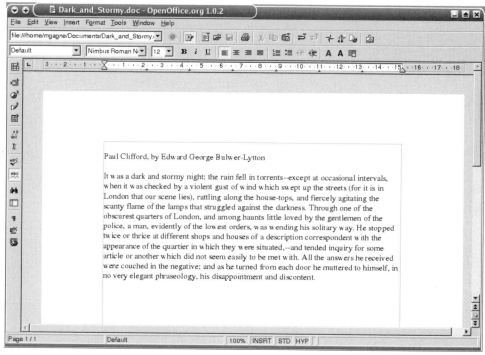

Figure 13–2   Your first document.

Paul Clifford, by Edward George Bulwer-Lytton

It was a dark and stormy night; the rain fell in torrents—except at occasional intervals, when it was checked by a violent gust of wind which swept up the streets (for it is in London that our scene lies), rattling along the house-tops, and fiercely agitating the scanty flame of the lamps that struggled against the darkness. Through one of the obscurest quarters of London, and among haunts little loved by the gentlemen of the police, a man, evidently of the lowest orders, was wending his solitary way. He stopped twice or thrice at different shops and houses of a description correspondent with the appearance of the quartier in which they were situated—and tended inquiry for some article or another which did not seem easily to be met with. All the answers he received were couched in the negative; and as he turned from each door he muttered to himself, in no very elegant phraseology, his disappointment and discontent.

Okay, you can stop there. Isn't that wonderful stuff? If you feel the need to read more, I've got links to the story and the famous Bulwer-Lytton fiction contest at the end of this chapter.

The Hunt for Typos

For years, I've been including the tag line *This massagee wos nat speel or gramer-checkered* in the signature section of my emails. Given that I continue to use this line, I am obviously amused by it, but never running a spell check is far from good practice when your intention is to turn in a professional document.

OpenOffice.org Writer can do a spell check as you go without actually correcting errors. Click Tools on the menu bar, then Spellcheck, and select AutoSpellcheck. Words that don't appear in the dictionary will show up with a squiggly red line underneath them, which you can then correct. Many people find this a useful feature, but some, like myself, prefer to just check the whole document at the end of our writing.

To start a full document spell check, click Tools on the menu bar, then Spellcheck, and click on Check. You can also just press <F7> at any time to start a spell check.

What Language Is That?

OpenOffice.org supports many different languages, and depending on where you picked up your copy, it may be set for a different language than your own. To change the default language, click Tools on the menu bar, then Options, Language Settings, and Writing Aids.

The dialog box that appears (Figure 13–3) should have OpenOffice.org MySpell SpellChecker checked on. You can then click the Edit button next to it and select your language of choice under the Default languages for documents drop-down box. When you have made your choice, click OK to exit the various dialogs.

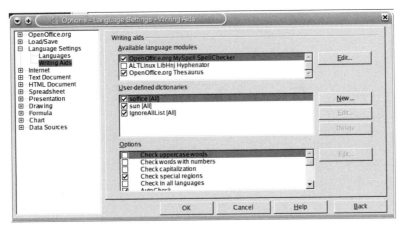

Figure 13 –3   Configuring writing tools.

Saving Your Work

Now that you have created a document (Figure 13–2), it is time to save it. Click File on the menu bar and select Save (or Save As). When the Save As window appears (Figure 13–4), select a folder, type in a file name, and click Save. When you save, you can also specify the File type to be OpenOffice.org's default format (.sxw), RTF, straight text, or Microsoft Word format.

If you want to create a new directory under your home directory, you can do it here as well. Click the icon that looks like a folder with a star beside it (near the right-hand corner), then enter your new directory name in the Create new folder pop-up window.

Should you decide to close OpenOffice.org Writer at this point, you can always return to your document at a later time by clicking File on the menu bar and selecting Open. The Open File dialog will appear, and you can browse your directories to select the file you want. You can specify a file type via a fairly substantial drop-down list of available formats. This gives you a chance to narrow the search to include only text documents, spreadsheets, or presentations. You can also specify a particular document extension (i.e., only * .doc files) or a particular pattern.

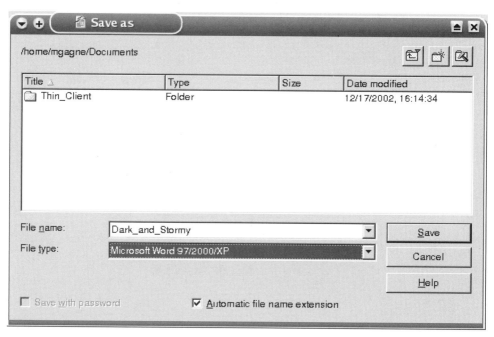

Figure 13–4   *It is always good to save your work.*

Printing Your Document

Invariably, the whole point of typing something in a word processor might be to produce a printed document. When you are through with your document, click File on the menu bar and select Print.

The Print dialog (Figure 13–5) has several options. The easiest thing to do after selecting your printer is just to click OK. The print job will be directed to your printer of choice and, in a few seconds, you'll have a nice, crisp version of your document. You can select a page range, increase the number of copies (one to all your friends), or modify the printer properties (paper size, landscape print, etc.).

You can also print to a file. This is particularly interesting in that you can filter that print job so that the result is a PDF file (readable with Adobe Acrobat Reader or Linux's own *xpdf*).

To print a PDF file, select the PDF Converter from the printer selection list. Click the Print to file check box, and the Save As dialog will appear (as in Figure 13–4). Choose a file name (make sure you add the .pdf extension), select PDF from the file type drop-down menu, and click Save. When the Print dialog returns, click OK, and your PDF document will be created.

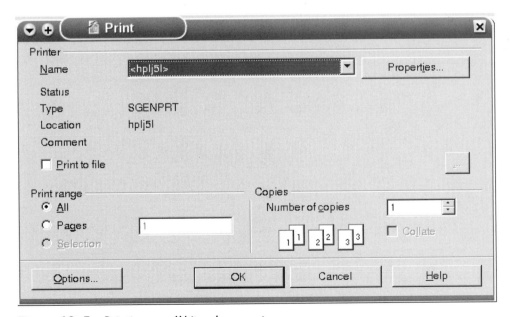

Figure 13–5   Printing your Writer document.

Toolbars of Every Kind . . .

Now that you are feeling comfortable with your new word processor, let's take a quick tour of the various toolbars, icons, and menus in Writer.

The icon bar directly below the menu bar is called the *Function bar*, and it contains icons for opening and creating documents, cutting and pasting, printing, and others. The Function bar is common to all the OpenOffice.org applications (Writer, Calc, Impress, etc.). On the left side of that Function bar is a combo box, a blank field where you can directly enter the path to a document you want to edit.

Below the Function bar is the *Object bar*. It provides common editing options, such as font selection, bolding, italics, centering, and so on. Select words or phrases in your document with the mouse (hold, click, and drag across the desired text), then click *B* for bold or *I* for italics. This bar will change from application to application, depending on what type of formatting is most needed.

At the bottom of the editing screen is the *Status bar*. What you'll see there is the current page number, current template, zoom percentage, insert (or overwrite) mode, selection mode, hyperlink mode, and the current save status of the document (if the document has been modified and not saved, an asterisk will appear).

Finally, off to the left is another icon bar. This one is called the *Main toolbar*, and it provides a quick method of inserting objects into the document, doing a search and replace, or running a spell check. Pause over each of the icons with your mouse cursor, and a tooltip will appear, describing the functions of the individual icons.

 Quick Tip Before we move on, let me tell you about a strange behavior you will encounter. After using OpenOffice.org a few times, you'll eventually get a pop-up asking you to register your software. This is completely voluntary, and you do not need to do this. If you do register, you can contribute by letting the OpenOffice.org team know about bugs, features you'd like, and so on. Unless you request a future reminder, this is the last time you will see this screen.

Help!

Under the Help heading on the menu bar, you'll find plenty of information. By default, tooltips are activated so that when you pause your mouse cursor over an item, a small tooltip will be shown. Click Help, and you'll see Tips checked on. Just below the word *Tips*, there is something else you might find useful. It's called *Extended Tips*. Turning that on will give you slightly more detailed tooltips.

If you are looking for help on a specific topic, choose Contents to open up the OpenOffice help screen. The various tabs at the top left of the help screen let you search for topics by application with the Contents tab, alphabetically using the Index tab, and by keyword using the Find tab. You can even set bookmarks under the Bookmarks tab for those topics you regularly access.

To Word or Not to Word?

Ah, that is the question indeed. OpenOffice.org's default document format is XML (eXtensible Markup Language), an open standard for document formats (although it is saved with an .sxw extension). The main reason for sticking with OpenOffice.org's native format is one of support and portability. XML is an emerging standard, and many applications in development either support XML or plan to.

Alternatively, the main reason for sticking with Word format is, *quite frankly*, that Word is everywhere. The sheer number of Word installations is the very reason that OpenOffice.org was designed to support Microsoft Office format as thoroughly as it does. That said, if you do want to switch to XML format, Writer provides an easy way to do that. Rather than converting documents one by one, the Document Converter speeds up the process by allowing you to run all the documents in a specific directory in one pass. It also works in both directions, meaning that you can convert from Word to OpenOffice.org format and vice versa. The conversion creates a new file but leaves the original as it is.

From the menu bar, select File, move your mouse to AutoPilot, then select Document Converter from the submenu. To convert your Microsoft Office documents (you can do the Excel and PowerPoint documents at the same time), click Microsoft Office on the menu, then check off the types of documents you want. The next screen will ask you whether you want both documents and templates or just one or the other. You will then type in the name of the directory you want to import from and save to (this can be the same directory). After you've entered your information and gone to the next screen, the program will confirm your choices and give you a final chance to change your mind. Click Convert to continue. As the converter does its job, it will list the various files that it encounters and keep track of the process.

When the job is done, you'll have a number of files with an .sxw extension in your directory. If you change your mind, don't worry. Your original files are still there, so you've lost nothing.

If working with Word documents in Word format is important, then read on. Ah, heck. Even if it isn't, you should read on.

Personalizing Your Environment

Every application you use comes with defaults that may or may not reflect the way you want to work, and this is true here, as well.

Click Tools on the menu bar and select Options. There are a lot of options here, including OpenOffice.org, Load/Save, Language Settings, Internet, Text Documents, HTML Document, SpreadSheet, Presentation, Drawing, Formula, Chart, and Data Sources. You've no doubt already noticed that although we are working with Writer here, the various components can be configured in this mode, as well. Because there are so many options here, I certainly can't cover them all, and besides, I don't want to bore you. Instead, I'll mention a few things that I *think* are important and let you discover the rest.

The main OpenOffice.org dialog covers a lot of general options regarding the look and feel of the applications. Take a moment to look at the *Paths* settings. If you keep your documents in a specific directory, you'll want to set that here. Under Type, choose My Documents, click Edit, then enter the new path to your directory of choice.

Let's move on to the very important *Load/Save* settings menu (Figure 13–6). If you are constantly going to move documents back and forth between systems running Microsoft Word and your own, you'll want to pay special attention here. Click the plus sign to the left of it, then click Microsoft Office.

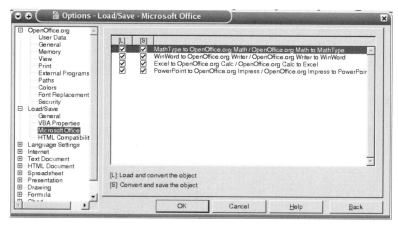

Figure 13–6   Load/Save defaults for Microsoft documents.

Click the Convert on Save (and load) check boxes on, and your OpenOffice.org Writer documents will be saved in Word format by default while your Calc sheets will wind up in Excel format. We're almost there. Although the conversion is pretty automatic here, when you try to resave a document that you have been working on, Writer may still disturb you with the occasional pop-up message informing you of the *minuses* of saving in Word format.

You get around this with one other change. In the same menu section, click General. Notice where it says *Standard file format* (Figure 13–7). For the Document type of Text document, click Microsoft Word in the Always save as drop-down list to the right. While you are here (assuming you are making these changes, of course), you probably want to change the Always save as format for *Spreadsheet* to be Microsoft Excel.

Click OK, and you are done.

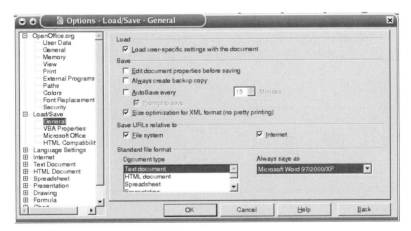

Figure 13–7   Defining the standard file format to be Microsoft Word.

Note I'm not saying that Microsoft's document format is in any way superior—it isn't—but if you have to move back and forth all the time, you don't want to be bothered with doing a Save as every time.

In the *Text Document* category (in the left-hand sidebar menu), the changes relate specifically to the Writer application. Whenever you start a new document, OpenOffice.org assigns a default font when you start typing. This may not be your ideal choice, and you don't have to accept it. Sure, you can change the font when you are writing, but why do this with every document when you can change it once? Under Text Documents, click Basic Fonts, and you'll have the opportunity to change the default fonts your system uses.

When you are done with the Options menu, click OK to return to the OpenOffice.org application.

Screen Fonts

Fonts aren't limited to your documents. They also define how those menu options in the menu bar look. This is also true for those little tooltips. The default menu font is Andale Sans UI, and quite honestly, I'm not particularly fond of it, so I changed it the first time I ran OpenOffice.org.

To change it, click Tools from the menu bar and select Options. From the OpenOffice.org category, select Font Replacement. On the left-hand side, choose Andale Sans UI from the list (or type it in), then select a replacement on the right-hand side. (I use Helvetica for my system.) Add the font by clicking on the green checkmark, make sure to click Always, and you are done. As you can see, doing the change isn't really a big deal.

Running on AutoPilot

OpenOffice.org comes with a number of templates that are available throughout the suite. The AutoPilot feature helps you choose and walk through the setup of some basic documents. The easiest way to understand what AutoPilots can do for you is to dive right in and try one.

On the menu bar, click File, and move your mouse over to AutoPilot. You'll see a number of document types here, from letters to faxes to presentations. We'll use Letter as an example. When the AutoPilot starts up (Figure 13–8), it will offer you two kinds of letters, business and personal, then will ask for a style, whether it be classic, modern, or decorative. As you progress through the various steps, you'll be asked to enter some basic information related to the type of document that you chose. In the case of a letter, this would involve a sender and recipient name and address. You can also add graphics to the document, decide on its position, change the margins, etc.

Figure 13–8   Writing on AutoPilot.

Navigating Style

Near the beginning of this chapter, I told you about the Stylist, that floating window (labeled *Paragraph Styles*) sitting above your document. I mentioned it then because it's there as soon as you start Writer. It made sense to explain it away, at least briefly. I'd like to give you some idea of how useful this little tool can be in formatting your documents. If you've banished the Stylist, bring it back by clicking its icon or pressing <F11>.

Whenever you start a new document, it loads with a default style. That style is actually a collection of formatting presets that define how various paragraphs will look. These include headings, lists, text boxes, and so on. All you have to do is select a paragraph, double-click on a style, and your paragraph's look—including font style and size—is magically updated. As an example of how to use this, try the following.

Start by reloading your dark and stormy document, then highlight your title text to select it. At the bottom of your stylist, it says *Automatic*. With your title highlighted, double-click on Heading 1. The heading changes to a large, bold, sans serif font. Now click the arrow at the bottom of the list, and change from Automatic to Chapter Styles. Double-click on Title, and your title is suddenly centered with the appropriate font applied (Figure 13– 9).

The Stylist is pretty smart, really. Look back to the bottom of the list at those categories—HTML Styles, Custom Styles, and so on. Depending on the document type that you are working on, the Stylist will come up with a pretty sane list for that Automatic selection. If you call up an HTML document, HTML formatting will show up in the Automatic list.

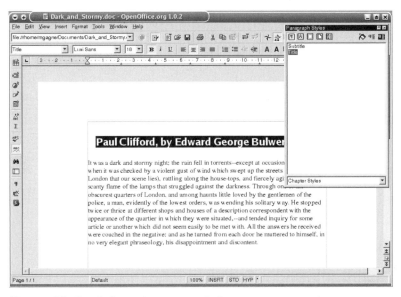

Figure 13–9   Styles make paragraph formatting easy and consistent.

Navigating the Rivers of Text

The second floating window is called the *Navigator*. This is a great tool for the power user or anyone who is creating long, complex documents. When you start up the Navigator by clicking Edit, then Navigator (or by pressing <F5>), you'll see a window listing the various elements in your document (Figure 13–10). These will be organized in terms of headings, tables, graphics, and so on.

What makes this a great tool is that you can use it to navigate a document quickly. Let's say that (as in this chapter) there are a number of section headings. Click on the plus sign beside the word *Headings*, and a treed list of all the headings in the document will be displayed. Double-click on a heading, and you will instantly jump to that point in the document. The same goes for graphics, tables, and other such elements in your document.

Speaking of Document Elements . . .

Take a look over at the far right of the Function bar. See the little icon that looks like a picture hanging on a wall? That's the *gallery* of graphics and sounds, decorative elements that can be inserted in your document. When you click the picture (or select Gallery from Tools on the menu bar), the gallery will open up with a sidebar on the left, listing the various themes.

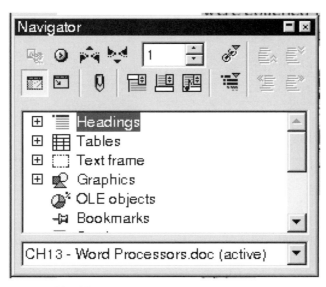

Figure 13–10   The Navigator.

Wander through the collection until you see something that suits your document, then simply drag it into your document, just as I did with that globe at the end of this paragraph. To banish the gallery, just click the icon again.

While you were using the Gallery, did you notice the words *New Theme…* at the top of the category sidebar? Click those words (which is really a button), and you'll be able to create a new category of images, clipart, or sounds. If you've got a directory of images you've collected, enter the path to that directory, pick a name for this collection, and you are done. Next time you bring up the Gallery, you can select from your own custom collection.

More! Give Me More!

OpenOffice.org comes with a limited number of templates, graphics, and icons. That's one of the advantages of its commercial (non-free) cousin, StarOffice from Sun Microsystems. However, if you find yourself in need of more templates than you already have or a richer gallery, take careful note of the following Web site. It's called *OO Extras*, and it may be the answer to your prayers.

```
http://www.ooextras.org
```

In addition to individual macros, icons, and templates, the goal of this Web site (created by Travis Bauer) aims to provide downloadable packages to enhance OpenOffice.org's suite.

Quick Tip If you enter a URL to a Web site in that combo box, you can actually open, view, and edit the Web page! Yes, Writer is an HTML editor, as well.

For those of you who are familiar with using your word processor as an HTML editor, this can be an extremely useful feature. Be warned, however, that the resulting code can be a little wordy and not altogether pleasant when working with other HTML editors.

Another Quick Tip In writing this book, I would occasionally switch among a handful of fonts. If you find yourself in that situation, here's a way to speed up the process. After selecting a word or phrase to change, click on the font selection list, type a portion of a font name, or scroll down the list to choose what you want. Note that if you press <Enter> to select a font, you will have to go through the whole selection process again next time. However, if you click on the font name with your mouse, that font will appear at the top of the list in a "recently used" group. This makes for faster access.

Other Options

I've concentrated on OpenOffice.org Writer perhaps because it is the real contender to Microsoft Office and the one that most people moving to Linux from the Microsoft Office world are likely to want to use. That's not to say that this is your only choice. For instance, the KDE suite comes with its own word processor, part of the KOffice suite. It is called *KWord*.

KWord is a frame-based word processing package. People who are used to working with desktop publishing packages such as FrameMaker will find this a familiar environment, just as those coming from Microsoft Word will experience somewhat of a learning curve. What KWord does is make it possible to create extremely precise documents where the layout of text and graphics must be accurate.

Another excellent word processor worth your consideration is *Abiword*.

You can probably find Abiword on your distribution CDs but you can always get the latest version on the Abisource Web site (`http://www.abisource.com`). What Abiword really has going for it is size and performance. This is a lightweight application that will perform well even on slower machines. It starts up fast and is excellent at what it does.

What KWord and Abiword have going against them (at least at the time of this writing) are compatibility issues with Microsoft Word documents. Both read the documents fairly well, but they do not export quite as well. As time goes on and development in import and export filters continues, this may not be an issue for long.

Resources

Abiword

http://www.abisource.com

Bulwer-Lytton fiction contest

http://www.bulwer-lytton.com

KDE's KWord

http://koffice.kde.org/kword/

OpenOffice.org Web Site

http://www.openoffice.org/

Sun Microsystems StarOffice

http://wwws.sun.com/software/star/staroffice/

14

Spreadsheets (Tables You Can Count on)

A spreadsheet, for those who might be curious, allows an individual to organize data into a table comprising rows and columns. The intersection of a row and a column is called a cell, and each cell can be given specific attributes, such as a value or a formula. In the case of a formula, changes in the data of other cells can automatically update the results. This makes a spreadsheet ideal for financial applications. Change the interest rate in the appropriate cell, and the monthly payment changes without you having to do anything else.

The idea of a computerized spreadsheet probably existed before 1978, but it was in that year that Daniel Bricklin, a Harvard Business School student, came up with the first real spreadsheet program. He called his program a visible calculator, then later enlisted Bob Frankston of MIT (Bricklin names him as co-creator) to help him develop the program further. This program would come to be known as VisiCalc. Some argue that with VisiCalc, the first so-called killer app was born.

Now that we have the definitions and history out of the way, let's get back to your Linux system and have a look at OpenOffice.org's very own spreadsheet program. It is called Calc—an appropriate name, given what spreadsheets tend to be used for.

Starting a New Spreadsheet and Entering Data

There are a few ways to start a new spreadsheet. If you are already working in OpenOffice.org Writer (as I am right now), you can click File on the menu bar, move your mouse to the New submenu, and select Spreadsheet from the drop-down list. Another way is to click the application starter (the big K) and select Calc from the OpenOffice.org or Office menu. When Calc starts up, you'll see a blank sheet of cells, as in Figure 14–1.

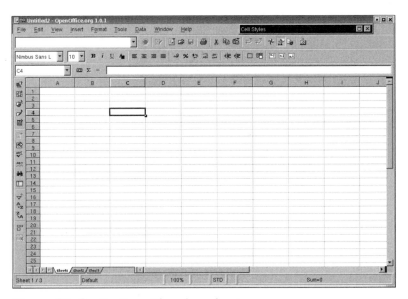

Figure 14–1   Starting with a clean sheet.

Directly below the menu bar is the *Function bar*. As with Writer, the icons here give you access to the common functions found throughout OpenOffice.org, such as cut, paste, open, save, and so on. Below the Function bar is the *Object bar*. Some features here are similar to those in Writer, such as font style and size, but others are specific to formatting content in a spreadsheet (percentage, decimal places, frame border, etc.).

Finally, below the Object bar you'll find the *Formula bar*. The first field here displays the current cell but you can also enter a cell number here to jump to that cell. You can move around from cell to cell by using your cursor keys, <Tab> (and <Shift+Tab>) key, or simply by clicking on a particular cell. The current cell you are working on will have a bold black outline around it.

Basic Math

Let's try something simple, shall we? If you haven't already done so, open a new spreadsheet. In cell A1, type *Course Average*. Select the text in the field, change the font style or size (by clicking on the font selector in the Object bar), then press <Enter>. As you can see, the text is larger than the field. No problem. Place your mouse cursor on the line between the A and B cells (directly below the Formula bar). Click and hold, then stretch the A cell to fit the text. You can do the same for the height of any given row of cells by clicking on the line between the row numbers (over to the left) and stretching these to an appropriate size.

Now move to cell A3 and type in a hypothetical number somewhere in the range of 1–100 to represent a course mark. Press <Enter> or cursor down to move to the next cell. Enter seven course marks so that cells A3 through A9 are filled. In my example, I entered 95, 67, 100, 89, 84, 79, and 93. (It seems to me that the 67 is an aberration.)

What we are going to do now is enter a formula in cell A11 to provide us with an average of all seven course scores. In cell A11, enter the following text.

```
=(A3+A4+A5+A6+A7+A8+A9)/7
```

When you press <Enter>, the text you entered will disappear and instead, you'll see an average for your course scores (Figure 14–2).

An average of 86.71 isn't a bad score (it is an A, after all), but if that 67 really was an aberration, you can easily go back to that cell, type in a different number and press <Enter>. When you do so, the average will automagically change for you.

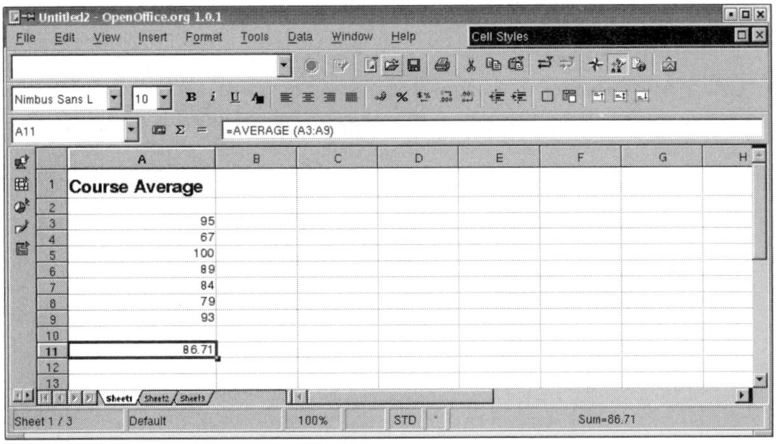

Figure 14–2   Setting up a simple table to determine class averages.

Calculating an average is a simple enough formula but if I were to add seventy rows instead of seven, the resulting formula could get *ugly*. The beauty of spreadsheets is that they include formulas to make this whole process somewhat cleaner. For instance, I can specify a range of cells by putting a colon in between the first and last cells (A3:A9) and using a built-in function to return the average of that range. My new, improved, and cleaner formula looks like this.

```
=AVERAGE (A3:A9)
```

Incidentally, you can also select the cell and enter the information in the input line on the Formula bar. I mention the Formula bar for a couple of reasons. One is that you can obviously enter the information in the field, as well as in the cell itself.

The second reason has to do with those little icons to the left of the input field. If you click into that input field, you'll notice that a little green checkmark will appear (to accept any changes you make to the formula), and to its left there will be a red *X* (to cancel the changes). Now look to the icon furthest on the left. If you hold your mouse over it, it should pop up a little tooltip that says *AutoPilot: Functions*. Try it. Go back to cell A11, then click your mouse into the input field on the Formula bar. Now click onto the AutoPilot Functions icon (you can also click Insert on the menu bar and select Function). You'll get a window such as the one in Figure 14–3.

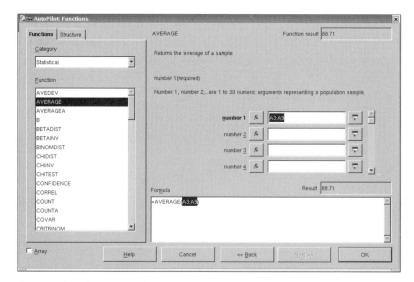

Figure 14–3 Using the AutoPilot to generate a function.

On the left side, you'll see a list of functions with descriptions of those functions off to the right. For the function called *AVERAGE*, the description is *Returns the average of a sample*. Because this is what we want, click the Next button at the bottom of the window. When the next screen appears, look at the window labeled *Formula* at the bottom of the screen. You'll see that the formula is starting to be built. At this point, it says *=AVERAGE()* and nothing else.

Near the middle of the screen on the right side are four data fields labeled *number 1* through *number 4*. The first field is required, whereas the others are optional. You could at this point enter *A3:A9*, click Next, and be done. Alternatively, you could click the button to the right of the number field (the tooltip will say *Shrink*), and the AutoPilot will shrink to a small bar floating above your spreadsheet (Figure 14–4).

Figure 14–4   The AutoPilot Formula bar.

On your spreadsheet, select a group of fields by clicking on the first field and dragging the mouse to include all seven fields. When you let go of the mouse, the field range will have been entered for you. On the left-hand side of the shrunken AutoPilots, there is a maximize button (move your mouse over it to activate the tooltip). Click it, and your AutoPilot will return to its original size. Unless you have an additional set of fields (or you wish to create a more complex formula), click OK to complete this operation. The window will disappear, and the spreadsheet will update.

Saving Your Work

Before we move on to something else, you should save your work. Click File on the menu bar and select Save (or Save As). When the Save As window appears (Figure 14–5), select a folder, type in a file name, and click Save. When you save, you can also specify the File type to be OpenOffice.org's default format (StarCalc), DIF, DBASE, or Microsoft Excel format.

Should you decide to close OpenOffice.org Calc at this point, you could always go back to the document by clicking File on the menu bar and selecting Open.

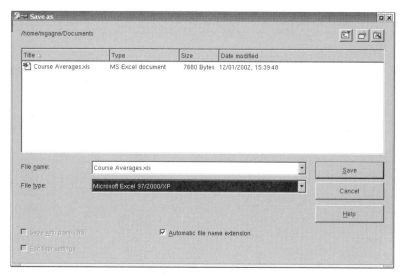

Figure 14–5   Don't forget to save your work.

Complex Charts and Graphs, Oh My!

This time, I'll show you how you can take the data that you enter into your spreadsheets and transform it into a slick little chart. These charts can be linear, pie, bar, and a number of other choices. They can also be two- or three-dimensional, with various effects applied for that professional look.

To start, create another spreadsheet. We'll call this one *Quarterly Sales Reports*. With it, we will track the performance of a hypothetical company.

In cell A1, write the title (Quarterly Sales Reports) and in cell A2, write the description of the data (in thousands of dollars). Now in cell A4, write the heading *Period*, then enter *Q1* in cell A6, *Q2* in cell A7, *Q3* in cell A8, and *Q4* in cell A9. Finally, enter some headings for the years. In cell B4, enter *1998*, then enter *1999* in cell C4, and continue on in row 4 right up to 2002. You should have five years running across row 4, with four quarters listed.

Time to have some virtual fun. For each period, enter a fictitious sales figure (or a real one if you are serious about this). For example, the data for 1999, Q2 would be entered in cell C7, and the sales figure for 2001, Q3 would be in cell E8. If you are still with me, finish entering the data, and we'll do a few things.

Magical Totals

Let's start with a quick and easy total of each column.

If you used the same layout as I did, you should have a 1998 column that ends at B9. Click on cell B11. Now look at the icon in the middle of the sheet area and the input line on the Formula bar. It looks like the Greek letter Epsilon. Hold your mouse pointer over it, and you'll see a tooltip that says *Sum*. Are you excited yet? Click the icon, and the formula to sum up the totals of that line, =SUM(B6:B10), will automatically appear (see Figure 14–6). All you need to do to finalize the totals is click the green checkmark that appears next to the input line.

Because a sum calculation is the most common function used, it is kept handy. You can now do the same thing for each of the other yearly columns to get your totals. Click on the sum icon, then click your beginning column and drag the mouse to include the cells you want. Click the green checkmark, and move on to the next yearly column.

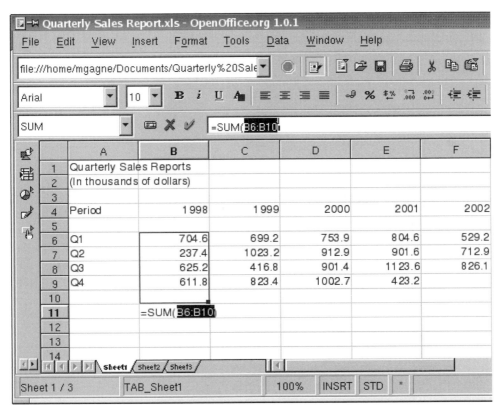

Figure 14–6   Select a series of cells, and Calc will automatically generate totals for you.

Nice, Colorful, Impressive, and Dynamic Graphs

Creating a chart from the data you have just entered is really pretty easy. Start by selecting the cells that represent the information you want to see on your finished chart, including the headings. You can start with one corner of the chart and simply drag your mouse across to select all that you want.

Warning If there are some empty cells in your table (in my example, row A3), you will want to deselect them. You can do this by holding down the <Ctrl> key and clicking those cells with the mouse.

Once you have all the cells you want selected, click Insert on the menu bar, and select Chart. The first window that appears (Figure 14–7) gives you the opportunity of assigning certain rows and columns as labels. This is perfect because we have the quarter numbers running down the left side and the year labels running across the top. Check these on.

Before you move on, notice the drop-down list labeled *Chart results in worksheet*. By default, Calc creates three tabbed pages for every new worksheet, even though you are working on only one at this time. If you leave things as they are, your chart will be embedded into your current page, though you can always move it to different locations. You have a choice at this point to have the chart appear on a separate page (those tabs at the bottom of your worksheet). For my example, I'm going to leave the chart on the first page. Make your selection, then click Next.

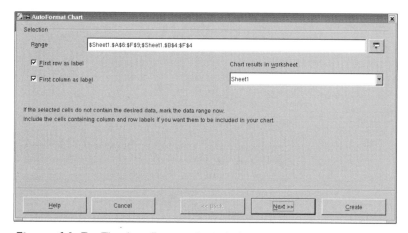

Figure 14–7   The AutoFormat chart dialog.

The next window (Figure 14–8) lets you choose from chart types (bar, pie, etc.) and provides a preview window to the left. That way, you can try the various chart options to see what best shows off your data. If you want to see the labels in your preview window, click on the check box for Show text elements in preview.

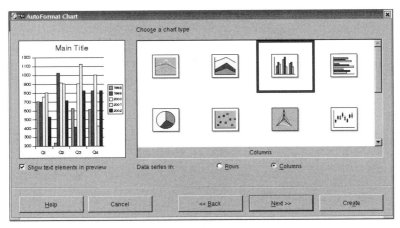

Figure 14–8   Lots of chart types to choose from.

You can continue to click Next for some additional fine-tuning on formatting (the last screen lets you change the title), but this is all the data you actually need to create your chart. When you are done, click the Create button, and your chart will appear on your page (Figure 14–9).

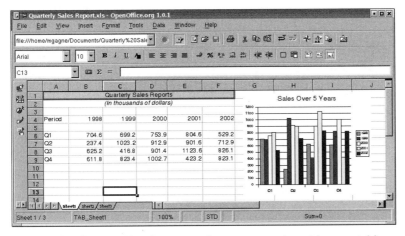

Figure 14–9   Just like that, your chart appears alongside your table.

To lock the chart in place, click anywhere else on the worksheet. You may want to change the chart's title, as well—double-click on the title, then make your changes. I'm going to call mine *Sales Over 5 Years*. If the chart is in the wrong place, click on it, then drag it to where you want it to be. If it is too big, grab one of the corners and resize it.

What's cool about this chart is that it is dynamically linked to the data on the page. Change the data in a cell, press <Enter>, and the chart will automatically update!

Final Touches

If you select (highlight) the title text in cell A1 and click the "center" icon, the text position doesn't change. That's because A1 is already filled to capacity, and the text is essentially already centered. To get the effect you want, click on cell A1, hold the mouse button down, and drag to select all the cells up to F1. Now click Format on the menu bar and select Merge Cells, then click Define. All six cells will merge into one, after which you can select the text and center it.

For more extensive formatting of cells, including borders, color, and so on, right-click on the cell, and select Format. (Try this with your title cell.) A Cell Attribute window (as in Figure 14–10) will appear, from which you can add a variety of formatting effects.

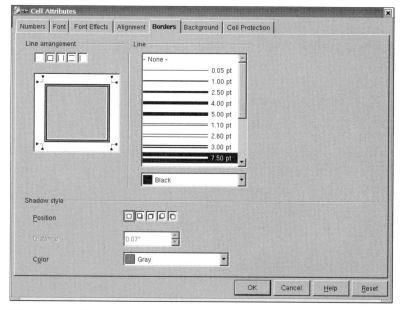

Figure 14–10   *Adding borders and fill to cell.*

A Beautiful Thing!

When you are through with your worksheet, it is time to print. Click File on the menu bar and select Print. Select your printer, click OK, and you'll have a product to impress even the most jaded bean counter.

Alternatives

Because OpenOffice.org is such an obvious and excellent replacement for Microsoft Office (including Word, Excel, and PowerPoint), it's easy to forget that there are other alternatives. One of the great things I keep coming back to when I talk and write about Linux is the fact that we do have alternatives, some costing no more than the time it takes to download and install them.

When it comes to spreadsheet programs, your Linux distribution CDs likely came with a few spreadsheet programs. The primary candidates are *Gnumeric*, *KSpread*, and the program we just looked at, OpenOffice.org's *Calc*.

Both Gnumeric and KSpread are certainly worth a look, but I've found Gnumeric to be particularly good when it comes to working with Excel spreadsheets.

Resources

Gnumeric

>   http://www.gnome.org/projects/gnumeric/

KSpread

>   http://www.koffice.org/kspread/

OpenOffice.org's Calc

>   http://www.openoffice.org/

chapter
15

Presentation Graphics
(For Those Who Need
No Introduction)

Once upon a time, even a simple business presentation could be quite a costly affair. The person putting together a presentation would create his or her presentation using a word processor (or pen and ink), then transfer all this to a business graphics presentation tool. Alternatively, a special design service might be hired to take that next step, but eventually, the whole thing would be sent to yet another service that would create 35-mm slides from the finished paper presentation.

On the day of the big meeting, the old carousel slide projector would come out, and the slides would be painstakingly loaded onto the circular slide holder. Then the lights would dim, and the show would begin. With any luck, the slides would all be in the right order, and the projector would not jam up.

These days, we use tools that streamline this process, allowing us to create presentations, insert and manipulate graphical elements, then play the whole thing directly from our notebook computers. The projectors we use simply plug into the video port of our computers. There are many software packages to do the job under Linux. The most popular (and the one I will cover here) is part of the OpenOffice.org suite. It is called Impress. For those of you coming from the Microsoft world, Impress is very much like PowerPoint. In fact, Impress can easily import and export PowerPoint files.

Getting Ready to Impress

After having worked with OpenOffice.org's Writer and Calc, you should feel right at home when it comes to using Impress. Working with menus, inserting text, spell checking, and customizing your environment all work in exactly the same way. The editing screen itself is probably more like Calc than Writer in some ways. The Impress work area will have tabbed pages so you can easily jump from one part of the presentation to the other. Each page is referred to as a *slide*. Given the history of business presentations—specifically, the making of these 35-mm slides—it's probably no wonder that we still use the same terms when creating presentations with software like Impress.

To start Impress, click on your application starter (the big K), select OpenOffice.org (or Office), and click on OpenOffice.org Impress in the sub-menu. You can also start a new presentation from any other OpenOffice.org application, such as Writer or Calc. Just click File on the menu bar, select New, and choose Presentation from the submenu.

When you start up Impress for the first time, you'll be presented with a number of choices. You can start with an empty presentation (Figure 15–1), work from a template, or open an existing presentation. Let's work through a new presentation together.

Quick Tip At the time of this writing, OpenOffice.org did not come with any Impress templates. As I've mentioned before, one of the differences between OpenOffice.org and StarOffice 6.0 (its commercial sibling) is that StarOffice 6.0 comes with a number of templates. That said, you can still download some free templates for OpenOffice.org from www.ooextras.org.

The AutoPilot allows you to select from existing presentations, as well as templates. For the moment, I'm going to stick with the very basics. Leave *Empty presentation* selected, and click Next. Step 2 (Figure 15–2) gives us the opportunity to select a slide design. Because we have none at this moment, it is safe to click Next, but pause first and have a look at the options for output medium. By default, Impress creates presentations designed for the screen (or a projector connected to your PC).

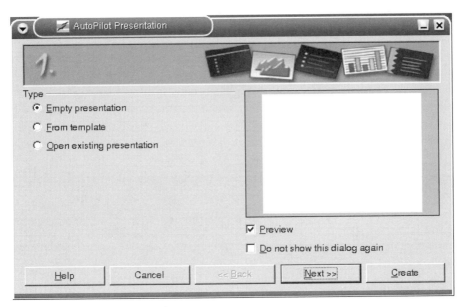

Figure 15–1 Starting up Impress.

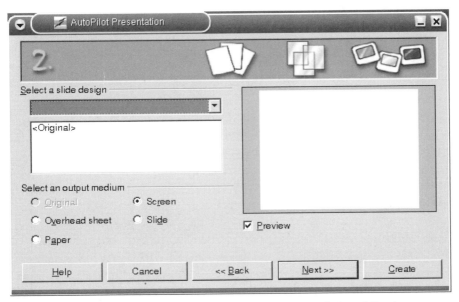

Figure 15–2 Impress defaults to creating presentations designed for the screen.

Step 3 (Figure 15–3) lets you define the default means for slide transition. You've all seen these presentations; as someone shows a presentation, slides dissolve to show the next one or fly in from the left or drop like a trap door closing. At this stage of the game, pick one of these effects from the drop-down box labeled *Effect*, then choose the Speed of that transition. On the right-hand side, there is a preview window that will show you what the effect looks like when you select it.

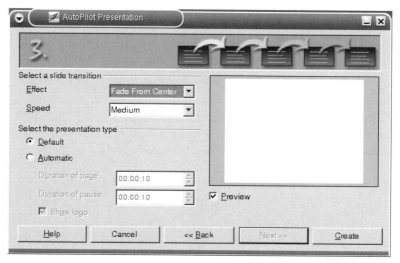

Figure 15–3   *Selecting slide transition effects.*

Directly below the slide transition selection, you will select the presentation type. Your choices are Default and Automatic. By default, transition from slide to slide is done by pressing a key, whether it be <Enter> or the spacebar (you can define this). Presentations can also run without any intervention from the person giving the presentation. By selecting Automatic, you can define the amount of time between slides or even between presentations. Accept the default setting here and click Create to start building your presentation.

We now have everything we need to start working on our presentation. A Modify Slide dialog box will appear (Figure 15–4) with a number of potential slide layouts having small preview images. From here, you can decide on the appearance of the slide, the number of columns, title locations, and so on. If you pause over one of the images with your mouse cursor, a tooltip till appear, telling you a little about the layout format. There's also space for the slide's

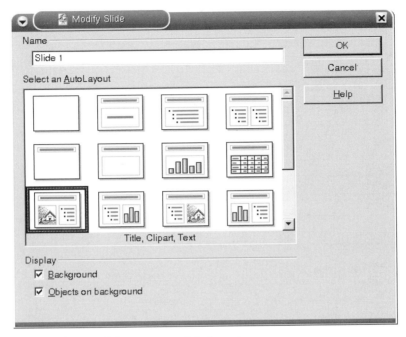

Figure 15–4   Selecting your slide layout.

title. By default, the title is *Slide*, followed by the slide's number in sequence. If you don't like this naming convention, you can easily override it by changing it in the Name field.

Follow along with me: Choose the Title, Clipart, Text layout and click OK to continue. Now that we are truly on our way, you'll notice that the editing window has a startling resemblance to that of both Writer and Calc (discussed in the last two chapters). The menu bar sits just below the title bar, and the function bar is directly below. You'll notice that the object bar has a number of different options unique to working in the Impress environment. On the left-hand side of the page, the main toolbar provides quick access to objects, drawing functions, 3D effects, and so on (Figure 15–5).

You can also click the last button in the list to start your slide show. There won't be much to see at this point, but you can click it at any time to see how your presentation is coming along. Another way to start the show is to click Slide Show on the menu bar and select the first option.

To start editing your slide, click (or double-click for images) the section you want to change. Make your changes by typing into that area. For the title, you might enter *Introducing Linux!* When you are happy with your changes, just

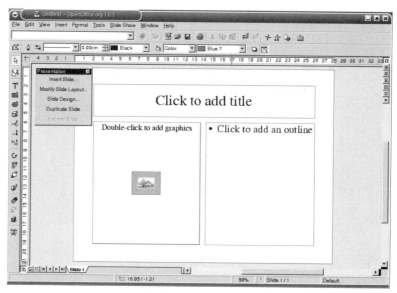

Figure 15–5   Starting with a slide template.

click outside of the frame area. Over on the right, in the frame that says *Click to add an outline*, insert these bulleted points.

- What is Linux?
- Is Linux really free?
- What can it do?
- Advantages?
- Disadvantages?

As you might have noticed, this outline serves as talking points that mirror the first chapter of this book. Now, over on the left-hand side, double-click on the frame (as instructed on the default slide) and insert a graphic. The Insert Graphics dialog will appear (Figure 15–6), allowing you to navigate your folders and look for the perfect image.

You can use any image you like here. For my image, I used Konqueror to surf over to Larry Ewing's Web site (`www.isc.tamu.edu/~lewing/linux/`), where I picked up my Tux graphic from the source (I'll tell you more about Tux at the end of this chapter). You may choose another image if you prefer. When you have your image selected, click Open, and it will replace the default text in the left-hand frame.

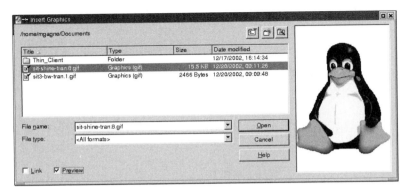

Figure 15–6   Inserting a graphic into the presentation.

Quick Tip Another option is to single-click the default image and press <Delete>. Then you can click Tools on the menu bar, select Gallery, and drag one of the included images onto your slide.

That's it. Your first slide is done. You might want to pause here and save your work before you move on. (Masterpieces must be protected.) Click File on the menu bar, select Save As, then enter a file name for your presentation. I used *Linux_Intro* as my title. Now click Save, and we'll continue building this presentation.

Inserting Slides

You might have already noticed the floating menu labeled *Presentation* on the page. From here, you can easily add another slide. If you choose this road, the slide selection dialog you used earlier (Figure 15–4) will reappear.

If you are just as happy to continue with the *same* slide design, I can show you a *really fast* way to add slides. Look at the tabs down at the bottom of the screen. For each slide, there will be one tab. Simply click to the right of the last tab (in the blank, gray area), and another blank slide (with corresponding tab) will automagically appear.

For the time being, click Insert Slide from the floating menu, and select the one called *Title, Text* (Figure 15–7).

We'll switch from two text frames to just one. Click OK, and a tab will appear, showing you Slide 2. Because we had five points (after our introductory

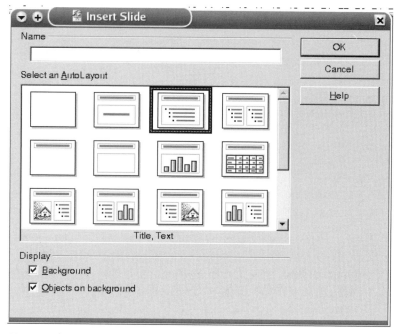

Figure 15–7 Our second slide.

slide), let's do a quick add of the next four slides by just clicking the gray area next to Slide 2. You should now have tabs labeled *Slide 1* through *Slide 6*.

Okay, click on the tab for Slide 2, then click the top frame where it says *Click to add title*. Enter the first bullet point from Slide 1. Then repeat the process for the next four slides, inserting the appropriate bullet point as the title.

Quick Tip You can give those tab labels more useful names by right-clicking on them and selecting Rename Slide.

As to what to enter in the text area of each slide, that I will leave to either your imagination or your memory of Chapter 1. When you have finished entering all the information you want, save your work. I'm going to show you how to dress up those plain white slides.

Adding Color

Right-click on your slide (not on the text), and select Slide from the pop-up menu. Now click on Page Setup (Figure 15–8).

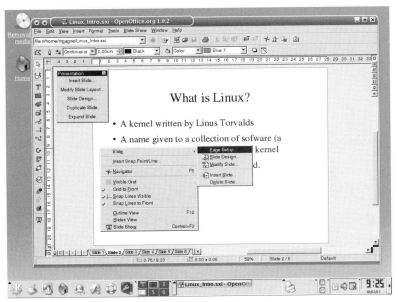

Figure 15–8   Modifying the page (slide) setup.

What you will see is a two-tabbed window (one says *Page* and the other *Background*). Click on the Background tab. Notice the five radio buttons (Figure 15–9). Each provides an option for background selection, whether it be plain white, colors, gradients, hatching, or bitmaps. Click on each to see the choices that they offer.

For example, you might choose the Linear blue/white gradient (a very business-looking background) or perhaps the Water bitmap. The choice is yours. When you click OK, you'll be asked whether you want this background setting to be for all slides. For now, click Yes.

All right. You've done a lot of work, so save it. It's time to see the fruits of your labors. Click Slide Show on the menu bar and select Slide show. You can also use the <Ctrl+F2> keyboard shortcut. The slides will transition with a touch of the spacebar.

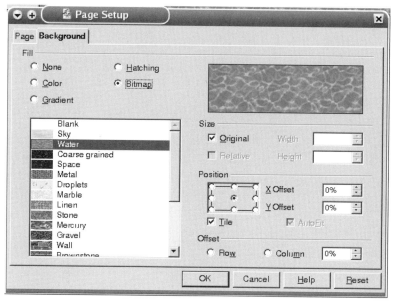

Figure 15–9   Impress background selection.

Printing Your Presentation

As with the other OpenOffice.org applications, click File on the menu bar and select Print from the menu (you can also click the small printer icon in the function bar). The standard OpenOffice.org print dialog will appear from which you can select your printer of choice.

Instant Web Presentations

Here's something you are going to find incredibly useful. Impress lets you export your existing presentation to HTML format. The beauty of this is that you can take your presentation and make it available to anyone with a Web browser. Best of all, the export functionality takes care of all the details associated with creating a Web site, including the handling of links and forward and back buttons.

To create an instant Web presentation, here is what you do. Make sure that your current Impress presentation is open and that your work is saved. Click File on the menu bar and select Export. The File Save dialog will appear. Because all the generated pages will appear in the directory you choose, it might make sense to create an empty directory into which to save your files before entering a file name. That file name, by the way, is the HTML title page, normally called `index.html`. If you would like a different name, choose it here, minus the `.html` extension (e.g., Linux_Intro), and click Save. A new window will appear. This is the HTML Export dialog (Figure 15–10).

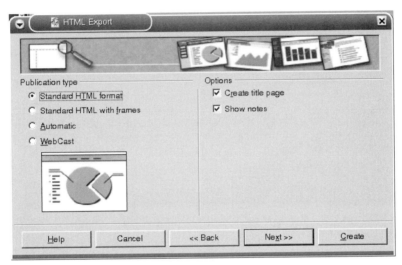

Figure 15–10   The HTML Export dialog in Impress.

To create a new design, make sure that the New Design radio button is clicked on, and click Next. You are given the choice of several publication types. The default choice (and probably a very good one) is Standard HTML format. You can also decide to create an HTML publication with frames, if you prefer. If you want to be totally in control of what your audience sees, you can also elect to create an automatic slideshow (using HTM refresh times of whatever you choose) or a WebCast. When you have made your choice, click Next.

On the next window (Figure 15–11), you must decide the *resolution of the images* created for your Web publication. The default is to use JPG images at 75% compression. You can elect to set this all the way up to 100% for the best quality possible, but be aware that the higher the quality, the larger the images and the slower the download time will be. If this presentation is meant to be viewed on your office network, it probably doesn't matter.

You are also asked to choose the *monitor resolution*. This is an excellent question that is probably worth more than a few seconds of configuration. At some point in your history of surfing, you must have come across a Web site

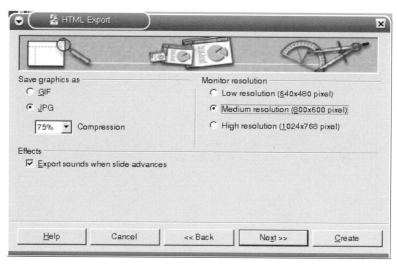

Figure 15–11   *Select your image resolution.*

where the Web page is larger than your browser window. To view the page, you needed to move your horizontal slide bar back and forth just to read the text. Although we are used to scrolling up and down to read text, left to right scrolling is somewhat more annoying. If you want to be as inclusive as possible for your audience, use 640x480. That said, most personal computer monitors these days will handle 800x600 without any problem. The same isn't true, however, of 1024x768 displays (however common). Is there a right answer? Probably not. Consider your target audience, make your decision based on those considerations, then click Next.

One last thing before we move on. Notice the check box under the label *Effects*. I'm not a big fan of Web pages that play sounds when I do things. You can choose to export sounds whenever slides advance. The best way to decide what you like is to try both. It's all for fun, anyhow.

On the next window that appears, fill in *title page information* for the Web presentation. This is the presentation title, your email address, and a link back to your own Web site, if you wish. Click Next, and you'll then have the opportunity to decide on the graphics you wish to use for the forward and back buttons. If you don't want to use graphical buttons, you don't have to. In fact, the default is to use Text only, so to use a particular button style, make sure you uncheck the check box (Figure 15–12), select your button style, and click Next.

We are almost there. The final window lets you decide on the *color scheme* for the presentation. The default is simply to use the colors from the original Impress publication but you can override this, as well as the color for hyperlinks

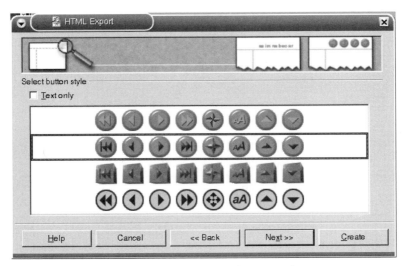

Figure 15–12   Pick a button style, any button style.

and the Web page background. Make your choices and click Create. One last window appears, asking you to name the HTML design. This is a free-form text field. Enter a brief description, and click Save.

The process of exporting your presentation may take a few seconds or a few minutes, depending on the speed of your machine and the complexity of your presentation. To view the presentation, open your browser and point to the title page. That is all there is to it.

So What's with the Penguin?

Having made you run off to Larry Ewing's site for a copy of Tux, I suppose I should take a moment to answer one of the most frequently asked questions in the Linux world. After all, every time you look at a Linux book, boxed set, or Web site, you stand a good chance of coming face to face with a fat, smiling penguin. You may well be wondering what Linux has to do with this penguin (Figure 15–13). Well, for starters, his name is *Tux*, and he is the Linux mascot. The most famous version of Tux (and there are many) is Larry Ewing's design.

The story behind Tux is the stuff of legend now and, like most legends, a little hard to pin down. Linus Torvalds was asked what he envisioned for a mascot. The answer from Linus was, "You should be imagining a slightly overweight penguin, sitting down after having gorged itself, and having just burped.

Figure 15–13   Tux, the Linux mascot.

It's sitting there with a beatific smile—the world is a good place to be when you have just eaten a few gallons of raw fish and you can feel another 'burp' coming."

There is also another story where Linus claims he was attacked by a killer penguin at the Canberra zoo, where he contracted "penguinitis," a disease whose main symptom is that you "stay awake at night just thinking about penguins and feeling great love towards them."

That's the thing about legends. They tend to get strange over time.

Some people have told me they don't think a fat penguin really embodies the grace of Linux, which just tells me they have never seen an angry penguin charging at them in excess of 100 mph. They'd be a lot more careful about what they say if they had.

—Linus Torvalds

Extra! Extra!

Before we move away from the classic office applications, I would like to take another moment to address the issue of templates. Although StarOffice, the non-free commercial sibling of OpenOffice.org, comes with a number of templates for word processing, spreadsheets, and presentation graphics, OpenOffice.org is still quite *light* in this area. As I mentioned earlier, the Impress package has no included templates at all.

To resolve this issue, the *OO Extras* Web site was born.

Travis Bauer has put together a great site with a number of community created and distributed templates for the OpenOffice.org suite. The site is laid out so that you can look for things specific to your application of choice, and screenshots are provided so that you can get a preview of what the document will look like. Because OO Extras has become an international affair, these extras come in different languages, as well.

A visit to OO Extras is well worth your time. Perhaps in time, you too will contribute to this growing body of work.

Resources

Larry Ewing's "Tux" (the Official Linux Penguin)

http://www.isc.tamu.edu/~lewing/linux/

Linux Logo Links at Linux.org

http://www.linux.org/info/logos.html

OO Extras

http://ooextras.sourceforge.net

chapter
16

Graphics and Art
(Just Call Me Leonardo)

Oddly enough, applications allowing users to work with graphics are among some of the most highly developed in the world. To see the truth in this rather bold statement, turn your eyes to Hollywood. Block-busters such as Titanic, Star Trek: Nemesis, Shrek, and others use Linux and Linux clusters to create the complex special effects.

In terms of graphical design and photo editing, your Linux system comes with one of the most powerful, flexible, and easy-to-use packages there is, regardless of what OS you are running. It's called the GIMP, and I'll be introducing you to its features a little later in this chapter.

Then we have digital cameras. In the world of your old OS, you needed special software to work with your particular camera. In the Linux world, you can do it all with a single interface. In fact, if you've come this far in this book, you probably already know almost everything you need to work with your camera.

Finally, I'll cover another of piece of graphical magic making when I show you how to use a scanner with your Linux system, from captur-ing your old photos to capturing and interpreting text.

Ready? Then smile!

Working with a Digital Camera

Behind the fancy graphical front end that takes photos from your camera and lets you work with them on your Linux system is a little package called *gPhoto2*. This package is actually a back end used by various other graphical programs, including, as you will see shortly, Konqueror.

A number of digital cameras are supported through gphoto2; 295 of them as I write this chapter. To discover whether your camera is supported directly, shell out and type the following command.

```
gphoto2 --list-cameras
```

You should see output similar to the following shortened list.

```
Number of supported cameras: 295
Supported cameras:
  "AEG Snap 300" (TESTING)
  "Agfa CL18"
  "Agfa ePhoto 1280"
  "Apple QuickTake 200"
  "Apple QuickTake 200"
  "Argus DC-100"
  "Barbie"
  "Canon PowerShot A20"
  "Canon PowerShot S10"
  "Canon PowerShot S100"
  "Chinon ES-1000"
  "DE300 Canon Inc."
  "Digitaldream DIGITAL 2000"
  "Epson PhotoPC 500"
  "Epson PhotoPC 550"
```

If your camera is not listed, don't despair. A visit to the gPhoto Web site for an updated version of the software may be all you need.

```
http://gphoto.sourceforge.net
```

Picture-Perfect Konqueror

Getting images from your USB digital camera is not at all difficult. Connect your camera to your Linux system via the USB cable. Every camera is a little different but all will have some kind of switch or setting to turn them on and allow transfer to the PC. Mine has a little jagged line with arrows at either side to represent a connection. Check your camera's manual for details.

Depending on your Linux distribution, you may find that a camera icon appears on your desktop when you plug in the camera. Click on that icon; Konqueror will open, and your camera's internal directories will be there for you to see. If such an icon doesn't magically appear, it's time for your old friend, Konqueror, to come to the rescue.

If it isn't already open, bring up Konqueror's navigation sidebar by pressing <F9>. Type *camera:/* in the Konqueror location field, and press <Enter>. You should see your digital camera listed in Konqueror's main window. On my system and with my USB-connected camera, it shows up as *Canon PowerShot S10* (Figure 16–1). Click on that icon, and you'll see folders corresponding to the way your camera stores its images. Just navigate down those directories until you get to your photo directories.

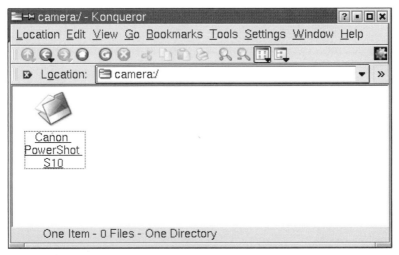

Figure 16–1   Konqueror is the easiest way to get pictures from your USB camera.

 Quick Tip If you want a preview of your images, click View on Konqueror's menu bar, select Preview from the menu bar, and check off Images in the drop-down list. You should now see little thumbnail images (Figure 16–2) corresponding to the images on your camera.

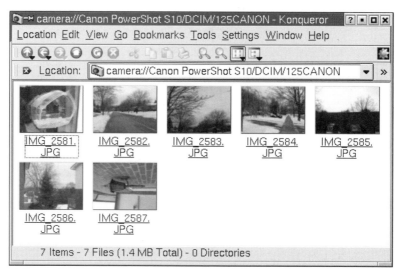

Figure 16–2   Pictures appear as thumbnails in Konqueror.

To move (or copy) your photos into a folder, select the images you wish (or press <Ctrl+A> for all the images) and drag them into a folder in the navigation window on the left-hand side. That is all there is to it.

Scanning . . .

There are many scanner options available, from old-fashioned parallel port devices to SCSI-connected scanners. These days, most people will choose a USB scanner for its low price and easy connection to the system. As with all devices, a visit to the USB devices for Linux Web site will save you time (and money) by helping you select a device that is well suited to run under Linux. If your scanner was connected to your system when you installed Linux, parts of the following section may not apply since your system may have already configured your scanner for you. Still, you should follow along to understand how all this happens.

Start by plugging in your scanner and, if necessary, turning it on (some scanners are on as soon as you plug them in). Any recent Linux distribution should do a very nice job of automatically noticing your scanner and loading the appropriate driver. Depending on your system, your USB scanner will be represented by the file name /dev/scanner0 or /dev/usb/scanner0. You may want to check for the existence of this file: Open a shell and type the following:

```
ls -l /dev/scanner0
 or
ls -l /dev/usb/scanner0
```

Another way to check for the existence of your scanner is to use the following command:

```
sane-find-scanner
```

You'll get several lines of text and information. In particular, you are looking for those lines that begin with the word *found*.

```
found USB scanner (vendor=0x04b8, product=0x0110) at
/dev/usb/scanner0
```

Before you can use your USB scanner, you may have to do a little setup work. Luckily, this is pretty simple, and *you only have to do it once*. For starters, it is possible that you *may have to* create the device file for your scanner manually. If the file isn't there, open a shell and switch to the root user.

```
su - root              .
```

Then use the following commands to create the USB scanner device file and make it usable by all users.

```
mknod /dev/usbscanner0 c 180 48
chmod 666 /dev/usbscanner0
```

You are almost there. Still running as root, change directory to /etc/sane.d and do an ls in that directory. You'll see a number of files ending in .conf, prefixed by a scanner brand name. In the case of my Epson scanner, I had to edit the /etc/sane.d/epson.conf file and change the following line.

```
#usb /dev/usb/scanner0
```

That "#" character at the beginning denotes a comment. *Removing* that character makes the line *real* (Figure 16–3). If you don't want to have to learn to use a programmer's editor, KDE has a very simple one that you can use. It is called *Kedit*, and you can run it from your current root shell by typing kedit. When the editor starts, click File on the menu bar, and select Open File. You've seen this open file dialog before, so this is nothing new now. If you know which

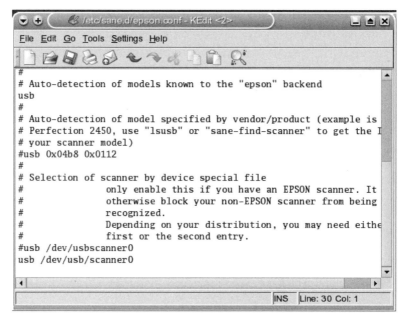

```
#
# Auto-detection of models known to the "epson" backend
usb
#
# Auto-detection of model specified by vendor/product (example is
# Perfection 2450, use "lsusb" or "sane-find-scanner" to get the I
# your scanner model)
#usb 0x04b8 0x0112
#
# Selection of scanner by device special file
#               only enable this if you have an EPSON scanner. It
#               otherwise block your non-EPSON scanner from being
#               recognized.
#               Depending on your distribution, you may need eithe
#               first or the second entry.
#usb /dev/usbscanner0
usb /dev/usb/scanner0
```

Figure 16–3   Using kedit to edit the scanner model file.

model file you need, just type it in the Location: field and press <Enter>. Otherwise, you can navigate your folders just as you would in Konqueror.

Make the changes as discussed above (Figure 16–3). Remove the comment character from the line that corresponds to your scanner device, then click File | Save, then File once again, followed by Quit, and you are done. It isn't necessary to reboot to get this new service running. Just load up the scanner module:

```
modprobe scanner
```

Type exit to leave the root shell, then exit again to close Konsole.

Scanning under KDE—Kooka

A number of scanning programs exist for Linux, and most are front ends to a package called *SANE* (Scanner Access Now Easy). One such front end is included with your Linux system. *Kooka*, part of KDE, is one such program.

Kooka is both a scan and optical character recognition (OCR) program. What this means is that you can use it to scan a document of text and export that text back into a word processing package of some sort for further editing.

You'll find Kooka under the main Multimedia or Graphics menu but you can also start the program from the shell or with your quicklauncher <Alt+F2>. The actual program name is kooka. When you start the program, you will see a dialog box similar to that in Figure 16–4. Kooka looks for available scanners and offers you a choice. If you have only one scanner on your system (as is usually the case), check the box labeled *Do not ask on startup again, always use this device* before clicking OK.

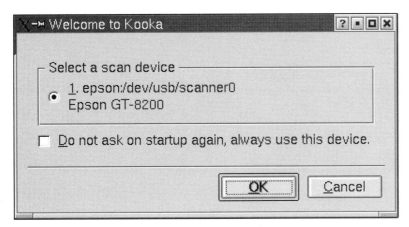

Figure 16–4 Kooka autodetects your connected scanner.

Once past this point, Kooka's main window will appear (Figure 16–5). It consists primarily of three areas, or *frames*: two horizontal frames to the left consisting of a navigation window up top and a Scanner Setting window at the bottom. The large right-hand side is the scan window itself. Along the top, you'll see a familiar-looking menu and icon bar. You can resize the main window to suit your tastes (and monitor size), as well as the individual frames.

Let's start by having a look at the navigation window. There are two tabs here, one labeled *Gallery* and the other *Preview*. Ignore the Preview tab for now and click on the Gallery tab. Now look directly beneath those tabs. You'll see a directory and file browser with a default directory called *Kooka Gallery*. You can create additional folders below this by right-clicking on the directory and selecting Create directory. As with all such dialogs, you can create directories inside of directories to organize your files efficiently. Scanned files will be saved in these directories.

Before scanning your first image, look down at the bottom left-hand window, where your scanner settings are set. What you see there will vary,

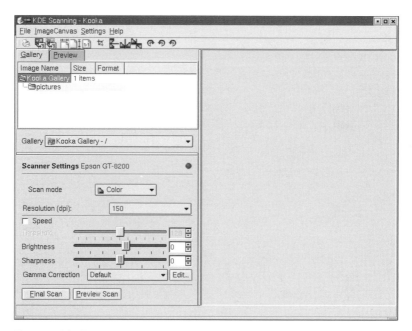

Figure 16–5   Kooka's main screen and work area.

depending on the model and type of scanner you are running. On my system, I used an Epson GT-8200. You can adjust scan mode (black and white, grayscale, or color), as well as resolution. Keep in mind that although higher resolution generally means higher quality, it also means a *much larger file* in terms of storage space. For Web page purposes, 75–100 dpi is probably ideal.

On my scanner, I can also adjust the brightness, sharpness, and gamma correction. The correct settings are somewhat of a trial-and-error affair. More than one scan may be necessary to decide what works (and looks) best.

Note These settings are scanner-specific, and different scanners may have different settings.

Find a photograph or picture you like, and put it on the scanner. Click the Preview Scan button in the Scanner Settings window. After the scan is complete, you can preview the results by clicking on the Preview tab in the top left-hand window.

In the image preview window, you can select the scan size to define the actual dimensions of the scanned file. If you want only a small portion of the photo, you can also drag the dotted lines in the preview window (with the mouse) to encompass only the part you wish to save. When you are happy with the preview, click Final Scan in the settings window.

When the scan is complete, the Kooka Save Assistant will appear (Figure 16–6). The various image formats available will be displayed, along with a description to help you make a decision on whether this is the format you wish to use. For instance, JPEG is described as "high compression, quality losing format for color pictures with many different colors." If you are always saving in the same format, you can elect to click the check box labeled *Don't ask again for the save format if it is defined*. Should you change your mind, click Settings on the menu bar, and select Configure Kooka. Under Image Saving, you can elect to bring back the Save Assistant.

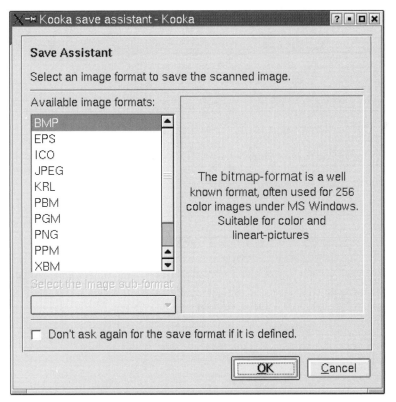

Figure 16–6 The Save Assistant helps you choose the file format.

Once you click OK, your scanned picture will appear in the scan window to the right (Figure 16–7). View options, such as *Scale to width*, *Set zoom*, or *Rotate image clockwise*, can be selected by right-clicking on the image. Switch back to the Gallery view by clicking the tab on the right side, and scanned images will appear with sequentially assigned names.

Figure 16–7   The final scan.

Saving Your Work

In a strange way, your images are already saved. In your home directory, you'll find another directory called .kde, where your KDE configuration files, Kmail address books, Konqueror bookmarks, and other files live. As it turns out, your scanned images are already saved there, although technically, they are still work files. If you want to have a look, check out .kde/share/apps/Scan-Images in your home directory. If you created new directories in your Gallery, you'll see them as well.

To *officially* save your work in Kooka, right-click on one of your scanned images in the Gallery frame (top left), and select Save Image. You'll be presented with the standard KDE save dialog. Choose a directory and a name for your image, and click Save (Figure 16–8).

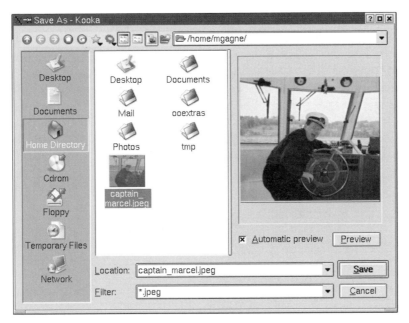

Figure 16–8   *Now it is time to save your images.*

You can now take that image, fire up the GIMP, and modify it at will.

The GIMP? I'll cover that very soon. I still have a little scanning magic to share with you.

Optical Character Recognition

Before I wrap up this discussion of Kooka, let me tell you about one other very cool thing the program does. Say you have an old document page that you want to transcribe. The obvious first choice is to sit it in front of you, open up a word processor, and start typing. Your second option is to pop that page on your scanner, use Kooka to scan it, then run it through OCR.

Here's how you do it. Because most people won't be using OCR, most distributions don't install the supporting software by default. Visit `jocr.source-forge.net` (that is not a typo) or check your distribution CDs for a package called *gocr* and install it. Kooka uses it to do OCR.

Start by scanning your page as you would any image. Binary scan mode is probably fine for straight text but this is one case where *the higher the resolution, the better your chances are of an accurate OCR*. When you are happy with the preview, click Final Scan, and you should see your page in the right-hand window. Now click ImageCanvas on the menu bar, and select OCR image. Alternatively, you can click the second icon from the left in the icon bar—it does the same thing.

A window labeled *Optical Character Recognition* will pop up (Figure 16–9), which allows you to specify a handful of settings to tune the character recognition software. Remember; OCR is not perfect by any means but with some tweaking, you can achieve fairly high levels of accuracy. For your first scan, simply leave it at the defaults and click Start OCR. The whole process of character recognition may take a few seconds, so be patient.

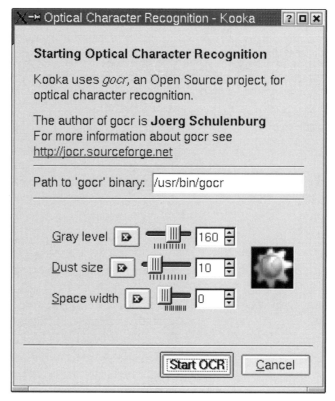

Figure 16–9   OCR settings.

After the process is complete, a window will appear showing you the results of the OCR process (Figure 16–10).

If you want to save the results, click Open in Kate, which will start KDE's multipurpose text editor. Once in the editor, click File from the menu bar, select Save As,

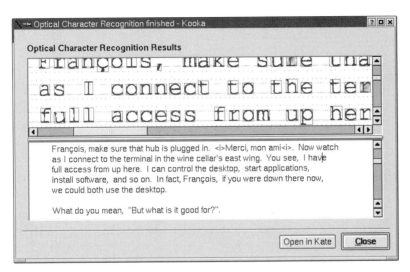

Figure 16–10   Kooka OCR results window.

and you'll be able to save the document in whatever directory you wish. Further editing can then be done with OpenOffice.org Writer or whatever word processor suits your needs.

Welcome to the GIMP

The GIMP is one of those programs that has helped create an identity for Linux. Of course, there are plenty of programs out there, as I'm sure I have demonstrated by this point in the book, but the GIMP is special in some ways. The Linux community has used it to create images, buttons, desktop themes, window decorations, and more. Even the Linux mascot, Tux the Penguin, as created by Larry Ewing (the mascot's best-known incarnation) was a product of the GIMP.

The GIMP is an amazingly powerful piece of software, yet it is very simple, as well. With a little bit of work, a lot of fun, and a hint of experimentation, anyone can use the GIMP to turn out a fantastic piece of professional-quality art. You doubt my words? Then follow along with me, and in just a few minutes, you'll have created a slick-looking logo for your Web page or your desktop. That said, with time, you can also learn to wield the GIMP with the power of a Hollywood special effects master.

Ladies and gentlemen, start your GIMP. Click on the application starter (the big K), scroll up to the Graphics submenu, and click on the GIMP. You can also use your program quickstart by pressing <Alt+F2> and entering `gimp` into the command field.

The First Time

If you are starting up the GIMP for the very first time, the GIMP User Installation dialog will appear (Figure 16–11). You'll be asked a number of questions regarding the location of your personal GIMP directory (defaults to a directory called *.gimp-version.no* under your personal home directory), how much memory you wish to allocate for the GIMP to do its work, and so on. For the most part, you can just accept the defaults by clicking Continue through the various screens.

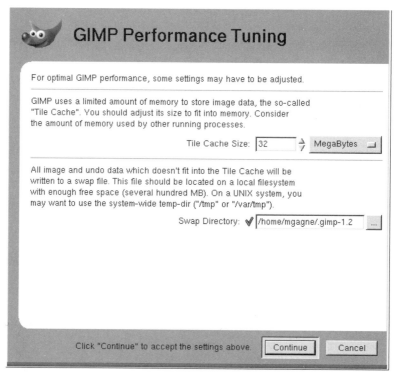

Figure 16–11   When you start the GIMP for the first time, you'll need to adjust a few settings.

Immediately after the performance tuning screen, you'll be asked for your monitor's resolution. If you plan on doing particularly fine work and you would like the GIMP to display images in their natural sizes, you should adjust your monitor's resolution. If you know the resolution, you can enter it manually or accept the default of 72 dpi.

Your final option for absolute accuracy is to click on the Calibrate button. A ruler will appear on your screen (Figure 16–12). Measure that ruler with a physical ruler and enter the actual size into the fields provided. When you are happy, click OK. This method can yield very different results from the defaults. My settings came in at 84.848 pixels per inch for the x axis (horizontal) and 85.106 pixels per inch for the y axis (vertical).

Once you have entered all this information, the GIMP proper will start up. You will probably get a number of panels aside from the GIMP's main screen. You will also likely get the GIMP Tip of the Day. As with all such tips, you can elect not to have them appear each time the program starts—just uncheck the Show tip next time GIMP starts button before you hit close, and you won't be bothered with them again. As for those additional windows (layers, tools options, and brush selection), closing them before you close the GIMP will make sure they don't come up by default.

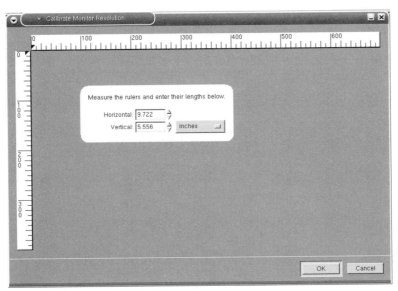

Figure 16–12   Fine-tuning the GIMP to match your monitor resolution.

The most important of those windows is the GIMP toolbox (Figure 16–13). Let us take a few moments to get familiar with it.

Along the top, directly below the title bar, is a familiar-looking menu bar labeled, quite simply, *File*, *Xtns*, and *Help*. Clicking on these will show you additional submenus. Below the menu bar is a grid of icons, each with an image representing one of the GIMP's tools. I will cover all of these things shortly, but first let's take the GIMP out for a spin.

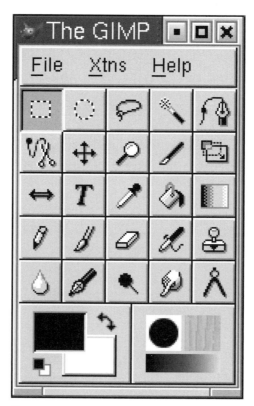

Figure 16–13   The GIMP toolbox.

Easy Logos with the GIMP

The nitty-gritty can wait. I think we should do something fun with the GIMP right now. I'm going to show you how to create a very cool-looking corporate or personal logo with just a few keystrokes. If you don't have the GIMP open yet, start the program now. From the main toolbox menu bar, select Xtns, scroll down to Script-Fu, and another menu will cascade from it.

Quick Tip Notice that the menus have a *dashed line* at the top. These are menu tear-offs, and you have seen them before when working with the KDE menus. By clicking on the dashed line, you can *detach the menu* and put it somewhere on your desktop for convenient access to functions you use all the time. In fact, all the menus, including submenus, can be detached.

From the Script-Fu menu, move your mouse to Logos. You should see a whole list of logo types, from *3D Outline* to *Cool Metal* to *Starscape* and more. For this exercise, choose *Cool Metal*.

Every logo has different settings, so the one you see in Figure 16–14 is specific to *Cool Metal*. *Particle Trace* will have a completely different set of parameters. To create your *Cool Metal* logo, start by changing the Text field to something other than the logo style's name. I'll change mine to read *Linux rocks!* The font size is set to 100 pixels, and we can leave it at that for now.

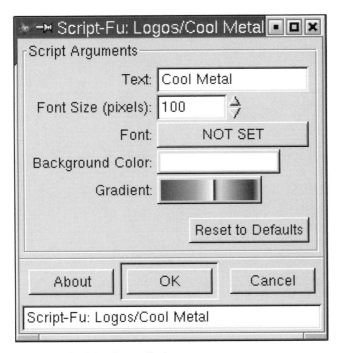

Figure 16–14 Script-Fu logo settings.

The font has not yet been set, so click the NOT SET button, and pick a font style and size from the list that pops up. The font select window shows you the various fonts available on your system and lets you try different font types, styles, and sizes. A preview window gives you an idea of what the font looks like (Figure 16–15). If you want, you can even change the text in the preview window from the default *abcdefghijk ABCDEFGHIJK* to your own words so that you can really see what it will look like.

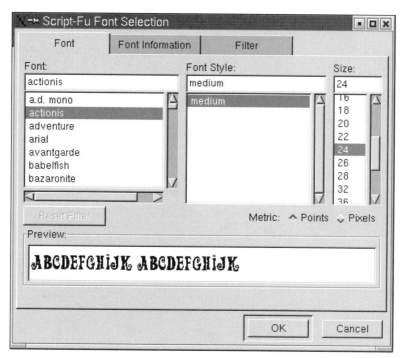

Figure 16–15   *Script-Fu font selection dialog.*

As I wrote this part of the book, I was working on a Mandrake test system and chose a font called *actionis* (actually, I used several distributions during the course of this book). You may choose whatever you like. When you have decided on a font, click OK. Then click OK again, this time in the Script-Fu:Logos/Cool Metal window. The result should be something similar to my own logo in Figure 16–16.

If you don't like the results, close the image by clicking the close button in the corner (usually an X unless you have changed your desktop theme or style).

Figure 16–16   Just like that! A professional-looking logo.

A warning box will pop up, telling you that changes have been made and that perhaps you might want to save your work (more on that in a moment). Click Close and it goes away. Then start over with another logo. You might try changing the background color or the gradient this time. You might even want to try a different type of logo altogether.

Saving and Opening Your Work

Now it is time to preserve your masterpiece. To save your work, right-click anywhere on the generated logo, select File from the pop-up menu, then click Save As. From the Save Image dialog box that appears, double-click on the directory you wish to save in.

Before you type in a file name, pay some attention to the Save Options. The default is indicated as *By Extension*. What this means is that I can save an image as JPG format simply by typing a file name such as *mylogo.jpg* (Figure 16–17) or as PNG format by typing *mylogo.png*. Most will do this, but you can also select from a number of supported file types (and there are many) by clicking the By Extension button and selecting your file type.

When you have entered your file name and selected a file type, click OK, and you are done.

Opening a file is similar. From the GIMP toolbox menu bar, select Open (or use the <Ctrl+O> shortcut) to bring up the Load Image dialog. The difference between this and the Save Image dialog is that when you click on a file name, you can also click on Generate Preview to display a small thumbnail preview in the Load Image dialog.

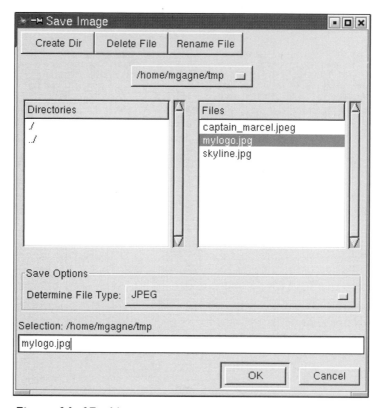

Figure 16–17 *Now it is time to save your work.*

Printing Your Masterpiece

You've created a masterpiece. You are infinitely proud of it, and you want to share it with your friends, who, alas, are not connected to the Internet. It's time to print your image and send it to them the old-fashioned, snail-mail way.

Okay, perhaps you aren't feeling quite that sharing, but there are times when you'll want to print the results of your work. Simply right-click on your image, move your mouse over to the File menu, and select Print. A printing dialog box will appear (Figure 16–18), from which you can specify a number of print options, including, of course, which printer you would like to use.

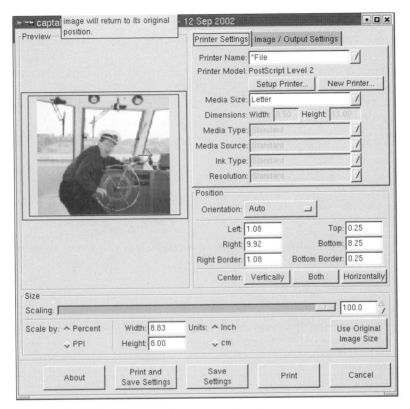

Figure 16–18   Time to print your masterpiece.

 Quick Tip Some distributions include the GIMP's printing functionality as a separate package, perhaps because images are usually imported into other applications, such as word processors. That package is called *gimpprint* and may have to be installed separately.

Tools, Tools, and More Tools

Now that we've had some fun and created some *true art*, it's time to find out what all those icons in the GIMP toolbox do. Before we do this, however, we should look at those two boxes at the bottom of the toolbox because what they offer affects what the icons do.

The block on the right is the color menu (Figure 16–19). It gives you quick and easy access to foreground and background colors. The black and white squares on the left can be changed to other colors by double-clicking on one or the other. If you click on the arrow between the two, you switch between foreground and background colors.

Figure 16–19   Color menu.

The box to the right is a quick dialog menu and really consists of three different tools: a brush selector, a pattern selector, and a gradient selector. Click on any of them to bring up the list of choices each provides (Figure 16–20).

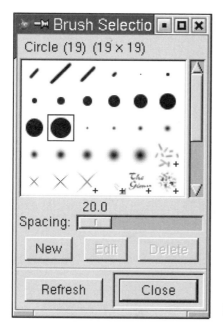

Figure 16-20   Brush selection.

If you select a different gradient, pattern, or brush from the resulting menus, you'll see them change on the dialog menu at the bottom of the GIMP toolbox, as well. This gives you a quick visual feedback on what brush, pattern, or gradient is active at the moment.

Now, on to the Tool Icons

Start by moving your mouse over the various icons, pausing over each one. Tooltips will appear, telling you what tool each of the icons represents (I'll go over these in a moment). If you double-click on any of these icons, a new window will appear, providing you with that tool's options (Figure 16–21).

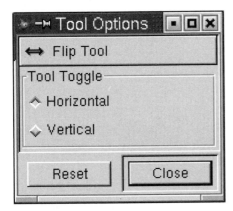

Figure 16–21   Tool options dialog.

So what are all those icons for? An excellent question. Let's look at them again, one row at a time, starting with—you guessed it—the first row (Figure 16–22).

Figure 16–22   First icon group.

The first icon, represented by a dotted rectangle, lets you select a *rectangular* area. Just hold down the left mouse button at whatever point you choose for a starting corner, and drag it across your image. A dotted line will indicate the area you've selected. If you hold down the <Shift> key at the same time as the left mouse button, your selections will always be perfect squares.

Quick Tip To undo changes, press <Ctrl+Z>.

The dotted circle icon next to it is much the same except that it selects *circular or elliptical* area. Similar to the rectangular select, you can hold down the <Shift> key along with the left mouse button to select only perfect circles.

Next, we have the *lasso* tool. This is another selection tool, but this one lets you select irregular or hand-drawn regions. Hold down the left mouse button and *draw* your selection around the object.

Quick Tip When you have selected an area on an image, you can right-click, move your mouse cursor over the Edit menu, and select Cut or Copy. You can then Paste your selection back to another part of the image.

Then comes the *magic wand*. This is a strange tool to get used to. It selects an area by analyzing the colored pixels wherever you click. Holding down the <Shift> key lets you select multiple areas. This is a very useful tool but also a little tricky. Double-click on the icon to change the sensitivity.

Finally, we wrap up the first row with the *Bezier tool*, which to be honest takes some getting used to. Once you get used to it, however, you'll be impressed with the flexibility it affords you in selecting both straight and curved areas. Click a point outside the area you want to select, and it creates an anchor point. Click again a little further along your outline, and you get new anchor points with a straight line connecting to the original. Click and drag an existing anchor point, and a *bar* will appear with control boxes on either end. You can then grab those control points and drag or rotate them to modify the straight line between the points. Once you have joined the final point, click inside the outlined region, and this completes your selection (you'll see an animated dotted line, as with the other selection tools).

That wraps it up for the first row of tools. It's time to look at the next set (Figure 16–23).

Figure 16–23   Second icon group.

We've still got one last selection tool to look at, the so-called *intelligent-scissors*. These will remind you somewhat of the Bezier tool, in that you select an area by clicking around it. What this tool does that the other does not is follow curved lines around an object. It does so by concentrating on areas of similar contrast or color. Simply click around the perimeter of the area you wish to select and watch the lines magically draw themselves. When you join the last dot, click inside the area to select it.

The second icon on the second row looks like a cross with arrows pointing in all directions. This is the *move tool*. It is really quite simple. Click the tool, then grab the selected area on the screen and move it to where you want. If you haven't selected an area, you can move the entire image in the window.

The *magnifying glass* does exactly what you expect it to. Click an area of the screen to zoom in. Double-click the icon to reverse the zoom. This doesn't actually scale the image, it just changes your view of things. Zoom is usually used to make it easier to work on a small area of the image.

On to the knife icon—the *crop tool*. I use the crop tool all the time when I am trying to get a small part of a larger image. It is what I used to separate the rows of icons from the GIMP toolbox image I captured. Click on a part of the screen, drag it to encompass the area you want to keep, and click Crop when asked to confirm. You can also fine-tune the settings (X and Y position, etc.) at this time.

The final item on this row is the *transform tool*, and it is really quite interesting. By default, this is a rotation tool. Click on an image (or a selection), and a grid will appear over your image or the selection. Grab a point on the grid, drag the mouse, and the grid rotates. When you have it in a position you like, click Rotate on the pop-up window that appears. The image will lock into place. But that's not all: Double-click on the transform tool icon, and three additional capabilities appear—scaling , shearing, and perspective.

On to row three (and Figure 16–24).

Figure 16–24   Third icon row.

The first box is the *flip tool*. By default, it flips the image horizontally. Double-click the icon to bring up the menu, and you can change it to flip vertically.

The next icon is the *text tool*. That's what the big *T* signifies. Click on your image, and the font selection box you used for your logo will appear. Select a font, type in your text in the Preview section, and click OK. Where the text appears on the screen, the move tool will be activated, allowing you to place the text accurately. The color of the text will be your current foreground color.

The third icon looks like an eyedropper. This is the *color picker*. Choosing an exact color can be difficult (if you need to get the tone just right), but if the color you want is on your existing image, click on that spot, and you've got it (your default active color will change).

Closely related to this is the fourth button on the third row, the paint can. This is the *fill tool*. It can fill a selected area not only with a chosen color but with a pattern, as well. To choose between color and pattern fill, double-click on the icon to bring up its menu.

The last item on this line is the *gradient fill tool*. Start by selecting an area on your image, then switch to this tool. Now click on a spot inside your selected area and drag with the tool. The current gradient style will fill that area. This is one of those things you almost need to try in order to understand what I mean.

And now . . . row 4 (Figure 16–25)!

Figure 16–25   Row 4 icons.

The first icon looks a *pencil*. In fact, this and the next three buttons all work with a brush selection (the bottom right-hand box). This pencil, as with a real pencil, is used to draw lines with sharply defined edges. Try drawing on your image with the different types to get an idea of what each brush type offers.

Quick Tip Would you like a blank canvas right about now? Click File on the GIMP toolbox menu bar and select New.

The next icon is the *paintbrush*. The difference between it and the pencil is that the brush has softer, less starkly defined edges to the strokes. Double-click the icon to bring up the paintbrush's menu and try both the Fade Out and Gradient options for something different.

If the next icon looks like an *eraser*, that's no accident. The shape of the eraser is also controlled by the current brush type, size, and style. Here's something kind of fun to try. Double-click on the icon to bring up its menu, then change the Opacity to something like 50%. Then start erasing again.

Now it's on to the *airbrush* tool. Just like a real airbrush, you can change the pressure to achieve different results. Hold it down longer in one spot, and you'll get a darker application of color.

Finally, we have the *clone tool* (the icon looks a bit like a rubber stamp). Sheep? No problem! We can even clone humans. Okay, that's a bit over the top. Where the clone tool comes in handy is during touch-ups of photographs. Open an image, hold down the <Ctrl> key, and press the left mouse button over a portion of the image—the tool will change to a crosshair. Let go of both the mouse button and the <Ctrl> key. This is your starting area for cloning. Now move to another part of the screen, click, and start moving your mouse button (the shape of the area uncovered is controlled by the brush type). As you paint at this new location, you'll notice that you are re-creating that portion of the image where you indicated with the <Ctrl+mouse-click> combination. Start with someone's head or body, and you can have twins on the screen.

And now, the last row of icons (Figure 16–26)!

Figure 16–26   The final group.

The droplet you see on the first item represents the *convolver tool*. It is used to blur or sharpen parts of an image. You switch between the two operations by double-clicking the icon and selecting the operation you want. Change the rate to make the effect more pronounced.

Next we arrive at another drawing tool, the pen, or *ink tool*. Double-clicking the icon brings up a menu that lets you select the tip style and shape, as well as the virtual tilt of the pen. The idea is to mimic the effect of writing with a fountain pen.

The *dodge and burn tool* looks like a stick-pin, but those who have worked in a darkroom might recognize it for something different—a stick with an opaque circle on the end of it. It is used to adjust the brightness or shade of various parts of an image (a photograph might have been partly overexposed).

On to the finger, or the *smudge tool*. Pretend that you are painting. You press your finger on the wet paint and move it around. The smudge tool has exactly the same effect on your virtual canvas.

Finally, we round up tools with the calipers, or *measuring tool*. This doesn't actually change anything on your image but reports. Click a starting point on the image, then drag the mouse pointer to another part of the image. Now look at the bottom of your image window. You'll see the distance in pixels from your starting location to where you let go of the mouse pointer. The angle of the line will also be displayed.

Touching up Photographs

I've mentioned the idea of touching up photographs on a few occasions while I discussed the tools. The GIMP is a wonderful tool for this and more than just a little fun. One of the most common functions I use is changing the light levels on photographs, automagically and instantly. After all, light levels are rarely perfect unless you are a professional photographer and paying attention to every shot. Here's what I do.

Right-click on the image to bring up the GIMP menu. Now move to the Image submenu, move over to Colors, and select Levels. You should see a window like the one in Figure 16–27. Notice the Auto button? That's where the magic is. I've found that more often than not, you can get a nice, dependable reset of levels just by doing this simple operation.

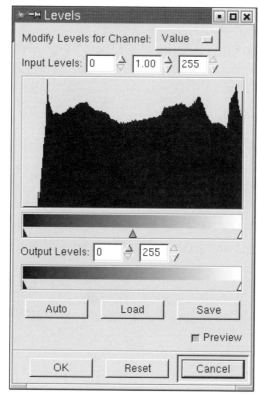

Figure 16–27   Adjusting levels with the GIMP.

We can also modify contrast, brightness, or color, but there are also the silly and *just plain fun* things we can do.

For instance, open an image in the GIMP, perhaps one you scanned in earlier. If you don't have something handy, grab an image from a Web site. This is just something to play with. Now right-click on the image and choose Filters by moving your mouse to that part of the menu. A submenu will open with even more options. You might want to detach this menu—you'll certainly want to play with what is there.

Try FlareFX under the Light Effects menu. If you've ever taken a flash picture through a window, you'll recognize this effect. Then try Emboss under the Distorts submenu. The effect is that of a metal-embossed picture (Figure 16–28).

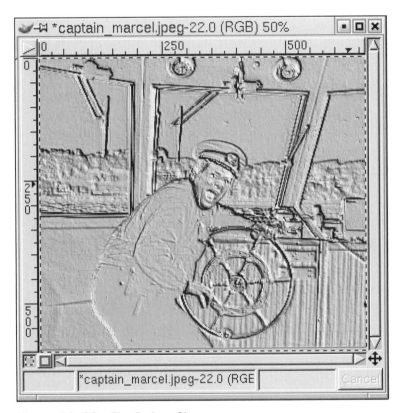

Figure 16–28 The Emboss filter.

Take some time to try the various filter options. When you are finished there, right-click on a fresh image and select the Script-Fu menu. There are other interesting effects available here, as well, such as Clothify under the Alchemy submenu. Your image will look as though it had been transferred to a piece of cloth.

So What Is Script-Fu?

Although it sounds like a strange form of martial arts, Script-Fu is in fact a scripting language that is part of the GIMP. With it, you can create scripts that automate a number of repetitive tasks to create desirable effects. When you created your logo, you might have noticed that a number of things were happening as it was being created. Try another logo and watch carefully what is happening. These steps are part of a Script-Fu script.

The GIMP comes with a number of Script-Fu scripts, and these are used for much more than just creating logos. Click Xtns on the GIMP toolbox, and scroll down to the Script-Fu menu. In addition to logos, you'll see options for creating buttons (for Web pages), custom brushes, patterns, and more. Play. Experiment. Don't be afraid.

Open an image. Then right-click on that image and scroll down to the Script-Fu part of the menu. Another menu drops down with selections such as Alchemy, Decore, Render, and so on. These are all pre-created effects that would ordinarily require many repetitious steps. Script-Fu is very much like a command script, where one command follows another. In this case, the commands just happen to be graphical transformations.

Becoming a GIMP Guru

You can make some pretty cool images with the GIMP with just a little knowledge, but with time and further exploration, you can take that cool to the level of amazing. Make no mistake, the GIMP is a professional-grade tool, and covering it in detail would fill a book of its own.

Consider a visit to the GIMP home page at `www.gimp.org` for the latest developments, software, and links to other GIMP documents. Some great books specifically cover the GIMP. Visit your local computer bookstore, and have a look through the titles. I'm particularly fond of Michael J. Hammel's book, *"Artist's Guide to the GIMP."* Another title I've enjoyed is Joshua and Ramona Pruitt's *"Teach Yourself GIMP in 24 Hours."*

chapter
17

Multimedia
(If Music Be the Food
of Love . . .)

Playing music on your Linux system is only the beginning of the multimedia experience. After all, multimedia isn't about just music. It represents a cornucopia of sensory experience delivered digitally, comprising text, audio, video, and endless combinations of the three.

Most modern Linux installations offer an impressive selection of programs to satisfy your cravings for the multimedia experience, from audio to video and everything in between. These programs include sound control systems, CD players, recorders, MIDI programs of varying flavors, music synthesizers, video players, music notation programs, and . . . the list goes on.

In this chapter, I'm going to cover some of the more popular multimedia tools for your Linux system. So, as old William Shakespeare might have said, "If music be the food of love, then multimedia must represent the smorgasbord."

Adjusting the Levels

Think back for a moment to those days of old when Mom or Dad would yell into your bedroom to "TURN THAT NOISE DOWN!" Doesn't that bring back memories? In particular, it brings back the memory that sometimes, you just have to crank the tunes.

Most music or multimedia players you are likely to use under Linux have some kind of a volume control. Your speaker system likely has one, as well. There is, however, a third set of controls you should know about—KMix, the master mixer controls on your system (Figure 17–1).

Figure 17–1 Kmix controls.

The various sliders correspond to various levels, from that of your CD player itself to the PCM output, microphone inputs, and so on. Pause your mouse pointer over the sliders, and a tooltip will tell you what that slider does. The left-to-right slider at the bottom is for your left-to-right speaker balance.

If you close KMix now (click the X in the top right-hand corner), you'll still have quick access to probably the most important item, the master volume control. Look down into the system tray at the bottom right corner of your screen, and you should see an icon that looks like a speaker (Figure 17–2).

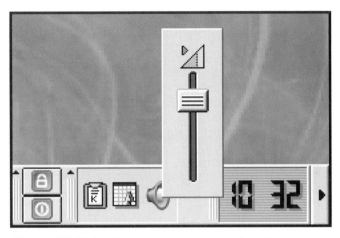

Figure 17–2 A volume control in your system tray.

Click on that speaker icon, and a volume control slider will appear. This provides you with a fast means of making volume-level adjustments.

Quick Tip If you find that the levels are still a bit low (particularly if you are running Mandrake), you may want to check out the global system settings. This is controlled by a program called `aumix`, which you can call from the command line or via your <Alt+F2> quicklaunch. This is a simple GUI from which you can drag the levels to something more to your liking. When you are done, click File on the menu bar, then Save, and Quit.

Now that you can easily modify the level of *noise* coming from your speakers, it's time to get some music on.

KsCD, the KDE CD Player

You might remember seeing a snapshot of KsCD earlier on in this book, when I was discussing command execution (Chapter 4). This is the default CD player included as part of the KDE desktop (Figure 17–3).

Figure 17–3   KsCD, the default KDE CD player.

If all you want to do is play your CDs and you want a simple, easy-to-use interface, look no further. Click the application starter (the big K), and look for KsCD under the Multimedia menu (the command name is `kscd`). Then push the play button, sit back, and enjoy.

XMMS

XMMS is pretty much the standard Linux media player but it is much more than a music player. Properly used, it is a spectacular light show, as well. It supports OGG Vorbis, MP3, and WAV formats. With the right extensions, you can also use it to play RealAudio and even MPEGs. More on that later.

Every major Linux distribution comes with XMMS, so you don't have to go far to find it. If it isn't already part of the installation, have a look on your distribution CD-ROM. If all else fails, you can always go to the source at `http://www.xmms.org` for the latest and greatest.

To start the program, look for XMMS under your Multimedia menu, or type `xmms &` (either from a shell or by pressing <Alt+F2>) and press the <Enter> key. If this is the first time that you start XMMS, you'll see something that looks like the amplifier on your home stereo system (Figure 17–4).

Notice that there are three *components* in my screen capture. If you are starting XMMS for the first time, you are likely to see only the amplifier module at the top left. Look at the buttons on the right of the amplifier. You'll see one labeled *EQ* (the equalizer) and *PL* (the playlist). Clicking these *buttons* will bring up the two additional modules for your stereo system. The buttons themselves may take some getting used to. They look more or less the same as you would expect on a home system and perform the same functions but, as you shall soon see when I explain *skins*, the *look* is very flexible.

Figure 17–4 XMMS amp, equalizer, and playlist.

 Quick Tip Before you try anything with XMMS, I should tell you that each of the three modules can be moved about individually on the screen. The arrangement I'm using, with the amplifier on top of the equalizer on the left and the playlist on the right, isn't the only variation. Consequently, you may find yourself readjusting their positions more often than you care to. The easy way to solve this is by right-clicking on the amplifier module, choosing Options from the menu, and choosing Easy Move. There's a <Ctrl+E> keyboard shortcut, as well.

If you want to play songs, click the +FILE button on the playlist editor, and select the songs you want from the file menu that appears. If you hold that button down for a second or two, you'll also have the opportunity to add a Web link (+URL) to a collection of songs, or a directory (+DIR). The button directly to the left of it (-FILE) lets you undo your choices. Once you have made your choices, press the play button.

XMMS Light Shows

XMMS has extensive plugin support for input, output, and visualization. To get at these, use the Preferences menu (the shortcut is <Ctrl+P)>. A new window will pop up, offering you tabs for various runtime options, fonts, and so on. This is also where you find the control for the various audio I/O, special effects, and visualization plugins (Figure 17–5). If you should find yourself having any problems with sound when you first start up XMMS, this is the place to start. Look under the audio section and check the output plugin. Running under KDE, you will likely use the aRts driver, but if XMMS is a little too silent, try the OSS Driver.

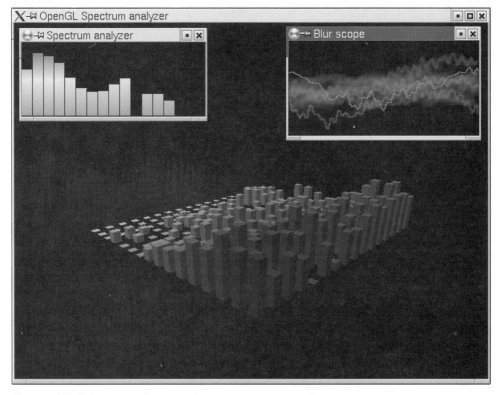

Figure 17–5 Some visualization plugins accompanying the music.

I could spend a great deal of time talking about the various options. Instead, I invite you to check out the various options on your own. What I wanted to talk about is the little light show effects, and these are the *visualization plugins*. To activate a plugin from Preferences, click on a plugin, then click the Enable plugin radio button.

We have things here such as Spectrum Analyzer and Blur Scope. Earlier on, I mentioned the OpenGL Spectrum Analyzer, another cool plugin that provides colorful 3D visuals to accompany your music—you can even launch that one full-screen; sit back, and enjoy the show.

Skinning XMMS

One of my favorite features of XMMS is its *skinability*, if you will. Using skins, I can change XMMS's look from its default black metal face to something more classic, such as cherry wood or a refined brushed aluminum. Using the <Alt+S> shortcut brings up the Skin Browser, which you can also select through the right-click menu. Mandrake Linux is *particularly nice* this way. This distribution includes a large number of skins for XMMS.

If you don't have any skins in your list, you need to get yourself some skins. For that, head to the XMMS Web site at www.xmms.org and click Skins on the menu. I guarantee you won't be getting bored anytime soon. There are literally tons of skins available.

So how do you install these skins? All of the skins on the Web site are in tar.gz format. Find one that appeals to you, download it, and save it to your $HOME/.xmms/Skins directory. You don't need to extract the file—just save it to the directory. Now right-click on the amplifier, select Options, and click on Skin Browser. Your installed skins should be available for you to select (Figure 17–6). To preview a skin, click on it, and XMMS will change to the new skin.

Figure 17–6 The XMMS Skins browser.

You can even click the Select random skin on play button if you'd like some automatic variety.

I'm going to leave XMMS behind on this topic of skins because the next application does skins in a great way, as well. I started off with XMMS, but KDE also has a great little program called *Multimedia Player*, or more rightly, *Noatun*.

Noatun

Sounds a bit like *know a tune*, doesn't it?

You can access the program by looking under the big K, choosing Multimedia, then clicking on the KDE Media Player or you can type `noatun &` at the command line. The problem is that when you fire it up for the first time, it tends to look a little boring, as in Figure 17–7.

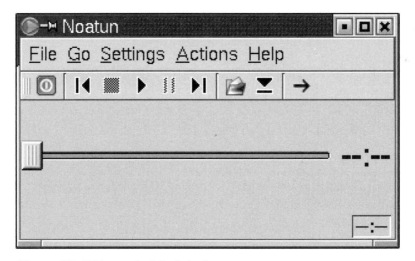

Figure 17–7 Noatun's default look.

Don't let that disappoint you. That is the default skin, named *Excellent*. Like XMMS, you can skin Noatun—in fact, some of Noatun's skins are downright wild. Before we get into that, however, let's just talk about playing songs with Noatun.

Click File on Noatun's menu bar and select Open. Navigate your directories until you get to a song you want to play. Select it, and click OK. In all likelihood, nothing will happen at this point. That's because you are loading songs into a playlist. To get to that playlist, click Settings and select Show Playlist.

You can also click the Playlist icon just under the menu bar, the second icon from the right. (The final icon lets you select between single play and playlist looping.)

At this point, you can just keep adding songs to the playlist (you can also add directories if you have collections you want to add). Eventually, you'll have your list. Click the diskette icon on the playlist (see Figure 17–8) to save your list. You are all set. Select a starting song in the playlist, and click the play button on Noatun's main screen (or click the starting song in the playlist).

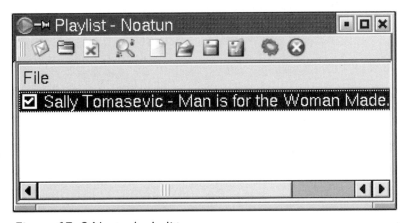

Figure 17–8 Noatun's playlist.

Noatun's slider is positional within the playing song. You can control volume using your KMix applet in the system tray, as well as through Noatun. To see the volume control, click Settings on the menu bar and select Show Volume Control.

 Quick Tip You can also use Noatun to play video clips.

Skinning Noatun

Let's get back to the subject of skinning Noatun.

Click on Settings, followed by Configure Noatun. From the pop-up menu that appears, choose Plugins, which will then give you a tabbed menu. Under Interfaces, you'll see four options for player styles. The skinable styles are *K-Jofol*

Figure 17–9   Noatun with a K-Jofol skin.

(Figure 17–9) and *Kaiman* (although there is also a Winamp skin loader). In both cases, you can find additional skins on the KDE-Look Web site at `http://www.kde-look.org`.

Start by clicking off the *Excellent* interface and clicking on the *K-Jofol* interface. You'll see the menu bar at the left change. It now shows a K-Jofol Skins option. The same would happen with the Kaiman interface but, obviously, with Kaiman skins. If you click on this menu option, you'll see a drop-down list on the right with a preview of the various installed skins.

 Quick Tip For the curious readers out there, Noatun skins live under the `$HOME/.kde/share/apps/noatun/skins` **directory.**

Noatun Lightshows!

When I told you about XMMS, I mentioned the variety of cool plugins you could use for visualization. KDE's media player, Noatun, has these as well. In the Configure Noatun Interfaces menu, select Plugins (from the left-hand sidebar), then click Visualizations.

Ripping and Burning Songs

Over the years, we have all purchased a lot of music CDs or, as some of us still call them, *albums*. Many of those albums, unfortunately, have only two or three songs we really liked, so playing the whole album wasn't what we wanted. As a result, we created collections of our favorite songs on tape and played the tapes, instead.

These days, with the help of our Linux systems, we can create our own collections from those albums we have purchased and create CD collections of those songs we want to hear. Furthermore, if you have lots of disk space and you spend a lot of time at your computer, nothing beats a collection of songs ready to play without having to change CDs all the time. Pulling songs from a CD and saving them to your system as digital images is what is commonly referred to as *ripping*.

Intermezzo: Digital Audio Formats

Before I get into the mechanics of ripping and burning songs, I'd like to spend a small amount of time discussing music formats. When you purchase a CD, the songs on that CD are in a format not generally used by your system. In fact, when we copy songs to disk from a CD, we always encode it into another, usually more compact format. The format we transfer to is identified by a three-letter extension on the file name. The most common formats are `.wav`, `.mp3`, and (more recently) `.ogg`.

The *wav* format is one originally created by Microsoft. It is extremely common but not the most efficient in terms of compression. The *mp3* format (from the Motion Pictures Experts Group, aka MPEG) on the other hand, owes its popularity to the high compression ratio it uses—about 12:1. The newcomer on the block is the *ogg* (or Ogg Vorbis) format. Like mp3, it boasts a high compression rate, but unlike mp3, it is completely unencumbered by patents.

To give you an idea of the compression values, I ripped a 3-minute, 46-second song to wav format. It came in at 39866444 bytes, while the same song in ogg format required only 3438407 bytes. If you do the math, that is a ratio of 11.6:1. Pretty impressive reasons for not using wav format files.

Grip

Most distributions will come with Grip, a CD ripper designed for the GNOME desktop. As I've explained before, being GNOME-based doesn't stop this program from doing its job under KDE. Using a library called *cdparanoia* (which I will discuss later), Grip makes it possible to create MP3s or OGGs easily from your favorite CD. If the program is installed, you will likely find it in your multimedia menu. You can also call it by its program name (using the shell or the <Alt+F2> program launcher), `grip`.

Grip consists of a single window with multiple tabs. Each tab presents you with a window from which various functions are performed (i.e., Tracks, Rip, and Config). The main Tracks tab features a list of the current CD's audio tracks, including track number, title, and length in minutes and seconds. The CD's title and artist appear just above the track window.

As you can probably tell by looking at Figure 17–10, Grip is also a CD player. Using the buttons at the bottom of the program window, you can play, pause, fast forward, or pause playback, just as you did with KsCD. The extra buttons let you open or close the CD-ROM drive, change the volume, edit tracks, perform track lookups, or switch to compact, player-only mode (Figure 17–11). If you move your mouse over the buttons and pause, tooltips will appear, informing you of the various button functions.

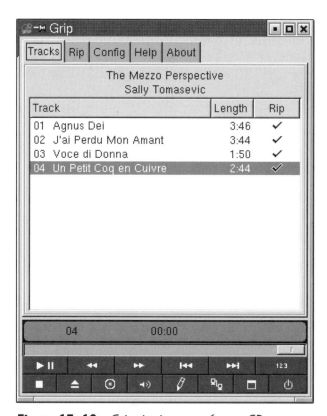

Figure 17–10   *Grip ripping songs from a CD.*

Figure 17–11   A more compact Grip.

To rip tracks to disk, either right-click on the track name or left-click under the Rip column heading at the track name's far right. In either case, a checkmark will appear, indicating that the track is ready for ripping. You can also quickly select all the tracks by clicking on the Rip column label. When you have selected the titles you wish to rip, click the Rip tab (Figure 17–12).

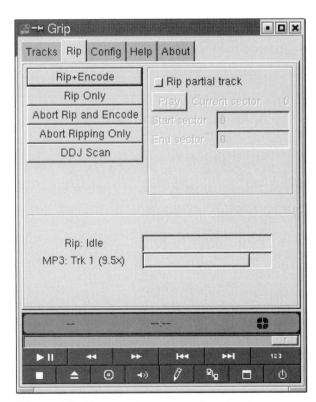

Figure 17–12   Ready to start extracting songs.

If you just go ahead and click Rip Only, the track will be saved in wav format (remember our discussion of compression). Click Rip+Encode, however, and Grip will encode and compress the disk file into ogg or mp3 format. The default encode is ogg format. To save as mp3, you will need an mp3 encoder, such as *bladeenc* or *lame* (check `rpmfind.net` for binary RPMs or check the resources section at the end of this chapter).

When the process starts, a progress indicator bar (about two-thirds of the way down) will detail the status of the rip. The resulting songs will be saved in your home directory under a folder called *mp3*, using the following format.

```
/home/username/mp3/artist_name/album_name/track_title.ogg
```

You can change this default by clicking the Config tab and selecting MP3, Encoder. There are a lot of possible settings here: dealing with the ripping process itself, MP3 encoders, online disc information servers, and file formats. The options are many, but the defaults are probably all you need if you are just writing songs to your disk. Grip comes with excellent help files for every part of this process. If you get stuck, just click the Help tab.

You'll notice I said *to your disk* at the end of the last paragraph? That's because Grip is strictly a ripping and encoding program. If you want to get those songs burned to CDs, you'll need a CD burning package. Luckily, this won't be a problem.

K3b for a Friendlier Burn

I still find it interesting to consider the terms that have entered the language when referring to creating CDs. We rip, then we burn.

Considering the violent-sounding nature of the process, anything that simplifies the process and makes things a little friendlier is certainly welcome. One of the friendliest tools for creating and copying audio and data CDs is called *K3b*. You may have K3b available on your system, but if it isn't, simply visit `www.k3b.org`. Both source code (it is GPLed, after all) and precompiled binaries are available. The program name (should you wish to run it from the shell or via the <Alt+F2> launcher) is `k3b`.

 Installation Note K3b depends on the cdrdao package.

When you fire up K3b for the first time, you'll get a little warning message alerting you to this fact and advising that you should consider running K3b

Setup. Click Yes here, and the setup program will automatically be started for you. Because, as you might expect, k3bsetup requires root permission, you will be asked for the password before continuing.

The K3b setup program is basically a wizard that takes you through a question-and-answer session to determine what drives you are using, who has access to the program, and so on. Click Next past the introductory screen, and you'll see the first of a few interesting dialogs (Figure 17–13)—this one deals with the external applications used by K3b. You should have *cdrdao*, *cdrecord*, and *mkisofs* listed among the available programs. Beyond that, you don't really need anything else. If these are listed, click Next.

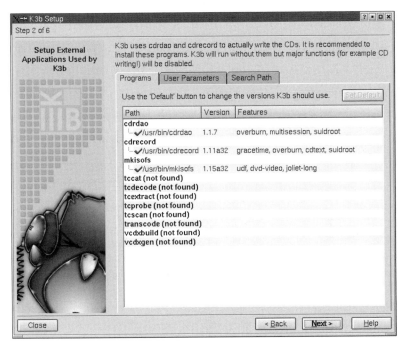

Figure 17–13 K3b setup for external programs.

On the following screen, the setup program will display the drives it has detected as being useful to burning CDs. For instance, if you have both a CD player *and* a CD writer, these should both be listed. On my system, I had a DVD player in addition to my CD writer (Figure 17–14). If a device appears missing and you believe it should be there, click Add Device and enter the information. Normally, you should only have to click Next past this screen.

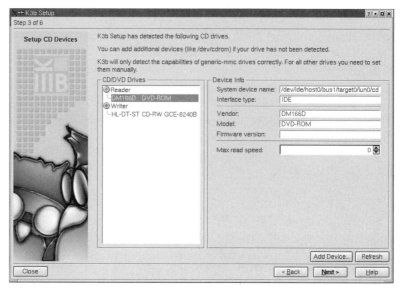

Figure 17-14   Device detection in K3b Setup.

The same holds true for the fourth screen. K3b will want to create mount points for the devices it chose in the previous step. Unless you feel things should be different, let K3b create the file system entries by clicking Next. The following screen (step 5 of the setup) is for user security, namely, which users are allowed to burn CDs. Click Add User and enter the name of the user to which you intend to grant permission. Keep adding until you have everyone. If you skip this step, only root will be able to create CDs.

The final screen is just a feel-good screen, congratulating you for a job well done. So are you ready to burn some CDs? Then let's get started.

Getting Familiar with K3b

K3b's interface is friendly and very easy to use. It is broken up into three main windows, with two top frames and one larger one at the bottom, all of which can be resized to your tastes. The top left-hand frame is your file navigator, showing your directories in the Konqueror-like tree format you are now familiar with. Just click the plus signs to open a directory or the minus sign to collapse it. The top right-hand frame will display the contents of whatever folder you have selected on the left-hand side.

Creating a CD of any kind in K3b is done with *projects*, and that is where the bottom window comes into play. If you are looking to create an *audio CD*, click File on K3b's menu bar and select New Project, then click on New Audio Project. If

≋-н K3b - The CD Kreator

File Project Tools Settings Help

📄 New Project 📂 Open 💾 Save ◐ Burn ◑ Copy CD ◉ Blank CD-RW

Figure 17–15 K3b's menu bar.

you were creating a data CD (which we will cover shortly), you would click on New Data Project. Have a look just below the menu bar, and you'll see a handful of quick-access buttons (Figure 17–15). You can click the New Project button there, as well. The additional buttons, labeled *Open, Save, Burn, Copy CD*, and *Blank CD-RW*, are also interesting, and I'll cover those things shortly.

Look to the bottom of the screen, and you'll notice that a tab labeled *Audio/* will appear under the Current Projects banner. You can create multiple projects, and each will appear with its own tab.

Backing up Your Data with K3b

K3b makes a quick and easy tool for backing up your important data. The best approach is to use CD-RW, or rewriteable CDs, because you can use them over and over again. Before you reuse your CD-RW, you'll want to blank it first. Pop the disk into your CD rewriter and click Blank CD-RW (just below the menu bar).

A window will appear (Figure 17–16), showing you some options for blanking the CD-RW. From there, you can select which CD writer you wish to use

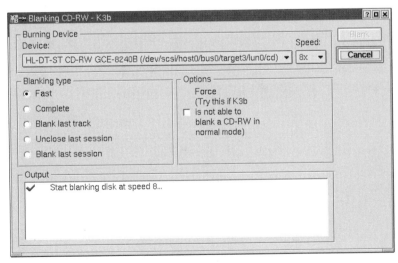

Figure 17–16 Preparing to blank a CD-RW.

(if you have more than one), the speed at which you want to perform the operation, and whether you want a fast blank or a complete erase. When you are happy with your choice, click the button labeled *Blank* at the top right-hand corner of the window. Just below all this is an Output window, where the progress of blanking will be displayed. After your successful completion message, you will still want to click Close to banish the window.

Now you are ready to back up your data. Start a New Data Project. A tab with a sequentially generated name will appear in the bottom projects window (Figure 17–17). It will be divided into two windows. On the left-hand side, you'll see a small icon representing a CD with the current project name next to it. On the right will be a blank list with headings for file Name, Type, Size, and Location.

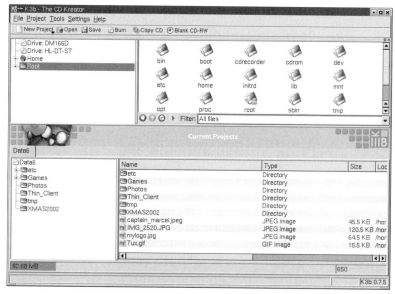

Figure 17–17   Creating a data CD.

To fill this project, simply drag directory or files onto the CD icon in the left-hand side project window. As each directory is added, K3b will calculate the amount of space all of this takes. Consequently, it may take a few seconds for a large directory to appear as these calculations are being made. A colored bar will stretch along the bottom, indicating the amount of space you still have left to create your data CD.

After you have added everything you want, click the Burn icon directly below the menu bar. You can also right-click the current project tab and select

Burn there. A new Write window will appear, with four tabs labeled *Burning*, *Volume Desc*, *Settings*, and *Advanced*.

I won't cover everything on every tab here, but I will tell you about a few of the more important settings, starting with the Burning tab. If your device is capable of high-speed burning, you may want to change the setting for Speed. The default speed of 1 is fine but very slow, and modern writers can handle much better performance. Part of this comes from the *Burn-Proof* technology built into many devices. If yours is capable, make sure you check this option on.

Quick Tip   A rather odd-sounding option is Simulate Writing, located on the Burning tab. After all, why go through the process and not do anything? The idea is to see whether a disc can be properly written at the current speed. Everything happens as it would, except that the laser is turned off. This is also where the Writing on the fly option will come into play. If your system performance is such that you can burn a disc without writing out an image first, make sure you check this option on.

The Volume Desc tab allows you to set some label information for your CD, such as the name, who created it, and what system it was intended for. You don't actually need to enter anything here. It is information only. Skip over the Settings tab for a moment and look under the Advanced tab, where you'll find a number of miscellaneous options related to how data is written on your CD. For most users, these can be left alone.

Did Someone Say "Backups?"

Not yet, but by now you must be thinking, "Hey, if I can copy data directories to my CD, surely I can use this thing to do backups," and you would be bang on. Other than the limitations of the CD's roughly 700 MB of storage, this is a great option. Use CD-RWs, and you can create a rotating set of discs for back-up purposes.

Taking all this into consideration, we're onto something here, but there are some things to consider.

Look under the Settings tab, and you'll find a couple of important settings related to data backups. The first has to do with whether you will ever be looking at this CD using a Windows system. If so, make sure you check on the Generate Joliet extensions box. Under Permissions, check on Preserve file permissions if this CD is a backup of your data. Should you ever need to recover from this CD, you'll want to have the proper ownership and permissions of files and directories maintained.

When you're done and ready to go, click on the Write button located in the top right-hand corner of this dialog box. A new progress window will appear with status information on the current CD creation (Figure 17–18).

That's it. With your data safely backed up, you can sleep soundly at night.

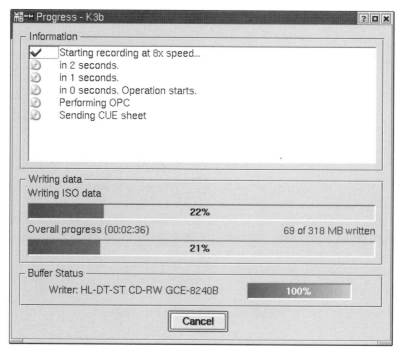

Figure 17–18 Watching the status of a burn in progress.

Creating a Music CD with K3b

Data is fine, of course, but I started this chapter talking about music. The good news is that if you've already mastered the art of creating a data CD with K3b, you are well on your way to doing the same with music.

When you start K3b again, select New Audio Project this time. In the upper left side window, click on the directory where your songs reside. You should see them appear in the top right-hand window. Simply click on a song, then drag it into the Audio project window at the bottom. Once again, a status bar at the bottom will let you know how much time this takes up on the CD. Just keep an eye on the total time as you add songs.

Don't worry about the order in which the songs appear on the list. When you have your selection complete, simply click on the songs in the lower pane, and move them up or down at will. If the song in position six would make a better opener, drag it up to position one. It is that easy.

When you are done, click Burn. As the window appears, you might notice that it looks a little different than the data burn window. For starters, there is one less tab. Of those tabs, the one originally labeled *Volume Desc* now says *CD-Text*. We'll start with that one in that, like its data counterpart, it is for information only. This is where you enter the CD label information, performer name, or other information related to this disc. Should you decide to simply leave this blank, your CD will still work.

The Advanced tab is much simpler than on the *data CD* dialog. The only option is a strange little trick to hide the first track of a song in the first pregap. If you do this, you won't find the song on a straight play. You'll have to seek backward from the first song.

Finally, we'll go back to the Burning tab. There's really nothing new here that you haven't already seen. Select your write speed and click Write.

 Quick Tip If you always use the same settings when burning either a data or a music CD, click the Save User Defaults button on the Write CD dialog.

Lights, Camera, Action: Moving Pictures

Believe it or not, you have already worked with one of the Linux video players in this chapter. It is Noatun, KDE's media player. It is just as adept at playing video clips, such as AVI or MPEG files. Try it!

If you have a DVD player installed on your system, you will likely want to take advantage of it. One of the more popular and slick-looking video players out there is *xine*. xine plays back video clips (such as AVI, MOV, or MPEG) and DVDs, as well. It can even handle URLs, meaning that you can play remote files on the Internet.

You can start xine from your Multimedia menu (command name *xine*) or by calling the command directly. Looking at Figure 17–19, you'll see xine's basic interface. Most of the buttons are pretty self-explanatory (play, forward, rewind, etc.). Others allow you to switch to full-screen mode. To see what everything does, move your mouse cursor over the various buttons, and tool icons and a helpful tooltip will appear.

Figure 17–19   xine's main controls are very approachable.

Now sit back and watch a movie (Figure 17–20)!

For more information on Linux videos and DVDs, visit the Linux Video Project at http://www.linuxvideo.org/.

Figure 17–20   Watching a movie on Linux with xine.

A Note on Encrypted DVDs

You may find as you play DVDs on your Linux system that some DVDs work and others do not. The reason for this is encryption. In an effort to protect against unlawful copying and distribution of movies on DVD, some companies in the motion picture industry have gone to extremes to protect themselves using a system called *Content Scrambling System* (CSS). The result of this overreaction curtails the freedom of those law-abiding individuals who are looking to play the DVDs that they legally bought and paid for on the DVD player that they legally bought and paid for on the computer they legally bought and paid for.

"There's a simple solution," you say. "Why not write or use software that decrypts the DVDs so you can watch them?"

Well, it isn't that easy.

In some countries, most notably the United States, it is illegal to use software that decrypts any form of encryption put in place by another individual or company, even when it is for private use (do a Google search on *DMCA*). As I write this, legal challenges to this law are currently in the courts and in some cases, have already upheld the right of the individual. This isn't to say that the motion picture industry will give up easily.

For instance, under the DMCA, a small handful of individuals have been charged for distributing a piece of software called *libdecss, libdvdcss* (or simply DeCSS), which lets you play encrypted DVDs on your Linux PC. The California Appeals Court ruled that the posting of source code (in this case, DeCSS) is upheld by the First Amendment.

Meanwhile, in Norway, a young man named Jon Lech Johanson was cleared of wrongdoing for distributing DeCSS software on the Internet. The 19-year-old "DVD Jon" faced two years in prison when the Motion Picture Association of America (MPAA) requested that Jon be arrested (he was only 15 at the time). In fact, the MPAA wanted both Jon *and* his father arrested.

Why am I telling you all this? I mention all of this because I want you to make yourselves aware of the laws in your area. Playing a DVD on your PC sounds like a perfectly normal and legal thing to do—I agree, but I must repeat myself—you should be careful and make yourselves aware of the laws regarding this as they apply to your state, province, or country. I don't want to hear that any of you are facing jail time just because you decided to watch your legal copy of the latest blockbuster on your Linux system.

Playing the MS-Only Plugin Game

Yes, despite the fact that Linux *is* the future, there are companies still producing plugins without a Linux equivalent. The obvious one here is Microsoft's own Windows Media Player. The benefits of running Linux far outweigh any possible downside to not having access to these players, but, as it turns out, you do not have to do without. Consider getting your hands on a copy of the *Codeweavers CrossOver Plugin*. This marvelous piece of software makes it possible to use native Windows plugins for Quicktime, ShockWave Director, Windows Media Player, and others seamlessly in your favorite Linux browser. For all those movie trailers that seem to be available only in Quicktime format, the CrossOver Plugin is a must, and although this isn't a free product, it is quite inexpensive. Installation is a piece of cake, and you won't need to feel left out when the next blockbuster preview shows up at a Web site near you. Still interested? Here's the address:

```
http://www.codeweavers.com
```

Furthermore, some CrossOver plugins can be used externally from your browser as stand alone programs. After installation, these will be made available in your KDE menu.

Then, There's Mplayer!

What the Codeweavers CrossOver Plugin has going for it is that you get to use the *actual* Windows plugin on your Linux system. It's the real thing and consequently looks just like the official product. Still, if you are willing to forego that *official* look, there is a freeware alternative that will do the job very nicely. It's called MPlayer. It is also a great media player that can handle both audio and video streams, play from a TV tuner card, record audio and video, and more. It works beautifully from the command line, but it also has a great, skinnable GUI. MPlayer requires a little more work up front, but the results are worth it, and it won't cost you a penny.

Some distributions such as Mandrake, already come with MPlayer, so check your distribution CDs first. In order to use the GUI, you'll want to install the `mplayer-gui` and `mplayer-skins` packages as well as `mplayer` itself. If you don't have it (or you want the latest and greatest), pay a visit to the MPlayer Web site at `http://www.MPlayerHQ.hu`. You'll find both source distributions as well as RPMs.

Tip Why not use your Konqueror shortcuts to search for a package:

```
rf: mplayer
```

MPlayer handles tons of video formats, from avi to mpg to Windows Media Player to Quicktime, and just about anything you can think of. The same is true for audio (think Ogg, MP3 and so on). MPlayer performs this magic by using a series of *codecs* (coder/decoders), little software translators that take a foreign video or audio format and let you enjoy it on your Linux system. To get the latest bundle of Win32 codecs, visit the following URL.

```
http://ftp.lug.udel.edu/MPlayer/releases/codecs/
```

You'll find different bundles there and for different video formats, but you may as well download the full set. The packages are tarred and compressed with bzip2. Open up a Konsole and cd to whatever directory you downloaded your codecs bundle. Once there, type this command:

```
tar -xjvf win32codecs.tar.bz2
```

This will create a subdirectory called `win32codecs`. Switch to that directory, and (as root) copy all the codecs to `/usr/lib/win32`. If the `/usr/lib/win32` directory doesn't already exist, you should create it.

```
cd win32codecs
su -c "mkdir -p /usr/lib/win32"
su -c "cp * /usr/lib/win32"
```

Notice the "`su -c`" before each of the commands. You might remember this from chapter 7. This command lets you quickly jump into root to perform the necessary steps, then jump back.

Once you've done all this, MPlayer is ready to use. Let's say that you have a movie clip called *"exciting_movie.avi."* To play that movie clip with MPlayer, you would open a shell and type the following:

```
mplayer exiciting_movie.avi
```

To use the graphical or GUI version of the player, run the command "gmplayer" instead.

Using the GUI is even easier because it provides a familiar interfrace for loading files as well as controlling all aspects of the playback (fast forward, pause, etc.). With the *Open* button, you can select the files you want to view, or point to your DVD drive and select the files you would like to view. Of course, the look of the interface will vary based on the skin you choose. Figure 17-21 shows off the default MPlayer skin.

When you first run the `mplayer` command, it will create a ".mplayer" subdirectory in your home directory. From there, it will read a file called "config" where you can add various configuration options, select audio and video output sources and so on. You can create or edit the `config` file with the Kate editor (covered in Chapter 16), and modify Mplayer to suit your needs. Here's what my `config` file looks like.

```
# Write your default config options here!
#
vo=xv,x11
ao=arts
```

Figure 17–21   Default MPlayer skin.

I'm asking Mplayer to use my X11 video for output and KDE's aRTs audio system for the sound. If you find yourself with no sound or with video problems, I recommend that you do the same.

When running MPlayer in GUI mode, you can switch to other skins by right-clicking on the interface. This will bring forward a menu with many options, one of which is to activate the skin browser.

MPlayer is powerful and flexible. You can do a lot more with it than I can cover here in a short period of time. For that reason, I do recommend that you read the accompanying documentation, or pay a visit to the MPlayer Web site to learn more. You can also type "`mplayer -h`" from the command line for a list of keyboard controls and options.

Using MPlayer as a Browser Plugin

You go visit your favorite movie preview Web site to watch a video clip only to discover that it is in Quicktime or Microsoft media format and that it doesn't work in your browser. I mentioned the Crossover Plugin as a solution, but you can use your MPlayer for viewing those clips as well.

You do this by using the *mplayerplug-in*, an open source plugin that uses Mplayer. Head over to `http://mplayerplug-in.sourceforge.net/` and download the latest source (RPM packages for RedHat are also availble there). If there are no packages available for your distribution and you need to build from source, have no fear. It's easy.

```
tar -xzvf mplayerplug-in_v0.80.tar.gz
cd mplayerplug-in
make
make install
```

What the last line really does is copy the resulting `mplayerplug-in.so` file into your home directory's `.mozilla/plugins` directory.

```
cp mplayerplug-in.so $HOME/.mozilla/plugins
```

If you want to make the plugin globally accessible, you'll need to know Mozilla's system-wide plugins directory (or Netscape's). For example, with my RPM-installed Mozilla, I would use this command:

```
cp mplayerplug-in.so /usr/lib/mozilla/plugins
```

I'm sure you are more than ready to try this out and you could do so with Mozilla immediately. Start Mozilla, and surf on over to your favorite movie preview site (I tend to like Apple's site for the latest trailers, *http://www.apple.com/trailers*). When you click on a movie clip to view, a window will appear in the browser with the words "mplayerplug-in – Loading movie …"

Sit back and enjoy the show.

It's a Wrap!

It sounds so base for me to say this, but multimedia *really is* about song and dance, dog-and-pony shows, and gratuitous flash and pizzazz. Judging from everything I've seen out there, our appetite for yet another adventure into sight and sound isn't abating anytime soon.

I've shown you a few of the more popular and useful tools to explore Linux sight and sound, but your own appetite for more will likely take you well beyond these pages. On that note, I'm going to give you another handful of Linux tools to excite the ears and eyes.

In the world of audio, check out *KMid* (command name `kmid`) for playing those MIDI files. What makes this program particularly fun is that it is a karaoke player, as well. Plug the words *karaoke*, *midi*, *files*, and *download* into a Google search form, and you should find plenty of files. Just load them up in KMid, click Play, and you are the next international singing sensation.

 Hint Why not enter the words:

      gg: karaoke midi files download

into Konqueror's Location field for a quick Google search?

In terms of video playback, another great DVD player is *Ogle* (command name `ogle`). This one probably isn't on your distribution disks, but you can pick it up at the following address:

    http://www.dtek.chalmers.se/groups/dvd/

What Ogle has going for it that xine doesn't (at this time, anyhow) is support for on-screen menus, such as you have with your home DVD player.

Feeling creative? Would you like to take a shot at writing your own music? A number of decent music notation programs are available for Linux. They include *NoteEdit* and *RoseGarden*, to name a couple. Links to each follow in the Resources section.

Just as there seems to be no end to the number of songs that humanity can create, so it is with software to manipulate sound. If I haven't mentioned it in this chapter, it certainly isn't because it doesn't exist. Check out the *Sound and MIDI Software for Linux* site at `http://linux-sound.org`.

Resources

Blade MP3 Encoder

http://bladeenc.mp3.no/

Grip

http://www.nostatic.org/grip/

K3b

http://www.k3b.org

Lame Encoder

http://lame.sourceforge.net

MPlayer

http://www.MPlayerHQ.hu/homepage/design4/news.html

NoteEdit

http://tan.informatik.tu-chemnitz.de/~jan/noteedit/noteedit.html

Ogg Vorbis

http://www.vorbis.com

RoseGarden

http://www.all-day-breakfast.com/rosegarden/

Sound and MIDI Software for Linux

http://linux-sound.org/

X-CD-Roast

http://www.xcdroast.org

xine video player

http://xinehq.de/

chapter
18
Fun and Games
(Very Serious Fun)

There's plenty to smile about when it comes to taking a little down time with your Linux system. A default KDE installation comes with a number of games, as does a standard GNOME installation. If you installed both desktops (Mandrake does just that by default), you will find yourself with plenty to keep you busy and happy for some time.

Expand your mind with one of the many puzzles. Do a little target practice in the arcade. Race down a dizzying mountain slope. Play golf. Sink someone's battleship. Board a space fighter and take on somebody halfway around the world. Play solitaire, backgammon, or poker.

There are tons of games available, and I'm just talking about the ones on your distribution disks. Head off to the Internet and you'll find yourself set for weeks, possibly months.

Sit back, relax, and get ready to enjoy a little fun, Linux style.

Security Revisited

"Is he crazy?"

You might be thinking that security is a strange topic to revisit when we are discussing fun and games. It's actually not, partly because this is one of the times when keeping certain people out of certain places is a plus. I'm talking about the kids.

As I mentioned earlier in the book, Linux is a multiuser operating system, meaning that one or more users can work on it at the same time. What this *also* means is that each person using your system is an individual, with his or her own home directories, files, menus, and desktop decorations. By creating a login for each member of your family or office, you not only protect the files that belong to each user, but you also protect yourself. If little Natika deletes all her icons or changes the desktop to a *garish green and purple*, it doesn't affect you. Similarly, this is a great opportunity to create a play world for the kids.

Each user is referenced by a username. Each username has a user ID (UID) associated with it and one or more groups. Like usernames, group names are also represented by a numeric identifier, this time called a *group ID* (GID). A user's UID is unique, as is a group's GID.

Adding users requires that you operate as root, so when you launch the KDE User Manager (command name `kuser`), you will be asked for the root password. When the program starts, a window will appear like the one in Figure 18–1. There will be two tabs, one for Users and the other for Groups.

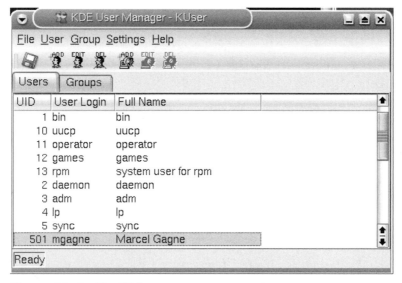

Figure 18–1   The KDE user management tool.

To add an additional user, click User on the menu bar, and select Add (you can also click the add user icon below the menu bar). A new window will appear asking you to enter the name of the new user. This username should be in lower case with a minimum of five characters and a maximum of eight characters.

When you press <Enter>, a new window will appear, the User Properties dialog (Figure 18–2). You don't really need to add anything new here, but there are fields provided to further identify the person for whom you are creating the login. For instance, you can choose to enter his or her full name, office location, or home address.

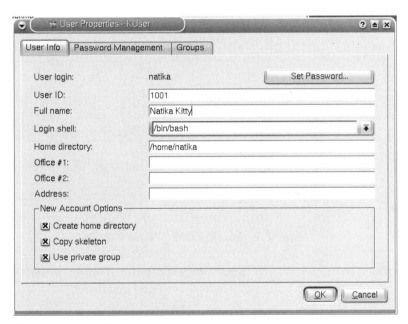

Figure 18–2   Setting user properties.

The most important item on this window is the Set Password button. Click that and you will be asked to enter a password (Figure 18–3). In fact, you will be asked to enter it twice, once for verification. Note that when you do enter the password, you won't actually see it, but rather stars will echo your keystrokes. When you are done, click OK.

This takes you back to the User Properties screen, where you can simply click OK to finish. To save your changes, click File on the menu bar and select Save. Alternatively, you can click the diskette icon just below the menu bar. When you are done adding users, just close KUser.

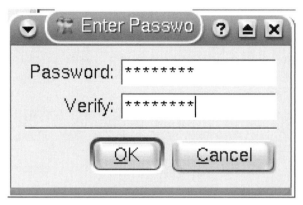

Figure 18–3　Setting a user password.

Now that you've made a nice place for everyone to play, let's get back to those games. You'll find most of these under your K menu (look for Amusements or Games) where they'll be ordered according to the type of game that each represents. In each case, I will also give you the command name so that you can either run them from the shell or start them with your program launcher <Alt+F2>.

Take Me out to the Arcade

Ah, the video arcade. I'm sure I spent far too much of my youth popping quarters into video game machines (yes, kids, it used to cost a mere 25 cents to play a game). Nevertheless, there was a real flavor associated with the kind of games you found there. In the heyday of the arcade (sorry kids, it is over), games tended to be fast but easy to learn. You didn't need to spend a small fortune just to get used to what it was the game did. Things came at you, you zapped them. Or you got out of the way.

With your Linux system, the arcade experience is alive and well. Let's take a look at the sorts of things you have at your disposal.

Cubes and Things that Drop

One of the most enduring games of that period was something called *Tetris*. The concept was simple. Colored geometric patterns would fall from above, and as they fell, you would rotate the pieces so that they fit (like a jigsaw puzzle) into the bottom row. Fill a row, and the pieces disappear. Miss too many of the pieces, and the top crushes the bottom—you lose. As simple as it sounds, this is an amazingly addictive game idea, and your Linux distribution probably came with several games of this type. KSirtet (command name `ksirtet`) is just one such game and an excellent clone of the original. KSirtet (Figure 18–4) can be played with more than one player or against the computer. If you loved Tetris, you will love KSirtet.

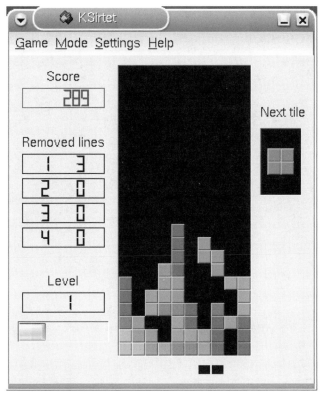

Figure 18–4   KSirtet, a Tetris-like game.

Variations included with the kdegames package are KSmileTris (command name `ksmiletris`) and KFoulEggs (command name `kfouleggs`). Both follow similar concepts (dropping pieces that you rotate), but each provides interesting variations on the game.

One of my favorite games from the arcade days also had a very simple concept—blast big rocks heading in your direction into smaller and smaller rocks. Did I mention that you are in command of a spaceship and the rocks are asteroids? KAsteroids (command name `kasteroids`) is a wonderful update of

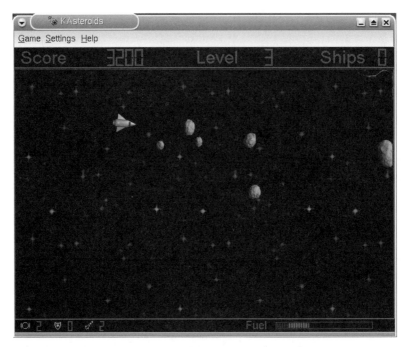

Figure 18–5   KAsteroids—break big rocks into smaller rocks.

the classic arcade game (Figure 18–5). Your spaceship and the oncoming asteroids are nicely rendered in 3D instead of the old vector graphics. Watch your fuel, your shields, and your back.

Perhaps my favorite arcade-style game under Linux also happens to be one of the most addictive games I have ever run across. It is called *Frozen-Bubble*. This is a bright, beautiful, and colorful game with dozens of levels featuring a great musical soundtrack, cool sound effects, and at least one penguin. You'll just have to trust me on this one—this game is a must have, and no, age doesn't enter into it. Still with me? Here's the premise.

Frozen, colored bubbles are arranged in various patterns against a wall at the top of your screen. Some kind of hydraulic press behind the wall slowly pushes the bubbles toward you (Figure 18–6). Your job is to guide your cute little penguin gunner (so to speak) to aim the bubble launcher at the oncoming wall of bubbles. If three of more bubbles of the same color are together, fire a similarly colored bubble at that group, and the arrangement collapses. Destroy all the bubble groups, and you win that level. If any of the bubbles at the wall touch you, everything freezes over, and your penguin cries a river of tears. It's silly. It's fun. You are going to love it.

Some Linux distributions do include Frozen-Bubble as part of the install, most notably Mandrake. If you don't find a copy on those CDs, head straight over to the main site at `http://www.frozen-bubble.org/` and pick yourself up a copy. You will be happy you did.

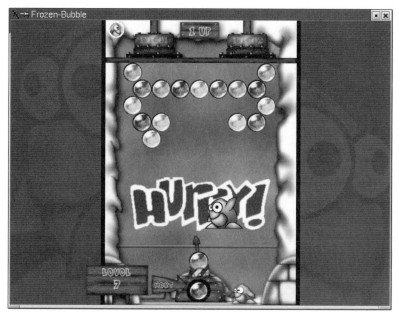

Figure 18–6   The incredibly addictive Frozen-Bubble.

Deal those Cards, Ace

If you find yourself with five cards in your hands, two of those cards being sevens and the other three being queens, and you call that a *full house*, you are my kind of person. We're talking poker, my friends, five-card stud and nothing wild.

The KDE games package comes with a nice poker game called *KPoker* (Figure 18–7; command name `kpoker`) that features sound effects, animated cards, and configurable card fronts and backs (just click Settings on the menu bar and select Configure Carddecks). It's a great way to waste some time gambling without losing a fortune. The only downside is that you can't bluff the computer.

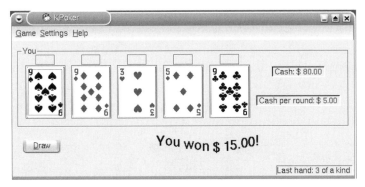

Figure 18–7   KPoker is fun. No bluffing.

Almost anyone who has held a deck of cards knows about solitaire, a one-person card game whose object is to reorder seven piles of cards, drawn at random, into four ordered piles, by suit and in numerical order. You may also know it as patience (as I did, growing up). There are, in fact, many solitaire or patience card games; the most famous and popular is also known as *Klondike*.

KPatience (command name `kpatience`) is more than just Klondike solitaire (Figure 18–8). Several games are included (click Settings on the menu bar and select Game Type), such as Freecell, Grandfather's Clock, Napoleon's Tomb, and others. As with KPoker, you can change the card styles for both the front and back. You can even change your background graphic.

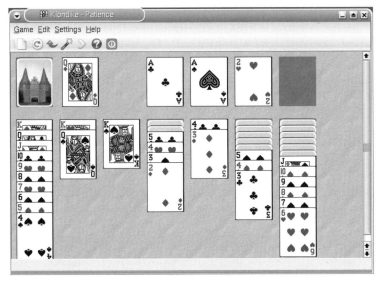

Figure 18–8   KPatience has several games, including the classic solitaire.

B-4. Miss. E-7. Hit!

What I find interesting is how many classic, low-tech games (you don't get much lower tech than playing cards) translate well to the computerized world. In the case of multiplayer board games, add a network connection and it all suddenly makes sense. You can play your favorite board games with the person sitting across from you or with someone halfway around the world. The following games can all be played on your local network or with friends in some distant part of the world.

A number of Linux games take full advantage of this capability, starting with KBattleship (command name `kbattleship`). As you might expect, this is a KDE version of the popular game Battleship. You need two networked computers to play this one. One person runs a server (under the File menu), and the other connects to it.

The rules are simple. You arrange your ships on a grid. In this version, the grid has no numbers or letters to indicate position. When it is your turn to fire, you simply click on a square, where you have to try to sink the opponent's ships. The game also has sound effects. A miss *splashes* into the water, whereas a hit *explodes* with the sound of the explosion.

One of the things I particularly enjoy about this game is the chat line. The bottom part of the game screen lets you send *instant messages* back and forth between yourself and your opponent (see Figure 18–9). Adding a little witty repartee to the game makes it even better.

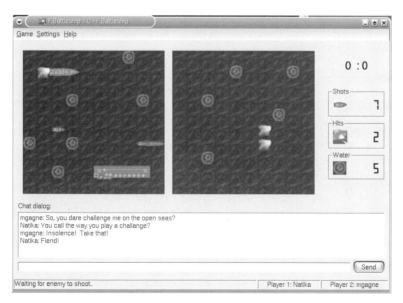

Figure 18–9   Network naval warfare with KBattleship.

Other network-playable games include KBackgammon (command name kbackgammon) and Atlantik, a network-playable, real estate, Monopoly-like game. It too features a chat area so that you can play with others around the world. Then there's *Tenes Empanadas Graciela*, or TEG, a network-enabled clone of the Risk world conquest game. Unfortunately, that one isn't on your disk, but if world conquest appeals to you, visit http://teg.source-forge.net and start building your empire.

Of course, one of the oldest and most popular board games in the world is chess. On your disks and perhaps already installed, you will almost certainly find xboard (and that is the command name). For the Mahjongg fans out there (the classic Eastern tile-matching game), there is a KDE version (command name kmahjongg) and a GNOME version (command name mahjongg).

Educational Games

Games can be educational, as well. As we all know, having a game that also happens to be educational doesn't automatically eradicate the fun factor. In fact, one of my favorite Linux games just happens to be an educational game (I'll tell you what it is shortly).

KStars

Kstars (command name, kstars), part of the kdeedu package, is a desktop planetarium program that displays the locations of stars and planets on your desktop. KStars is amazing fun but much more than a toy. With a database of the planets, 40,000 stars, and 13,000 deep-sky objects, KStars is an astronomical treasure. With it, you can visually identify the position of stars, galaxies, nebulae, and other glories of the night sky (see Figure 18–10). You can control what is displayed, zoom in on objects, and (I love this part) download images from online resources, such as Hubble and the Space Telescope Science Institute. Just right-click on an object of interest, and the pop-up will offer you both additional information and links to high-resolution images of those objects when appropriate.

When you start KStars, it will assume your location as Greenwich, United Kingdom, which is probably not what you want (unless, of course, you live near Greenwich). Start by clicking Location on the menu bar and selecting Geographic. A dialog box will appear with a world map (Figure 18–11).

Click an area on the map close to where you live. This will provide you with a list of geographical points in a list to the right of the map. Make your

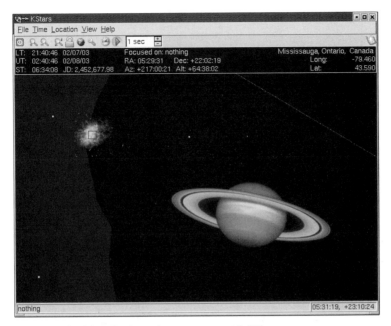

Figure 18–10 Explore the universe with KStars.

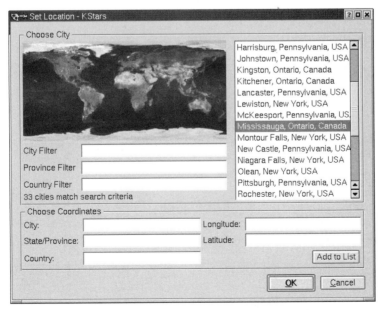

Figure 18–11 Choosing your geographical location for viewing.

selection and click OK. Should you happen to know your latitude and longitude, you can simply enter that at the bottom of the window.

Explore. Learn. The universe is yours!

Learn to Type

In this day and age, learning to type is a life skill. From what I have seen, a foolproof voice recognition system is still some time off. For years, it has been my dream to be able to speak my thoughts and have them appear in my word processor or text editor, but I have seen nothing that works faster than just typing. What I'm saying is that everyone, including kids, should learn to type.

As part of the kdeedu package, you'll find a package called *KTouch* (command name `ktouch`), a great little typing program. Besides being a nice typing tutor, KTouch looks great while doing the job. The display highlights which key to press as you go along, and the color coding tells you which finger to use (Figure 18–12). It supports multiple keyboard layouts, tracks your performance, and automatically changes levels, based on that performance.

If the kids are particularly young, KTouch may not seem like a great deal of fun. Another way to get them into the spirit of learning is with a game called

Figure 18–12   Learn to type with KTouch.

Figure 18–13   Learning to type becomes a game with TuxTyping.

TuxTyping (Figure 18–13). This one isn't likely to be on your distribution disk, but head on over to the Web site and pick up a copy at `http://www.geek-comix.com/dm/tuxtype`.

TuxTyping features a pleasant musical soundtrack, friendly graphics, colorful background images, and multiple levels of increasing difficulty. Furthermore, when you complete a level, TuxTyping rewards you with applause that can be quite raucous at times. There's also a free-type mode where Tux stands inside something that looks like the holodeck. You might find this the ideal level for the beginner. I particularly like waiting until the letters are almost at ground level before I let Tux go for them. It's great fun to see him run for it. Otherwise, he just lazily makes his way over to the fish. If you have kids and you want to teach them to type, get TuxTyping. They will love you for it.

That Potato Guy

I can't honestly say whether this qualifies as educational (although it does force you to use your imagination), but it does qualify as fun. What I am talking about here is Potato Guy (command name `ktuberling`), a computerized version of the potato-head game where you plug various plastic eyes, ears, noses, and hats into a plastic potato to create a funny-looking potato person (Figure 18–14). The *official* Mr. Potato Head is, of course, the famous store-bought version of this game, sold by Hasbro. I'm old enough to remember when the potato wasn't included with the game. You used a *real* potato.

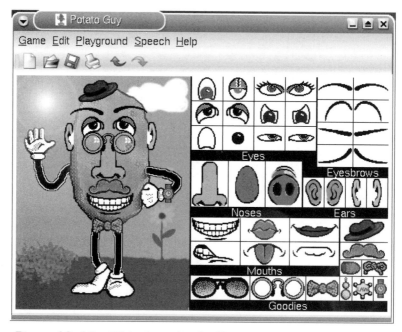

Figure 18–14   KTuberling, aka the "Potato Guy."

As you add the various pieces to the potato guy, a friendly voice speaks out the names of those parts. *"Nose." "Eye." "Spectacles."* Change the playground (click Playground on the menu bar), and you can dress up Tux the penguin or create an aquarium scene in the same way.

Yes, I know it is a kid's game, but I have had a lot of fun with this simple diversion.

The Edutainment Pack

I'm going to wrap up this section on educational games by telling you a bit more about one of the packages that comprises KDE, the one called *kdeedu*. In it, you will find a scrambled word-guessing game called *KMessedWords* (command name kmessedwords), as well as *KHangMan* (command name khangman), another word-guessing game.

The package also contains some more advanced items, including KPercentage (command name `kpercentage`), a math testing game using (what else?) percentages; KGeo (command name `kgeo`), an interactive geometry program; and KAlzium (command name `kalzium`), an interactive periodic table of the elements with a Web lookup.

There is quite a lot of work going on in this area. For more details (and to see what else is in the works) visit `http://edu.kde.org`.

3D Accelerated Fun

To truly appreciate the following pastimes, you will require a 3D accelerated video card and OpenGL or Mesa 3D video libraries. Many manufacturers sell these cards, and some are extremely well supported under Linux. Even when the card is supported, the manufacturer of the card may not distribute the accelerated driver for inclusion with the Linux distributions themselves. That doesn't mean they aren't available, but you may have to visit the vendor's site and download them. With some cards, full 3D acceleration is directly supported under XFree86, the graphical environment on which your desktop runs.

A quick way to test for the presence of 3D support is with the following command:

```
glxinfo | grep rendering
```

The system should respond with this:

```
direct rendering: Yes
```

Another nice little test you can perform involves running a program called *gears* (part of the Mesa-demos package). To do this, you need to shell out (open a terminal or Konsole window), type the command name (`gears`), and press <Enter>. A window will appear with three gears spinning on your screen (Figure 18–15).

Don't get too distracted by the spinning gears. Look back at your terminal window, and you will see some statistics regarding the performance of your 3D hardware.

```
1778 frames in 5.001 seconds = 355.529 FPS
```

Figure 18–15   gears, a 3D acceleration measuring tool.

That result comes from my test (play) system running with an NVIDIA GeForce2 card, and it is reasonably impressive hardware performance. In contrast, my notebook, which does not have accelerated hardware, yields this result:

```
312 frames in 5.004 seconds = 62.350 FPS
```

Not having acceleration for your card doesn't stop the program from working, it's just that it will run very slowly. On that note, let's have a look at our selection of 3D accelerated games, starting with a personal favorite.

FlightGear

You may not know this (well, you do now), but your humble author is also a pilot. Consequently, I have a warm spot in my heart for FlightGear, an extremely impressive open source flight simulator (Figure 18–16). The developers of this incredible package have produced a beautiful thing. The scenery itself is breathtaking, and the coloration of land and sky is verging on photorealistic. You can also download scenery packs for every bit of land mass in the world, allowing you to fly and explore distant lands from the comfort of your own room. Fancy a lazy flight through the Grand Canyon? With FlightGear, it's not a problem.

FlightGear comes with a number of different aircraft models, from a single-engine Cessna to a Boeing 747, an A4 fighter (Figure 18–16), or even a Sopwith Camel.

Figure 18–16   FlightGear, a great flight simulator.

Now that I have sold you on this (hopefully), I should tell you that this is one you will have to get online (`http://www.flightgear.org`)—many distributions will not include it (partly because it can be a huge program). Multiple packages are also involved in this one (and don't forget the scenery), so make sure you read the information on the Web site carefully. Despite the extra work, the rewards for this one are well worth it.

TuxRacer

These days, the *official* TuxRacer game (Figure 18–17) is actually a proprietary game (available at `www.tuxracer.com`), although it did start out as an open source project. Because of those GPL'ed, open source roots, you can still get

Figure 18–17　Fast, frozen fun with TuxRacer.

your hands on the original TuxRacer from many different download sites. In fact, many distributions include it on the disk, so look there first. If you can't get enough of the free game, perhaps you'll pay the official site a visit.

The idea is simple. Tux races down snow or ice covered mountains on his belly. As the speed increases, you try to dodge obstacles while picking up herring along the way. The action is fast-paced and exciting, with Tux taking flight off the occasional cliff or ramp. All this as you race against the clock.

More Games! I Need More Games!

Well, it was bound to happen. As you can imagine, there are tons of games out there. Some are commercial packages, and others are free for the download (or compile). Still more are in various stages of development and playability.

To satisfy your hunger for Linux games, you might take a little time browsing in the games section on either SourceForge (`www.sourceforge.net`) or FreshMeat (`www.freshmeat.net`). You'll find plenty there.

One of my favorite sites for games is the Linux Game Tome at `happypenguin.org`. Although not a download site, the Linux Game Tome organizes, reviews, and lets users rate games. It's organized and searchable, and it should be on your list when it comes to adding some new diversions to your system. If you are looking specifically to find games for the younger kids, check out Linux for Kids at `http://www.linuxforkids.com`.

Play on!

Resources

FlightGear

http://www.flightgear.com

KDE Edutainment Site

http://edu.kde.org

KDE Games Center

http://games.kde.org

Linux for Kids

http://www.linuxforkids.com

Linux Game Tome

http://happypenguin.org

A

The GNU General Public License

This is a copy of the GNU General Public License. Those wishing to see the original can do so by visiting the Free Software Foundation Web site. The direct link to the license is as follows.

http://www.gnu.org/copyleft/gpl.html

On that Web site, you may also want to check out the comparative list of license types (both commercial and noncommercial) and how they compare with the GNU GPL. Most interesting here is the definition of whether a license qualifies as free and whether it is compatible with the GPL. That address is here.

http://www.gnu.org/philosophy/license-list.html

Now, without further ado, here is the GNU GPL.

GNU General Public License

Version 2, June 1991

Copyright (C) 1989, 1991 Free Software Foundation, Inc.
59 Temple Place, Suite 330, Boston, MA 02111-1307 USA

Everyone is permitted to copy and distribute verbatim copies of this license document, but changing it is not allowed.

Preamble

The licenses for most software are designed to take away your freedom to share and change it. By contrast, the GNU General Public License is intended to guarantee your freedom to share and change free software—to make sure the software is free for all its users. This General Public License applies to most of the Free Software Foundation's software and to any other program whose authors commit to using it. (Some other Free Software Foundation software is covered by the GNU Library General Public License instead.) You can apply it to your programs, too.

When we speak of free software, we are referring to freedom, not price. Our General Public Licenses are designed to make sure that you have the freedom to distribute copies of free software (and charge for this service if you wish), that you receive source code or can get it if you want it, that you can change the software or use pieces of it in new free programs; and that you know you can do these things.

To protect your rights, we need to make restrictions that forbid anyone to deny you these rights or to ask you to surrender the rights. These restrictions translate to certain responsibilities for you if you distribute copies of the software, or if you modify it.

For example, if you distribute copies of such a program, whether gratis or for a fee, you must give the recipients all the rights that you have. You must make sure that they, too, receive or can get the source code. And you must show them these terms so they know their rights.

We protect your rights with two steps: (1) copyright the software, and (2) offer you this license which gives you legal permission to copy, distribute and/or modify the software.

Also, for each author's protection and ours, we want to make certain that everyone understands that there is no warranty for this free software. If the software is modified by someone else and passed on, we want its recipients to know that what they have is not the original, so that any problems introduced by others will not reflect on the original authors' reputations.

Finally, any free program is threatened constantly by software patents. We wish to avoid the danger that redistributors of a free program will individually obtain patent licenses, in effect making the program proprietary. To prevent this, we have made it clear that any patent must be licensed for everyone's free use or not licensed at all.

The precise terms and conditions for copying, distribution, and modification follow.

GNU General Public License

Terms and Conditions for Copying, Distribution and Modification

0. This License applies to any program or other work which contains a notice placed by the copyright holder saying it may be distributed under the terms of this General Public License. The "Program," below, refers to any such program or work, and a "work based on the Program" means either the Program or any derivative work under copyright law: that is to say, a work containing the Program or a portion of it, either verbatim or with modifications and/or translated into another language. (Hereinafter, translation is included without limitation in the term "modification".) Each licensee is addressed as "you."

Activities other than copying, distribution, and modification are not covered by this License; they are outside its scope. The act of running the Program is not restricted, and the output from the Program is covered only if its contents constitute a work based on the Program (independent of having been made by running the Program). Whether that is true depends on what the Program does.

1. You may copy and distribute verbatim copies of the Program's source code as you receive it, in any medium, provided that you conspicuously and appropriately publish on each copy an appropriate copyright notice and disclaimer of warranty; keep intact all the notices that refer to this License and to the absence of any warranty; and give any other recipients of the Program a copy of this License along with the Program.

You may charge a fee for the physical act of transferring a copy, and you may at your option offer warranty protection in exchange for a fee.

2. You may modify your copy or copies of the Program or any portion of it, thus forming a work based on the Program, and copy and distribute such modifications or work under the terms of Section 1 above, provided that you also meet all of these conditions:

a) You must cause the modified files to carry prominent notices stating that you changed the files and the date of any change.

b) You must cause any work that you distribute or publish, that in whole or in part contains or is derived from the Program or any part thereof, to be licensed as a whole at no charge to all third parties under the terms of this License.

c) If the modified program normally reads commands interactively when run, you must cause it, when started running for such interactive use in the most ordinary way, to print or display an announcement including an appropriate copyright notice and a notice that there is no warranty (or else, saying that you provide a warranty) and that users may redistribute the program under these conditions, and telling the user how to view a copy of this License. (Exception: if the Program itself is interactive but does not normally print such an announcement, your work based on the Program is not required to print an announcement.)

These requirements apply to the modified work as a whole. If identifiable sections of that work are not derived from the Program, and can be reasonably considered independent and separate works in themselves, then this License, and its terms, do not apply to those sections when you distribute them as separate works. But when you distribute the same sections as part of a whole which is a work based on the Program, the distribution of the whole must be on the terms of this License, whose permissions for other licensees extend to the entire whole, and thus to each and every part regardless of who wrote it.

Thus, it is not the intent of this section to claim rights or contest your rights to work written entirely by you; rather, the intent is to exercise the right to control the distribution of derivative or collective works based on the Program.

In addition, mere aggregation of another work not based on the Program with the Program (or with a work based on the Program) on a volume of a storage or distribution medium does not bring the other work under the scope of this License.

3. You may copy and distribute the Program (or a work based on it, under Section 2) in object code or executable form under the terms of Sections 1 and 2 above provided that you also do one of the following:

a) Accompany it with the complete corresponding machine-readable source code, which must be distributed under the terms of Sections 1 and 2 above on a medium customarily used for software interchange; or,

b) Accompany it with a written offer, valid for at least three years, to give any third party, for a charge no more than your cost of physically performing source distribution, a complete machine-readable copy of the corresponding source code, to be distributed under the terms of Sections 1 and 2 above on a medium customarily used for software interchange; or,

c) Accompany it with the information you received as to the offer to distribute corresponding source code. (This alternative is allowed only for noncommercial distribution and only if you received the program in object code or executable form with such an offer, in accord with Subsection b above.)

The source code for a work means the preferred form of the work for making modifications to it. For an executable work, complete source code means all the source code for all modules it contains, plus any associated interface definition files, plus the scripts used to control compilation and installation of the executable. However, as a special exception, the source code distributed need not include anything that is normally distributed (in either source or binary form) with the major components (compiler, kernel, and so on) of the operating system on which the executable runs, unless that component itself accompanies the executable.

If distribution of executable or object code is made by offering access to copy from a designated place, then offering equivalent access to copy the source code from the same place counts as distribution of the source code, even though third parties are not compelled to copy the source along with the object code.

4. You may not copy, modify, sublicense, or distribute the Program except as expressly provided under this License. Any attempt otherwise to copy, modify, sublicense or distribute the Program is void, and will automatically terminate your rights under this License. However, parties who have received copies, or rights, from you under this License will not have their licenses terminated so long as such parties remain in full compliance.

5. You are not required to accept this License, since you have not signed it. However, nothing else grants you permission to modify or distribute the Program or its derivative works. These actions are prohibited by law if you do not accept this License. Therefore, by modifying or distributing the Program (or any work based on the Program), you indicate your acceptance of this License to do so, and all its terms and conditions for copying, distributing or modifying the Program or works based on it.

6. Each time you redistribute the Program (or any work based on the Program), the recipient automatically receives a license from the original licensor to copy, distribute or modify the Program subject to these terms and conditions. You may not impose any further restrictions on the recipients' exercise of the rights granted herein. You are not responsible for enforcing compliance by third parties to this License.

7. If, as a consequence of a court judgment or allegation of patent infringement or for any other reason (not limited to patent issues), conditions

are imposed on you (whether by court order, agreement or otherwise) that contradict the conditions of this License, they do not excuse you from the conditions of this License. If you cannot distribute so as to satisfy simultaneously your obligations under this License and any other pertinent obligations, then as a consequence you may not distribute the Program at all. For example, if a patent license would not permit royalty-free redistribution of the Program by all those who receive copies directly or indirectly through you, then the only way you could satisfy both it and this License would be to refrain entirely from distribution of the Program.

If any portion of this section is held invalid or unenforceable under any particular circumstance, the balance of the section is intended to apply and the section as a whole is intended to apply in other circumstances.

It is not the purpose of this section to induce you to infringe any patents or other property right claims or to contest validity of any such claims; this section has the sole purpose of protecting the integrity of the free software distribution system, which is implemented by public license practices. Many people have made generous contributions to the wide range of software distributed through that system in reliance on consistent application of that system; it is up to the author/donor to decide if he or she is willing to distribute software through any other system and a licensee cannot impose that choice.

This section is intended to make thoroughly clear what is believed to be a consequence of the rest of this License.

8. If the distribution and/or use of the Program is restricted in certain countries either by patents or by copyrighted interfaces, the original copyright holder who places the Program under this License may add an explicit geographical distribution limitation excluding those countries, so that distribution is permitted only in or among countries not thus excluded. In such case, this License incorporates the limitation as if written in the body of this License.

9. The Free Software Foundation may publish revised and/or new versions of the General Public License from time to time. Such new versions will be similar in spirit to the present version, but may differ in detail to address new problems or concerns.

Each version is given a distinguishing version number. If the Program specifies a version number of this License which applies to it and "any later version", you have the option of following the terms and conditions either of that version or of any later version published by the Free Software Foundation. If the Program does not specify a version number of this License, you may choose any version ever published by the Free Software Foundation.

10. If you wish to incorporate parts of the Program into other free programs whose distribution conditions are different, write to the author to ask for

permission. For software which is copyrighted by the Free Software Foundation, write to the Free Software Foundation; we sometimes make exceptions for this. Our decision will be guided by the two goals of preserving the free status of all derivatives of our free software and of promoting the sharing and reuse of software generally.

NO WARRANTY

11. BECAUSE THE PROGRAM IS LICENSED FREE OF CHARGE, THERE IS NO WARRANTY FOR THE PROGRAM, TO THE EXTENT PERMITTED BY APPLICABLE LAW. EXCEPT WHEN OTHERWISE STATED IN WRITING THE COPYRIGHT HOLDERS AND/OR OTHER PARTIES PROVIDE THE PROGRAM "AS IS" WITHOUT WARRANTY OF ANY KIND, EITHER EXPRESSED OR IMPLIED, INCLUDING, BUT NOT LIMITED TO, THE IMPLIED WARRANTIES OF MERCHANTABILITY AND FITNESS FOR A PARTICULAR PURPOSE. THE ENTIRE RISK AS TO THE QUALITY AND PERFORMANCE OF THE PROGRAM IS WITH YOU. SHOULD THE PROGRAM PROVE DEFECTIVE, YOU ASSUME THE COST OF ALL NECESSARY SERVICING, REPAIR OR CORRECTION.

12. IN NO EVENT UNLESS REQUIRED BY APPLICABLE LAW OR AGREED TO IN WRITING WILL ANY COPYRIGHT HOLDER, OR ANY OTHER PARTY WHO MAY MODIFY AND/OR REDISTRIBUTE THE PROGRAM AS PERMITTED ABOVE, BE LIABLE TO YOU FOR DAMAGES, INCLUDING ANY GENERAL, SPECIAL, INCIDENTAL OR CONSEQUENTIAL DAMAGES ARISING OUT OF THE USE OR INABILITY TO USE THE PROGRAM (INCLUDING BUT NOT LIMITED TO LOSS OF DATA OR DATA BEING RENDERED INACCURATE OR LOSSES SUSTAINED BY YOU OR THIRD PARTIES OR A FAILURE OF THE PROGRAM TO OPERATE WITH ANY OTHER PROGRAMS), EVEN IF SUCH HOLDER OR OTHER PARTY HAS BEEN ADVISED OF THE POSSIBILITY OF SUCH DAMAGES.

END OF TERMS AND CONDITIONS

How to Apply these Terms to Your New Programs

If you develop a new program, and you want it to be of the greatest possible use to the public, the best way to achieve this is to make it free software which everyone can redistribute and change under these terms.

To do so, attach the following notices to the program. It is safest to attach them to the start of each source file to most effectively convey the exclusion of warranty; and each file should have at least the "copyright" line and a pointer to where the full notice is found.

\<one line to give the program's name and a brief idea of what it does.\>
Copyright (C) \<year\> \<name of author\>

This program is free software; you can redistribute it and/or modify it under the terms of the GNU General Public License as published by the Free Software Foundation; either version 2 of the License, or (at your option) any later version.

This program is distributed in the hope that it will be useful, but WITHOUT ANY WARRANTY; without even the implied warranty of MERCHANTABILITY or FITNESS FOR A PARTICULAR PURPOSE. See the GNU General Public License for more details.

You should have received a copy of the GNU General Public License along with this program; if not, write to the Free Software Foundation, Inc., 59 Temple Place, Suite 330, Boston, MA 02111-1307 USA.

Also add information on how to contact you by electronic and paper mail.

If the program is interactive, make it output a short notice like this when it starts in an interactive mode:

Gnomovision version 69, Copyright (C) year name of author

Gnomovision comes with ABSOLUTELY NO WARRANTY; for details type 'show w.' This is free software, and you are welcome to redistribute it under certain conditions; type 'show c' for details.

The hypothetical commands 'show w' and 'show c' should show the appropriate parts of the General Public License. Of course, the commands you use may be called something other than 'show w' and 'show c'; they could even be mouse-clicks or menu items—whatever suits your program.

You should also get your employer (if you work as a programmer) or your school, if any, to sign a "copyright disclaimer" for the program, if necessary. Here is a sample; alter the names:

Yoyodyne, Inc., hereby disclaims all copyright interest in the program 'Gnomovision' (which makes passes at compilers) written by James Hacker.

\<signature of Ty Coon\>, 1 April 1989

Ty Coon, President of Vice

This General Public License does not permit incorporating your program into proprietary programs. If your program is a subroutine library, you may consider it more useful to permit linking proprietary applications with the library. If this is what you want to do, use the GNU Library General Public License instead of this License.

appendix

B

Take Command of Linux

Welcome to the extended "Shell Out" section of the book. In deciding to join me here, you have identified yourself as one of the bold and curious explorers who really want to know their Linux systems. Sure, it is possible to work day in and day out with your Linux system and rarely use the command line, but the command line is power. Your reward for continuing to this next level will be a deeper understanding of your system and the power to make it do whatever you want.

An Easy Start

Start by opening a Linux shell. You can start KDE's Konsole by clicking on the terminal icon in the Kicker panel or by running `konsole` from your <Alt+F2> quickstart.

Trivia time There are many ways to start a shell with your system. Other terminal programs include xterm, rxvt, and eterm, just to name a few. Konsole just happens to be KDE's terminal application.

From the shell prompt, why not try entering each of the following commands? Notice what they do.

A few simple commands

`date`	Date and time.
`df`	Show me how much free space my disks have
`who`	Who is logged onto the system?
`w`	Similar to *who* but with different information.
`cal`	Show me a calendar
`tty`	Identify your workstation.
`echo`	Hello, ello, llo, lo, o, o, o . . . .
	Try typing: `echo "Hello world."`
`last`	Who last logged in and are they still logged in?
	You may need root access for this one.

Working with Files

Let me tell you the secret of computers, of operating systems, and of the whole industry that surrounds these things: Everything is data. Information is the be-all and end-all of everything we do with computers. Files are the storehouses for that information and learning how to manipulate them, use and abuse them, and otherwise play with them will still be the point of computers 20 years from now.

You might remember a few of these commands from chapter 5.

A few file related commands:

`ls`	LiSt files
`cat`	conCATenate files
	Try `cat /etc/profile`

sort	SORT the contents of a file (or any output for that matter)
	Try `sort /etc/passwd`
uniq	Return only the UNIQue lines—you do this after sorting
wc	Word Count (returns a count of words, characters, and lines)
cp	CoPy files
mv	MoVe, or rename, a file
rm	ReMove, or delete, a file
more	Easy paging of large text files
less	Like the `more` command but with serious attitude

File Naming Conventions

Valid file names may contain almost any character. You do have to pay some attention to the names you come up with. Your Linux system will allow file names up to 255 characters in length. How you define file names can save you a lot of hassle, as I will soon demonstrate.

Some valid file name examples include the following:

```
fish
duck
program_2.01
a.out
letter.to.mom.who.I.dont.write.often.enough.as.it.is
.bash_profile
```

Notice the last name in particular. It starts with a period. Normally, this type of file is invisible with a default listing. To see these so-called dotfiles, use the `ls` command with a -a (`ls -a`).

Listing Files with Emotion!

The ls command seems so simple, yet it has a number of options that can give you tons of information. Change to something such as the `/etc` directory and try these options if you never have:

```
cd /etc
ls —color
ls -b
ls -lS
ls -lt
```

The first listing will show different types of files and directories in color. The second (-b) will show octal representations for files that might have been created with control characters. Depending on the terminal you are using, the default is to show question marks or simply blanks. If you need to access (or delete) the file, it helps to know what it is really called. The third and fourth options control sorting. The -1S option gives you a long listing (lots of information) sorted by file size. The last option (-1t) sorts by time, with the newest files at the top of the list and the oldest at the bottom.

A Peek at Metacharacters

Metacharacters are special characters that have particular meaning to your shell—that dollar sign or hash mark. The two I want to look at are the asterisk and the question mark. The following shows what they mean to the shell.

       *   Match any number of characters
       ?   Match a single character

Extending our talk of listing files, you could list all files containing `ackle` by using this command:

```
$ ls *ackle*
hackle hackles    tackles
```

Similarly, you could find all the words that start with an h like this:

```
$ ls h*
hackle   hackles
```

Now, if you want to see all the seven-letter words in your directory, use this command:

```
$ ls ???????
hackles  tackles
```

Each question mark represents a single letter position.

File Permissions in the Shell

Back in Chapter 5, I showed you how to look at file permissions with Konqueror. When you use the `ls -l` command, you are doing the same thing—looking at basic Linux security at the file (or directory) level. Here is an example of a long ls listing:

```
$ ls -l
total 3
drwxr-x--    5 root     system    512   Dec 25 12:01   presents
-r-xr-r-     1 zonthar  users     123   Dec 24 09:30   wishlist
-rw-rw--     1 zonthar  users     637   Nov 15 09:30   griflong
```

The first entry under the total column shows a directory (I'll talk about the next nine characters in a moment). The first character is a d, which indicates a directory. Right at the end of each line, you'll find the directory or file name—in my example, they are presents, wishlist, and griflong. The first character in the permissions field is d, so presents is a directory.

On to those other nine characters (characters 2 through 10). These indicate permissions for the user or owner of the file (first three), the group (second group of three), and others or everyone else (last three). In the first line, user root has read (r), write (w), and execute (x) permissions, whereas the system group has only read and execute. The three dashes at the end imply that no one else has any permissions. The next two files are owned by the user called *zonthar*.

Standard Input and Standard Output

It may sound complicated, but it isn't. Standard in (STDIN) is simply where the system expects to find its input. This is usually the keyboard, although it can be a program or shell script. When you change that default, you call it *redirecting from STDIN*.

Similarly, standard out (STDOUT) is where the system expects to direct its output, usually the terminal screen. Again, redirection of STDOUT is at the discretion of whatever command or script is executing at the time. The chain of events from STDIN to STDOUT looks something like this:

```
standard in -> Linux command -> standard out
```

STDIN is often referred to as *fd0*, or file descriptor 0, and STDOUT is usually thought of as *fd1*. There is also standard error (STDERR), where the system reports any errors in program execution. By default, this is also the terminal. To redirect STDOUT, use the greater-than sign (>). As you might have guessed, to redirect from STDIN, you use the less-than sign (<). But what exactly does that mean? Let's try an experiment. Randomly search your brain and pick a handful of names. Got them? Good. Now type the *cat* command and redirect its STDOUT to a file called random_names.

```
cat > random_names
```

Your cursor will just sit there and wait for you to do something, so type those names, pressing <Enter> after each one. What's happening here is that cat is taking its input from STDIN and writing it out to your new file. When you are done with your list of names, press <Ctrl+D> to finish. <Ctrl+D>, by the way, stands for *EOF*, or end of file.

```
Marie Curie
Albert Einstein
Mark Twain
Wolfgang Amadeus Mozart
Stephen Hawking
Hedy Lamarr
^D
```

If you cat this file (`cat random_names`), the names will be written to STDOUT—in this case, your terminal window. You can also give cat several files at the same time. For instance, you could do something like this:

```
cat file1 file2 file3
```

Each file would be listed one right after the other. That output could then be redirected into another file. You could also have it print out the same file over and over (`cat random_names random_names random_names`). cat isn't fussy about these things and will deal with binary files (programs) just as quickly. Beware of using `cat` to print out the contents of a program to your terminal screen. At worst, your shell session will lock up or reward you with a lot of beeping and weird characters.

Quick Tip If you do get caught in such a situation and all the characters on your screen appear as junk, try typing echo, then pressing <Ctrl+v> and <Ctrl+o>. If you can still type, you can also try typing `stty sane`, then pressing <Ctrl+j>.

Redirecting STDIN works pretty much the same way, except that you use the less-than sign instead. Using the sort command, let's take that file of random names and work with it. Many commands that work with files can take their input directly from that file. Unless told otherwise, cat and sort will think that the word following the command is a file name. That's why you did the STDIN redirection thing. Yes, that's right: STDIN is just another file. Sort of.

```
sort random_names
```

The result, of course, is that you get all your names printed out in alphabetical order. You could have also specified that sort take its input from a redirected STDIN. It looks a bit strange, but this is perfectly valid.

```
[mgagne@testsys tmp]$ sort < random_names
Albert Einstein
Hedy Lamarr
Marie Curie
Mark Twain
Stephen Hawking
Wolfgang Amadeus Mozart
```

One more variation involves defining your STDIN (as you did previously) and specifying a different STDOUT all on the same line. In the following example, I am redirecting from my file and redirecting that output to a new file called sorted_names.

```
sort < random_names > sorted_names
```

Pipes and Piping

Sometimes the thing that makes the most sense is to feed the output from one command directly into another command without having to resort to files in between at every step of the way. This is called *piping*. The symbolism is not that subtle: Imagine pieces of pipe connecting one command with another. Not until you run out of pipe does the command's output emerge. The pipe symbol is the broken vertical bar on your keyboard, usually located just below or (depending on the keyboard) just above the <Enter> key and sharing space with the backslash key. Here's how it works:

```
cat random_names | sort | wc -w > num_names
```

In the preceding example, the output from the cat command is piped into sort, whose output is then piped into the wc command (that's word count). The -w flag tells wc to count the number of words in random_names. So far, so good.

That `cat` at the beginning is actually redundant, but I wanted to stack up a few commands for you to give you an idea of the power of piping. Ordinarily, I would write that command as follows:

```
sort random_names | wc -w > num_names
```

The `cat` is extraneous because sort incorporates its function. Using pipes is a great time saver because you don't always need to have output at every step of the way.

Working with Directories

There is another batch of commands suited to working with directory files (directories being just another type of file).

pwd	Print Working Directory
cd	Change to a new Directory
mkdir	MaKe or create a new DIRectory
mv	MoVe directories or, like files, rename them
rmdir	ReMove or delete DIRectories

One way to create a complicated directory structure is to use the `mkdir` command to create each and every directory.

```
mkdir /dir1
mkdir /dir1/sub_dir
mkdir /dir1/sub_dir/yetanotherdir
```

What you could do instead is save yourself a few keystrokes and use the -p flag. This tells mkdir to create any parent directories that might not already exist. If you happen to like a lot of verbiage from your system, you could also add the `−verbose` flag for good measure.

```
mkdir -p /dir/sub_dir/yetanotherdir
```

To rename or move a directory, the format is the same as you used with a file or group of files. Use the `mv` command.

```
mv path_to_dir new_path_to_dir
```

Removing a directory can be just a bit more challenging. The command `rmdir` seems simple enough. In fact, removing this directory was no problem:

```
$ rmdir trivia_dir
```

Removing this one, however, gave me this error:

```
$ rmdir junk_dir
rmdir: junk_dir: Directory not empty
```

You can use `rmdir` only to remove an empty directory. There is a -p option (as in *parents*) that enables you to remove a directory structure. For instance, you could remove a couple of levels like this:

```
$ rmdir -p junk_dir/level1/level2/level3
```

Warning Beware the of `rm -rf *` command. Better yet, never use it. If you must delete an entire directory structure, change directory to the one above it and explicitly remove the directory. This is also the first and best reason to do as much of your work as possible as a normal user and not root. Because root is all-powerful, it is quite capable of completely destroying your system. Imagine that you are in the top-level directory (`/`) instead of `/home/myname/junkdir` when you initiate that recursive delete. It is far too easy to make this kind of mistake. Beware.

All the directories from `junk_dir` on down will be removed, but only if they are empty of files. A better approach is to use the *rm* command with the -r, or recursive, option. Unless you are deleting only a couple of files or directories, you will want to use the -f option, as well.

```
$ rm -rf junk_dir
```

More on File Permissions

What you can and can't do with a file, as defined by your user or group name, is pretty much wrapped up in four little letters. Each of these letters in turn can be referenced by a number. They are r, w, x, and s. Their numerical representations are 4, 2, 1, and "it depends." To understand all that, you need to do a little binary math.

Reading from right to left, think of the *x* as being in position zero. The *w*, then, is in position 1, and the *r* is in position 2. Here's the way it works:

2 to the power of 0 equals 1   (x is 1)
2 to the power of 1 equals 2   (w is 2)
2 to the power of 2 equals 4   (r is 4)

To specify multiple permissions, you can just add the numbers together. If you want to specify both read and execute permissions, simply add 4 and 1, and you get 5. For all permissions (*rwx*), use 7.

File permissions are referenced in groups of three rwx sections. As you might expect, the *r* stands for "read," the *w* means "write," and the *x* denotes that the file is executable.

Although these permissions are arranged in three groups of three *rwx* combinations, their meaning is the same in all cases. The difference has to do with who they represent, rather than the permissions themselves. The first of these three represents the user, the second trio stands for the group permissions, and the third represents everybody who doesn't fit into either of the first two categories.

The commands you will use for changing these basic permissions are `chmod`, `chown`, and `chgrp`.

chmod	CHange the MODe of a file (aka its permissions)
chown	CHange the OWNer of the file or directory
chgrp	CHange the GRouP of the file or directory

User and Group Ownership

To change the ownership of the file `mail_test` from root to natika, you first have to log in as root because only root can change root's ownership of a file. This is very simple.

```
chown natika mail_test
```

You can also use the `-R` option to change ownership recursively. Let's use a directory called `test_directory` as an example. Once again, it belongs to root, and you want to make every file in that directory (and below) owned by natika.

```
chown -R natika test_directory
```

The format for changing group ownership is just as easy. Let's change the group ownership of test_directory (previously owned by root) so that it and all its files and subdirectories belong to group accounts:

```
chgrp -R accounts test_directory
```

You can even combine the two formats. In the following example, the ownership of the entire finance_data directory changes to natika as the owner and accounts as the group. To do so, you use this form of the chown command:

```
chown -R natika.accounts finance_data
```

 Quick Tip You can use the -R flag to recursively change everything in a subdirectory with chgrp and chmod, as well.

So now files (and directories) are owned by some user and some group. This brings us to the next question.

Who Can Do What?

From time to time, you may need to modify file permissions. One reason has to do with security. The most common reason, however, is to make a shell script file executable. This is done with the chmod command.

```
chmod mode filename
```

For instance, if you have a script file called list_users, you make it executable with the following command:

```
chmod +x list_users
```

That command will allow execute permissions for all users. If you want to make the file executable for the owner and group only, you specify it on the command line like this:

```
chmod u+x,g+x list_users
```

The *u* means "user" (the owner of the file, really), and *g* stands for "group." The reason you use *u* for the owner instead of *o* is that the *o* is being used for "other," meaning everyone else. The `chmod +x list_users` command can then be expressed as:

```
chmod u+x,g+x,o+x list_users
```

Unfortunately, this starts to get a bit cumbersome. Now let's look at a much more complicated set of permissions. Imagine that you want your list_users script to have read, write, and execute permissions for the owner, read and execute for the group, and read-only for anybody else. The long way is to do this is as follows:

```
chmod u=rwx,g=rx,o=r list_users
```

Notice the equal sign (=) construct, rather than the plus sign (+). That's because the plus sign adds permissions, and in this case you want them to be absolute. If the original permissions of the file allowed write access for "other," the plus sign construct would not have removed the execute permission. Using the minus sign (-) removes permissions. If you want to take away execute permission entirely from a file, you can do something like this:

```
chmod -x list_users
```

One way to simplify the chmod command is to remember that *r* is 4, *w* is 2, and *x* is 1, and add up the numbers in each of the three positions. *rwx* is then 4 + 2 + 1, or 7; *r-x* translates to 4 + 1; and *x* is simply 1. That monster from the second-to-last example can then be rewritten like this:

```
chmod 751 list_users
```

Finding Anything

One of the most useful commands in your arsenal is the `find` command. Generally speaking, find is used to list files and redirect (or pipe) that output to do some simple reporting or backups. The basic form of the command is as follows.

```
find starting_dir [options]
```

One of those options is `-print`, which makes sense only if you want to see any kind of output from this command. You could easily get a listing of every file on the system by starting at the top and recursively listing the disk.

```
find / -print
```

Although that might be interesting and you might want to redirect that to a file for future reference, it is only so useful. It makes more sense to search for something. For instance, look for all the JPEG-type image files sitting on your disk. Because you know that these images end in a *.jpg* extension, you can use that to search.

```
find / -name "*.jpg" -print
```

Depending on the power of your system, this can take a while, and you are likely to get a lot of Permission denied messages (particularly as you traverse a directory called `/proc`). If you are running this as a user other than root, you will likely get a substantial number of Permission denied messages. At this point, the usefulness of find should start to become apparent because a lot of images stashed away in various parts of the disk can certainly add up as far as disk space is concerned. Try it with an *.avi* or *.mpg* extension to look for video clips (which can be very large).

Faster Finds Using Locate

Depending on the power of your system (and the number of files), running a find can take quite a long time, and as I mentioned earlier, you are likely to get a lot of Permission denied messages.

Luckily, there is a faster way. On most Linux systems, you have a process that runs once a day (or once a week on some systems). That process builds a database of all the files on your system for quick and easy searching. The command is called `locate` or `slocate`. The process that runs on your system is located in `/etc/cron.daily` (or `/etc/cron.weekly`) and called `slocate.cron`. If your system is not up 24 hours, you can rebuild the slocate database any time you wish by running the cron script manually or with the command `updatedb`. Let us try to find those .jpg files again.

```
slocate jpg
```

Amazingly fast, isn't it? I should tell you that the `find` command is still quite a bit more powerful than `slocate`, but if you need to lay your hands on a file quickly and you have no idea where it has gone, try `slocate`.

Using grep

`grep`: Global regular expression parser.

That definition of the acronym is one of many. Don't be surprised if you hear it called the "gobble research exercise program" instead of what I called it. Basically, `grep`'s purpose in life is to make it easy for you to find strings in text files. This is its basic format:

```
grep pattern file(s)
```

As an example, let's say you want to find out whether you have a user named *natika* in your `/etc/passwd` file. The trouble is that you have 500 lines in the file.

```
[root@testsys /root]# grep natika /etc/passwd
natika:x:504:504:Natika the Cat:/home/natika:/bin/bash
```

Sometimes you just want to know whether a particular chunk of text exists in a file, but you don't know which file, specifically. Using the `-l` option with grep enables you to list file names only, rather than lines (grep's default behavior). In the next example, I am going to look for Natika's name in my e-mail folders. Because I don't know whether Natika's name is capitalized in the mail folders, I'll introduce another useful flag to grep: the `-i` flag. It tells the command to ignore case.

```
[marcel@testsys Mail]# grep -i -l natika *
Baroque music
Linux Stuff
Personal stuff
Silliness
sent-mail
```

As you can see, the lines with the word (or name) *Natika* are not displayed—only the files. Here's another great use for `grep`. Every once in a while, you will want to scan for a process. The reason might be to locate a misbehaving terminal or to find out what a specific login is doing. Because `grep` can filter out patterns in your files or your output, it is a useful tool. Rather than trying to scan through 400 lines on your screen for one command, let grep narrow down the search for you. When grep finds the target text, it displays that line on your screen.

```
[root@testsys /root]# ps ax | grep httpd
1029 ?        S       0:00 httpd
1037 ?        S       0:00 httpd
1038 ?        S       0:00 httpd
1039 ?        S       0:00 httpd
1040 ?        S       0:00 httpd
1041 ?        S       0:00 httpd
1042 ?        S       0:00 httpd
1043 ?        S       0:00 httpd
1044 ?        S       0:00 httpd
30978 ?       S      0:00 httpd
1385 pts/2  S     0:00 grep httpd
```

Notice the last line that shows the grep command itself in the process list. You'll use that line as the launch point to one last example with grep. If you want to scan for strings other than the one specified, use the -v option. Using this option, it's a breeze to list all processes currently running on the system but ignore any that have a reference to root.

```
ps aux | grep -v root
```

And speaking of processes....

Processes

All you have to remember is that any command you run is a process. Processes are also sometimes referred to as *jobs*.

The session program that executes your typed commands (the shell) is a process. The tools I am using to write this chapter are creating several processes. Every terminal session you have open, every link to the Internet, every game you have running—all these programs generate one or more processes on your system. In fact, there can be hundreds, even thousands of processes running on your system at any given time. To see your own processes, try the following command:

```
[root@testsys /root]# ps
  PID TTY          TIME CMD
12293 pts/5    00:00:00 login
```

```
12316 pts/5    00:00:00 su
12317 pts/5    00:00:00 bash
12340 pts/5    00:00:00 ps
```

For a bit more detail, try using the u option. This will show all processes owned by you that currently have a controlling terminal. Even if you are running as root, you will not see system processes in this view. If you add the a option to that, you'll see all the processes running on that terminal—in this case, revealing the subshell that did the su to root.

```
[root@testsys /root]# ps au
USER       PID %CPU %MEM   VSZ  RSS TTY       STAT START    TIME COMMAND
root     12293  0.0  0.4  2312 1196 pts/5      S    21:23   0:00 login -
mgagne
mgagne   12294  0.0  0.3  1732  976 pts/5      S    21:23   0:00 -bash
root     12316  0.0  0.3  2156  952 pts/5      S    21:23   0:00 su - root
root     12317  0.0  0.3  1736  980 pts/5      S    21:23   0:00 -bash
root     12342  0.0  0.2  2400  768 pts/5      R    21:24   0:00 ps au
```

The most common thing someone will do is add an x option. This will show you all processes, controlled by your terminal or not, as well as those of other users.

Killing Processes

Sometimes, a process (or program) gets hung and needs to be terminated. You can interrupt a foreground process (one you are running from the shell) by pressing <Ctrl+C>, but that does not work with background processes. The command used to terminate a process is called kill, which as it turns out is an unfortunate name for a command that does more than just terminate processes. By design, kill sends a signal to a job (or jobs). That signal is sent as an option (after a hyphen) to a process ID.

```
kill -signal_no PID
```

For instance, you can send the SIGHUP signal to process 7612 like this:

```
kill -1 7612
```

Signals are messages. They are usually referenced numerically, as with the ever-popular kill -9 signal, but there are a number of others. The ones you are most likely to use are 1, 9, and 15. These signals can also be referenced symbolically with these names.

Signal 1 is SIGHUP. This is normally used with system processes such as `xinetd` and other daemons. With these types of processes, a SIGHUP tells the process to hang up, reread its configuration files, and restart. Most applications will just ignore this signal.

Signal 9 is SIGKILL, an unconditional termination of the process. Some people I've worked with over the years call this *"killing with extreme prejudice."* The process is not asked to stop, close its files, and terminate gracefully. It is simply killed. This should be your last-resort approach to killing a process, and it works 99% of the time. Only a small handful of conditions will ever ignore the -9 signal.

Forging on . . .

I'm going to leave this extended Shell Out section here. Given the sheer number of Linux commands and the incredible flexibility of the shell language, I could write an entire book on the subject. Who knows?

I hope you enjoyed this foray into the nongraphical world of Linux. Furthermore, I hope it has whetted your appetite for more.

Once you get comfortable with the shell, nothing is impossible.

Meanwhile, if you want to learn more about the shell and what can be done with it, I will point you to a couple of excellent bash shell references at the Linux Documentation Project website. They are the *Bash Prompt HOWTO*, and the *BASH Programming—Introduction HOWTO*. Look for the links in the reference section, which follows.

References

BASH Programming - Introduction HOWTO

http://www.tldp.org/HOWTO/Bash-Prog-Intro-HOWTO.html

BASH Prompt HOWTO

http://www.tldp.org/HOWTO/Bash-Prompt-HOWTO/index.html

Index

About the CD-ROM

The CD-ROM included with *Moving to Linux: Kiss the Blue Screen of Death Goodbye!* contains the following:

WFTL Edition Knoppix: this is a Debian-based distribution that runs entirely from your PC's CD-ROM drive (though much slower than if you actually *install* Linux). That's right. You can run Linux on your personal computer system without having to change your system or uninstall Windows®. This CD is full of great software, some of which is covered in this book. You'll have access to email applications, web browsers, word processors, spreadsheets, games, and more. In fact, you should be able to follow along with this book and do many, *though not all*, of the things covered without having to install Linux at all.

Note The version of Knoppix included with this book is *not* the official version, but one that has been slightly modified by your humble author. I wish to express my admiration and thanks to Klaus Knopper, the creator of Knoppix, for his fine work, but any questions regarding the included disk should be directed to myself. Visit http://www.marcelgagne.com.

Minimun Suggested Requirements and Instructions

For best performance, your system should have at least a 350 Mhz Pentium class CPU with at least 128 Megabytes of RAM. WFTL Edition Knoppix supports a wide variety graphics cards, monitors, sound cards, network cards, and other hardware. The odds are pretty good that the WFTL Edition Knoppix CD will work with your system if the minimum requirements are met.

Using the CD should be as simple as shutting Windows® and doing a re-boot. Make sure your PC is set to boot from the CD. WFTL Edition Knoppix boots up to a nice, graphical screen with a simple `boot :` prompt from which you can simply press `Enter` and let the CD do the rest; this is an amazingly simple *install*. As the system comes up, you'll see a number of prompts as hardware is detected and your environment is created. This can take a few minutes, so please be patient.

Additional details on your WFTL Edition Knoppix CD can be found in Chapter 1 of this book in the section titled "About the CD."

License Agreement

Nearly all of the software on the CD is licensed under the GPL or other OSI ap-proved licenses, but there are some exceptions (see http://www.gnu.org/copy-left/gpl.html or the Appendix for a copy of the GPL). While you are free to copy and redistribute this CD, use of the software accompanying *Moving to Linux: Kiss the Blue Screen of Death Goodbye!* is subject to the terms of the Li-cense Agreement and Limited Warranty, found in Appendix A.

CD *website* and excerpts from *Linux System Administration: A User's Guide* are copyright Marcel Gagné and Addison Wesley Professional.

Technical Support

Addison-Wesley does not offer technical support for any of the programs on the CD-ROM. However, if the CD-ROM is damaged, you may obtain a re-placement copy by sending an email that describes the problem to: disc_ex-change@prenhall.com.